Great Australian
FLOOD
STORIES

Great Australian
FLOOD
STORIES

Ian Mannix

ABC
Books

The ABC 'Wave' device is a trademark of the
Australian Broadcasting Corporation and is used
under licence by HarperCollinsPublishers Australia.

First published in Australia in 2012
by HarperCollins*Publishers* Australia Pty Limited
ABN 36 009 913 517
harpercollins.com.au

HarperCollins*Publishers*
Level 13, 201 Elizabeth Street, Sydney NSW 2000, Australia
31 View Road, Glenfield, Auckland 0627, New Zealand
1–A Hamilton House, Connaught Place, New Delhi — 110 001, India
77–85 Fulham Palace Road, London W6 8JB, United Kingdom
2 Bloor Street East, 20th floor, Toronto, Ontario M4W 1A8, Canada
10 East 53rd Street, New York NY 10022, USA

National Library of Australia Cataloguing-in-Publication data:
Mannix, Ian.
Great Australian flood stories / Ian Mannix.
978 0 7333 2530 4 (pbk.)
Floods – Australia – Anecdotes.
Natural disasters – Australia – Anecdotes.
363.34930994

Cover design by HarperCollins Design Studio
Cover image © Newspix
Typeset in 10/15pt ITC Bookman by Kirby Jones
Printed and bound in Australia by Griffin Press
70gsm Classic used by HarperCollins*Publishers* is a natural, recyclable product made
from wood grown in sustainable forests. The manufacturing processes conform to the
environmental regulations in the country of origin, Finland.

5 4 3 2   12 13 14 15

Contents

Acknowledgements

It is not easy for people to describe their response to natural disasters, and I am grateful to all the people mentioned in this book for inviting me to hear their experiences and thoughts. I have been privileged to share people's emotions, fears, and vulnerabilities. None of these people want to be described as heroes; all believe that if they can share a small part of their story, their own fight against nature and circumstances will not have been in vain.

Chas Keys gave me a great deal of his time and helped me understand the history of flooding and mitigation. He provided insights into the professional's response, as well as advice about recovery. Chas offered invaluable direction and support.

The Australian Bureau of Meteorology is an institution with a wonderful group of professionals who see their first role as to help our community and, if possible, to provide information to help keep them safe. It is a role they take seriously, and we can be proud of their wonderful work. Peter Baddiley at the Bureau of Meteorology in Queensland provided enormous assistance for this book, just as he has done for many years for all the people of Queensland.

The Bureau of Meteorology web site contains an archive of material about every major flood in Australia since the Bureau was set up, and most of the factual elements in this book, particularly in the introduction, relied on that web site. Congratulations to all who had a hand in compiling this wonderful national resource.

ABC Local Radio staff throughout Australia assisted me with items of interest. ABC Managers Tony Rasmussen and Michael Mason have been very encouraging and supportive.

This book took three years to complete, as personal matters and the Black Saturday Bushfires and then Queensland weather crisis of 2010-2011 intervened. In that time Associate Publisher Jo Mackay was very patient and provided wonderful support and encouragement. Thanks to Jacquie Kent for whipping it all into shape.

Writing this book took up time I would otherwise have given to my family. Thanks for all your love, Sue, Liam and Hayley.

Ian Mannix
ABC Local Radio Manager
Emergency Broadcasting and Community Development
October 2011

Introduction
A long and terrible history

Flooding is a serious problem in this country; Australia's flood history speaks for itself. Floods occur in coastal regions due to storm surge and river outflow, along both sides of the Great Dividing Range from riverine flooding, along all major escarpments and in all catchments. Even slow-moving and widespread riverine flooding has dramatic effects on farmland and infrastructure and, while farmers welcome the regular water and silt deposits, flooding also causes great personal and economic hardship.

Though floods described and recorded before the last hundred or so years were undoubtedly dramatic and occasionally catastrophic, the twentieth century has seen some of the worst and most widespread flooding in Australia's European history.

The so-called La Niña years of 1916–17, 1954 through 1956, 1973 through 1975 and 2010–2011 featured some of the worst and most widespread flooding ever recorded. A feature of the climate pattern during the La Niña years is the widespread and prolonged rainfall that soaks catchment areas.

Australia's whole eastern seaboard is at risk of storm surge, flash flooding and riverine flooding. Particularly intense rainfall occurs during weather systems known as 'east-cost lows', when water is apparently pulled out of the Pacific Ocean and dumped over coastal areas. These derive much of their energy from the warm waters of the Tasman or Coral Seas, which also provide moisture for rain that can be torrential.

In August 1986, an east-coast low was responsible for Sydney's heaviest recorded daily rainfall. That winter had been the driest in almost a century. But early on Monday 4 August light rain began to fall. It became heavier overnight and heavier still next morning. Between midday and three in the afternoon on

Wednesday it reached its peak, when 100 millimetres cascaded down. Rain continued throughout the evening, finally easing by about 2am on the Thursday. The twenty-four-hour rainfall total to 9am on the Wednesday was a record 327.6 millimetres: even in the western suburbs, which are normally drier, the totals exceeded 250 millimetres.

The torrential rains created chaos. Motorists abandoned their cars, bus services were severely disrupted and flooded tunnels caused trains to grind to a halt. Faced with difficulties and danger in getting home, many people stayed in the city. In the western suburbs, creeks rose rapidly, flooding houses. There were six deaths, and in one case the floods tore two young children from their father's arms.

The rain eased in Sydney, but then shifted to the southern escarpment of the Blue Mountains. The Coxs and Grose rivers had their largest floods on record; and heavy rains extended south to the Illawarra escarpment west of Wollongong.

Intense rain can persist over an area for several hours, especially where the topography serves to 'anchor' storms. This is what happened in the Illawarra escarpment on 18 February 1984. More than 800 millimetres fell on the escarpment in twenty-four hours — the heaviest falls registered in Australia outside the tropics or subtropics. As the water flowed from the escarpment it swept across farmland and the Princes Highway and through parts of the suburb of Dapto. Water overturned cars and damaged houses, and 600 people had to be evacuated. Remarkably, nobody was killed.

This type of weather, caused by low-pressure systems, had caused chaos on the eastern side of the continent before. In June 1952 a low-pressure system developed and intensified east of Bass Strait. Tanybryn in Victoria's Otway Ranges registered 587 millimetres in three days. The surge of water down narrow and steeply sloping river valleys washed away parts of the Great Ocean Road, isolating Apollo Bay and flooding businesses in Geelong. Flooding in the surf town of Barwon Heads left hundreds homeless.

The same system generated vast amounts of rain in eastern Victoria and southeastern New South Wales, causing major flooding on every river in Gippsland and adjacent southern coastal New South Wales. In Walhalla, an old gold mining town in a narrow valley, disaster struck as an avalanche of water, rocks, silt and logs swept over the town. Residents barely had time to escape: their town was covered in more than a metre of debris. (There are eerie parallels with the flood damage at Grantham in Queensland in 2011.) Meanwhile in New South Wales the town of Forbes became three islands, isolated by the rising of the Lachlan River, and there were two metres of water in the Commercial Hotel. Further southeast in Wagga Wagga, 1200 people were evacuated when the Murrumbidgee rose; and forty homes were flooded in Narrandera some 100 kilometres further northwest.

No state is immune from flooding and floods can occur in any month of the year. In 1929, Tasmania had what is known as 'the flood year'. Heavy rainfall occurred throughout Derby in the north east, Ulverstone in the north west, and Launceston in the north. Gale force winds destroyed roads and buildings and damaged farmland, causing flooding and stock losses as far south as Hobart and New Norfolk.

This resulted in the only fatal dam failure in Australia's history. According to *The Companion to Tasmanian History*, after the heavy rains in 1929

> The once prosperous tin mining centre of Derby was practically wiped out when the Cascade Dam {containing 188 million gallons of water} burst on 5 April and flooded the Briseis Tin Mine. Fourteen lives were lost in the only dam burst in Australia's history to have taken human life. Houses were crushed like matchsticks as a twelve-foot wave of water swept through the town. A ten-ton granite boulder which had travelled two miles was among the mountain of debris left in its wake. The influx of water caused the Ringarooma River above Derby to run uphill for nearly six hours ... In Launceston the post office bells rang out in the

early morning to warn residents of Inveresk and Invermay to evacuate their homes immediately. Volunteers in boats transported thousands of refugees to the shelter of the Albert Hall. All this occurred in pitch darkness, as power supplies to the city were cut off when the Duck Reach power station was washed away.

Widespread and extreme flooding also occurred throughout Tasmania in 1960, with the Macquarie, Elizabeth, Lake and Liffey rivers particularly affected. Part of the Lake Highway bridge was carried away when the river rose one metre in thirty minutes. The Macquarie Plains–New Norfolk area saw the greatest damage, with several people being rescued from rooftops, twelve houses destroyed and an estimated 650 made homeless. Hobart sustained record losses estimated at millions of dollars as the Hobart Rivulet flooded: water ran knee-deep in Liverpool Street, and the army was called out to help in the rescue.

Flooding is comparatively common in the northwest of Western Australia, due to the wet-season rains occasionally accompanied by cyclones. However, as the area is sparsely populated, there has not so far been a great deal of threat to life or damage to the economy. This is likely to change as the mining industry grows and money returns to the pastoral and tourism industries.

Perth has not often suffered heavy rain and flooding, especially in recent years. But it is after all on the Swan River and therefore cannot be immune. The city suffered major floods in 1926, 1945 and 1963: in July 2001 it received 99 millimetres in a day, not a large amount by Australia's experience, but enough to cause serious problems. Perhaps the risk is made worse by the lack of flood events in recent memory.

Storm surge is a flood risk in Perth, according to the Bureau of Meteorology. Most storm-surge events there, are driven by sustained westerly gales caused by intense low-pressure systems and cold fronts during the cooler months. A strong westerly gale on 20 July 1910 caused damage along the west coast as far north as Geraldton. The Fremantle North Mole was damaged, while on the Swan River all the surrounding low-lying lands and many of the jetties were submerged. During a storm on 23 May 1994 the tidal elevation measured at Fremantle showed a storm surge of 0.98 metres. Fortunately the peak occurred at low tide.

When floods occur, they are generally spectacular: during the twentieth century they broke many records and caused much heartbreak.

Heavy rain fell over much of eastern Australia from October 1954 and on 23 February 1955 an intensifying monsoon depression moved south from Queensland. Torrential rain developed over the area of New South Wales covering the Macintyre, Gwydir, Namoi, Castlereagh, Macquarie and Bogan rivers, all tributaries of the Barwon-Darling. Rainfall totals exceeded 250 millimetres in twenty-four hours between Nevertire and Dunedoo 350 kilometres northwest of Sydney. Heavy rains then moved east across the Liverpool Ranges and down the Hunter Valley.

With such intense rain falling on already saturated ground from the unusually wet summer, the rivers reached unprecedented heights. More than 5000 homes were flooded, in some cases submerged, by up to five metres of muddy water. About 15,000 people were evacuated, some plucked from rooftops by boat or helicopter. The floodwaters destroyed thirty-one homes in Maitland; and more than a hundred others were so badly damaged that they had to be demolished. Eleven lives were lost, including four or five due to electrocution during rescue operations. In the Singleton region, about fifty kilometres away, another 1600 homes were flooded and three more people died.

The 1990 floods in southern Queensland, northern New South Wales and southeast Victoria inundated an area larger than Germany. On 23 April the Bogan River overtopped the levee protecting the town of Nyngan. Desperate attempts were made to raise the levee with sandbags. The bags were punched through by the weight of the water and virtually the whole town was inundated. Almost all the population of 2500 were evacuated by helicopter and bus to Dubbo, 160 kilometres away.

Even in South Australia, the driest state in the driest continent, floods have caused great distress. In Adelaide in 1923 heavy rain inundated parts of the city and caused serious damage to market gardens along the River Torrens. More recently, intense rainfall over the Adelaide area on 7 and 8 November 2005 led to major flooding in several streams, with extensive flash flooding in several suburbs.

Semi-arid Australia is not immune to flooding either. Broken Hill has been targeted at least twice, usually by intense thunderstorms causing flash flooding. In one day in 1992, storms produced around 100 millimetres of rain in isolated locations around the city. Four houses were hit by a metre-high wall of water and their occupants were evacuated. More than eighty homes and businesses were flooded. On 1 January 1998 a severe thunderstorm passed over Broken Hill early in the afternoon, producing heavy rain and localised flash flooding. More than 25 per cent of Broken Hill's annual rainfall of 255 millimetres was dumped on the city in forty-five minutes. About fifty homes, shops and the fire station were flooded, with the State Emergency Services helping to cover rain-damaged roofs with tarpaulins and sandbag houses in low-lying areas.

The Red Centre is normally associated with drought, but Alice Springs has been flooded in the past. More than 300 millimetres of rain fell in the western MacDonnell Ranges in the twenty-four hours to 9am on 31 March 1988, with more than 150 millimetres at stations around Alice Springs. The normally dry Todd River burst its banks, flooding large areas of Alice Springs, killing three people and causing a lot of damage. That flood on the Todd was thought to be the second highest since Europeans settled there in the 1870s. Geological evidence suggested that the flooding in the region was the worst for about 850 years.

In January 1998 three people drowned as record floodwaters from ex-tropical cyclone Les swamped Katherine and inundated 1000 square kilometres. It was Katherine's worst recorded flooding. The event also triggered a state of emergency among the indigenous communities and pastoral regions of the Daly River as the floodwaters moved downstream.

As most Australians know and remember, in January 2011 there appeared to be a disastrous series of violent floods affecting three states. After months of persistent rain in Queensland floods swept down the Condamine, Balonne, Mary, Burnett, Fitzroy, Herbert, Nogoa, Darling and Brisbane Rivers, inundating homes and businesses; almost thirty towns were declared disaster zones, with floodwaters covering almost 70 per cent of the state.

The Gascoyne River in Western Australia 'blew up' to record heights at about the same time, affecting hundreds of farmers and wiping some small communities off the map. About 30 per cent of rural Victoria, which had also seen a long period of heavy rainfall going back to the previous September, underwent flooding. And in southern New South Wales the Molonglo and Queanbeyan rivers flooded, as did the Murrumbidgee and Billabong Creek. There is occasionally a period of several months when there is repeated flooding over a wide area in a number of states, but of course statistics are no consolation when individual Australians have to come to terms with the devastation caused.

The impact of these floods is often devastating, both in economic terms and in their effect on communities.

The Federal Bureau of Infrastructure Transport and Regional Economics estimates that flooding in Australia between 1967 and 2005 cost the country an average of about $377 million per annum.

More locally, the cost of the June 2007 storm and flood in the Hunter Valley and the New South Wales central coast has been estimated at $1.3 billion, and 49 per cent of the home-related damage was not covered by insurance. And the Queensland Reconstruction Authority has estimated that the damage from floods in that state in 2010–2011 exceeded $5 billion. This flooding affected 478,000 homes, which underwent everything from simple loss of electrical power to total destruction. In the first four months after the floods insurance companies had paid out nearly $2 billion to Queensland home owners and businesses, and there was massive loss affecting the coal and agricultural sectors.

In Brisbane during the flood of 2010–2011, when the Brisbane River peaked at 4.46 metres on 13 January, sixty-seven suburbs were flooded to some extent and 1200 homes were completely submerged, with 9500 damaged. One thousand people were evacuated to relief centres and tens of thousands more fled to relatives and friends.

This was not the worst flood to affect the Brisbane River, however. In 1893, the river peaked at 8.3 metres and in 1841 at 8.4 metres. But in the nineteenth century, the water caused nothing like the same damage, simply because the population, and thus the value of homes and businesses, is so much greater now than it was then.

And even so, the events of 2010 and 2011 were not the most calamitous that have ever affected this part of Australia. Between 25 and 29 January 1974 near-record rainfall associated with tropical cyclone Wanda caused the greatest flooding ever suffered in an Australian capital city. One-third of the Brisbane metropolitan area, covering about forty suburbs, was inundated, forcing 9000 from their homes. During the floods fifty-six houses were swept away, with at least another 1600 damaged, while 6007 were flooded to some degree. Overall 13,000 buildings in Brisbane, Ipswich and other towns along the river were damaged or affected in some way; and many vehicles were damaged or destroyed. Thirteen people were drowned, while three others suffered fatal heart attacks.

Floods in the summer of 1998–1999 in Queensland, the Northern Territory and New South Wales affected 83,500 people, including the 6710 who were temporarily left homeless. The Bureau of Meteorology reported that the floods resulted in fifteen deaths, with at least 169 injured. The total estimated cost was $990 million, of which only $184 million was covered by insurance. This is because insurance is not yet compulsory or even universally available in flood-prone areas.

Many people interviewed for this book said that the rise of floodwaters took them by surprise. But death in floods is hardly unknown in Australia's European history. Lucinda Coates in 1996, presented an overview of fatalities from some natural hazards in Australia, at a conference on Natural Disaster Reduction on the Gold Coast, and reported: 'Between 1788 and 1996 at least 2213 people were killed'. About a dozen places have recorded more than twenty deaths in a single episode of flooding, including in Queensland's Lockyer Valley in January 2011.

'Flash flooding' is a hazard common to many parts of the country. In tropical areas 100 millimetres a day falls regularly, and low-lying areas around creeks and rivers are quickly flooded, with drains unable to handle the volume of water. Residents of northern Australia are readily able too cope with a few days or weeks of this, with grassy areas too sodden to walk on, pot plants and dog bowls constantly full of water — and lots of mosquitoes. Creeks and rivers rise and fall rapidly. The danger is that drivers will not heed the caution signs and so find themselves stranded in low-level crossings. This is not only a nuisance for local government and emergency agencies but a real danger to motorists.

For those not involved, and who get their information from media reports, flooding is alarming. Trees can fall across power lines, electricity goes off and driving becomes hazardous. And once water enters homes, its effects can be devastating. According to a report put out by Emergency Management Australia there are about 170,000 residential properties susceptible to severe flooding. EMA suggested that the total value of the assets at risk in Australia during the biggest floods 'considerably exceeds $100 billion'. Flooding may therefore be Australia's most damaging and costly natural hazard. And the costs rise as more and more people are affected, as we create further investment in housing and other land use on flood plains.

Having your home flooded unexpectedly can be terrifying. People interviewed for this book recall waking up to find themselves surrounded by floating furniture. The water movement inside homes in these cases is not usually dangerous in itself, but for the elderly and frail, as well as young children, the shock and temperature of the water can create serious problems.

Floodwater moves quickly and can float fridges, even cars and containers. These rogue objects then become battering rams, smashing into other items and breaking them. Donna Reynolds, a resident of Charleville, described hearing her house shake as the relentless debris–laden water pounded it.

The residual effects of the flooding are almost worse. The water brings with it mud, silt, slime and toxic waste. Few houses recover well from water lying in them for a period. Gyprock walls need to be torn down and thrown out, chipboard cupboards swell and rot, carpets soak up silt and waste and can rarely be salvaged. Water is trapped under lino, floorboards buckle, window–sills warp.

Yards are trashed. Vegetation lying under water for a prolonged period starts to rot and the stench from the mud is sickening. For many people who are already despairing that they cannot save their property and belongings, the smell becomes the trigger for an outpouring of grief and hopelessness.

And when the water recedes the problems remain. Rebuilding homes takes months at best, years at worst — and even longer if the owner is broke or has no insurance or an already chaotic lifestyle. Many people interviewed for this book did not return to their homes for more than a year.

A graphic description of what a flood means and what heartbreak it can cause, as well as how it can bring communities together, was written by Lyn Berlowitz. The first woman member of the Northern Territory Legislative Council (from 1960 to 1963), she and her husband Happy bought Bullita Station near Timber Creek, 650 kilometres southwest of Darwin, in 1965. They ran it profitably for a few years as a cattle property, but by the late 1970s the USA had banned Australian frozen beef exports and the bottom dropped out of the industry. The station was struggling to survive when in April 1977, the East Baines River flooded massively, with water rising fifteen metres in a matter of hours. Lyn was alone in the house. A few days later, she wrote to her sister describing what had happened:

Our trouble really started on Tuesday night of the 15 March. During the month of February which is usually our heavy monsoonal rain month, only 117 millimetres or nearly 5 inches of rain registered. Normally 20 to 24 inches falls, so we all concluded the 'wet' was to be a very dry one. The month of March to 15th (am) only 256 mm, or just over ten inches had registered, and no one was concerned.

Happy and the menfolk were away on their job about fifty miles from here and were not due home until Saturday night. On the 15th I went to bed about 8pm. (The insects are such a pest one can't do anything at night.) It had rained on and off all day, but fairly lightly, and the river was at normal height.

About 2am I was wakened by a bit of a crash, and thinking it was a big frog hopping in the kitchen, I ignored the noise. Within ten minutes there was a big crash of glass so I grabbed my torch to investigate. Just in front of my elevated stove was a terrible mess of cornflakes, sugar and All Bran mixed in with broken jars. When I raised the torch higher to the mantelshelf over the stove I just about fainted, for there was the longest and fattest brown snake I had ever seen. Of course by this time the rain was falling heavily and steadily and a beaut electrical thunderstorm was right over the station (Bullita). Couldn't put the generator on as it's housed away from the cottage, and I would have got sopping wet, and also the lightning was playing all around the hills and might have struck the engine.

I went and got my Browning pistol. And holding the torch took aim, but missed the snake which slithered down from the shelf down under our dresser in the kitchen. Sent off a couple of more shots but as I was trembling so much I am never sure that I hit the beastly thing. There seemed to be quite a bit of blood oozing out so I was hoping it would bleed to death. Couldn't bear to go back to bed knowing the snake was still alive so got a chair and holding the pistol sat and watched until daylight came and I could see what I was doing.

By this time the rain had really set in, so as soon as it was light enough to see, went out to look at the rain gauge and got quite a shock as it had evidently been raining over some considerable time, as there was quite a lake around the galvanised iron container [Bullita is a registered rainfall observer's reporting station], and at 9am each morning we telegraph in the amount measured. I think the gauge holds about 10 inches of rain. Noting this I went to look at the river (East Baines) which is only 40-50 yards from the cottage. The river had risen and was running swiftly and had broken its banks on both sides, and was almost up to our windmill which stands 15 yards from the back door. Even then I didn't panic as each year this has happened, but the water had not gone beyond the windmill.

I quickly went down and opened the doors to the fowl and duck pen which already had 12 inches of water through them. Our pet dog Princess has five week-old puppies which we used to bed down in our bathroom each night for fear of snakes. I grabbed a strong mail bag and put the puppies in but unfortunately the load was too heavy over my back, so took three out, intending to go back and get the others. Called the Royal Flying Doctor Service Base at Wyndham and reported the river was very high and that I was leaving for higher ground. I slung the mail bag and the two puppies over my shoulder and set off to wade up to the goat yard. I had on an old plastic raincoat of Happy's and white 'wet proof' bowling hat and your brown desert boots for which later on I was very thankful.

The water was only to my knees in the breakaway 'overflow' from the river, and I was in no way concerned. Each year this area in front of the cottage needed to be negotiated when the river flooded and broke its banks.

I dumped the two puppies down in the goat yard and made their mother Princess stay with them and set off again back to the cottage which is about a short quarter mile away. I tried to follow the road but the rushing waters pushed me into a deep rut where I lost my footing and was swept away downstream in the overflow of the river, which by this short time, had spread almost up to the goat yard. I got very frightened at the noise and the water swept me along ... but kept saying to myself 'Don't panic'. Hampered by the big mail bag I let it go and within seconds the water swept it out of sight.

It was too deep for me to stand so when I came near to a big dead tree lying on its side (it was a white gum which had only collapsed six months previously in a wind blow) I grabbed it and held on, climbing up and wedging myself in the fork with my right foot. This is where I was grateful for your desert boots. I was wearing only a sleeveless seersucker button-down-the-front dress. And as the thunder, lightning and rain didn't let up, you can imagine how cold I was. As the river rose and rose I needed to climb up the slippery crumbling bark. Afterwards I found my knees, arms and thighs were all lacerated, and my right foot having to be so tightly wedged in the fork got very cramped and sore.

When it became unbearable I just had to lift it for relief, and when I did the raging river tried to snatch me, and I went under twice, but each time grimly I held on to the lower end of the fork by one arm. Big logs and living trees 30 to 40 feet long were all being uprooted and were swirling past at a terrific pace. It was a wonder I wasn't struck by one. Smaller trees and logs I managed to steer off and they got tangled in my big tree roots.

By this time all of the huge fencing posts near the cottage 4'6" above the ground could not be seen, and looking up I could see I only had 9 inches of my right fork. If the river rose further than that I knew I wouldn't make it.

From 8.20am till dark I was standing bent over the fork with both arms hugging my chest, with only my head above water, saying my prayers and talking with God. He felt very close and I knew He would support me in this old tree I called my 'Rock of Ages cleft (especially) for me'. Twice I tried to board a huge living tree just to my side and to the rear of mine, but just could not make it. This turned out to be lucky as towards the late afternoon the living tree was uprooted and joined the throng of trees, cattle, drums, snakes, etc racing down the river towards the sea.

Having notified the Flying Doctor Services base I felt sure a helicopter would be sent to rescue or even check if I was okay. But amid the storm, no one came. Late afternoon the rain stopped and the river was starting to go down. I was amazed how quickly the water was receding and just before dusk I was able to see the top of the fence posts. Feeling the water receding I waited another hour before I left my 'Rock' and waded back to the cottage.

What a dreadful scene of wreckage and devastation greeted me. I couldn't open the door because of the 18 cubic foot freezer, which was lying on its side together with the refrigerator and another small fridge.

The kitchen dresser, sideboard, buffets, were all over and smashed, louvres broken, fly-wire torn, beds upended and the innerspring mattress all lying in the filthy evil slime. My dresses in the wardrobe were ruined up to the waistline, badly marked and oh, so smelly.

Clearly everything has to be burned. Even my precious piano. The Viscount Caravan was torn from its moorings and swept up towards the native quarters where it lies a complete writeoff. The Toyota Landcruiser lies amongst dozens of upended trees torn out by the roots. The house paddock is now denuded of trees, and at the back of the fowl and duck pen where there were very thick trees, the course of the river has cut a channel which now takes the river much nearer the homestead.

We lost most of the fowls — only six hens and a rooster left, and most of our fifty goats went. The ducks died, and also my dear little puppies I tried to save.

When I arrived at the cottage so wet and shivering with cold I made up my mind to have a hot rum and milk to warm my body and stop my teeth from chattering, but of course everything was caught up in the flood with nothing warming left. You can imagine how shocked and ghastly I felt. All I wanted was to lie down somewhere, but there was nowhere to lie and nowhere to go. How totally alone I felt.

To my complete surprise Princess ran whimpering into the house having swum the now shallow lake out the front, then thinking I could hear faint yelping I went out to the gate where happily I could definitely hear a puppy crying. I asked myself: 'Will I or wont I?' knowing I needed to wade up to the cattle yards, but of course I had to go. When I eventually spotted the pup it went mad with joy, and strangely it was the little runt of the litter. How it survived is a mystery. It was so cold and hungry like myself. I picked it up and cuddled it, taking it back to the house.

Back at the house with the rain still falling steadily I found an old loll-about wedged near the gate and set it up in one of the evil-smelling rooms. Searching for anything dry I found a woollen cardigan that only the sleeves had touched the flood, and wrapped my feet in it, then tried to sleep with the puppy on my lap. Then the vomiting and purging started and went on all night. Princess looked so worried. Early the next morning I heard a plane overhead, struggling outside and waved trying to tell them I needed help.

Unbeknown to me it was a charter plane with Happy on board. Happy said later when he saw me standing and waving the cloth he assumed I was OK. In the afternoon another plane circled and I did the same thing, only this time the pilot flew very low over me and dropped a note saying 'Get a sheet and make a minus sign if OK, or a cross if help is needed'. The note also said Happy was on his way. I naturally made a minus sign. Happy arrived and the men arrived at about 9.20pm and couldn't believe the chaos and wreckage. The big generators, pumps, piano, all our furniture and personal possessions, photos, were all ruined … it means trying to start all over again.

Since the ordeal I haven't been well. My whole body took such a battering from the rushing water, debris and logs that my arm, chest, back and legs are exceedingly painful.

It's agony to turn over in bed or even get up. However I am getting there. Today my right foot which was wedged in the fork of the tree has swollen and flared up. I can hardly walk. I have been turning to God for comfort and support. I feel sure he won't let me suffer.

We thank you for your telegram with Robin's offer of accommodation but we have to remain here as we owe the bank $20,000 and could hardly walk off not honouring our commitment. We believe something will unfold.

Now Min darling I have tried to give you a true and accurate picture of what happened. Four days later a family of six, three men and a woman and two children on Dorisvale Station on the Daly River all lost their lives when the big flood struck (and they had a boat), so it's one of God's miracles that I survived.

Bullita Station never fully recovered. It was eventually purchased by the Northern Territory government and is now part of Gregory National Park, the biggest in the Northern Territory after Kakadu. The old tin homestead is now a display centre in the park.

Most of Australia's worst floods can be predicted in advance. The Bureau of Meteorology can accurately forecast low-pressure systems laden with moisture, monsoonal troughs bringing torrential rain for hours or days, sequences of fronts crossing parts of the continent and bringing bad floods. Long-term forecasting can predict the advance and eventual onset of a La Niña weather pattern.

While the bureau's flood warning equipment may be compromised by the quantity of water around, people should not wait until water heights become alarming before they start preparing for possible disaster.

But in fact most people don't prepare for floods, says Chas Keys, former Deputy Director-General of the New South Wales State Emergency Service. 'Floods are quite frequent overall, but not in individual areas,' he says. 'The Brisbane River had seen no severe flooding for thirty-seven years before January 2011, though some tributaries had.

'Flooding is irregular in most local areas, and that's a problem. If they were regular, like the Indian monsoon, we would probably be more ready because we would be expecting them in the appropriate season.'

Flood warning is also a problem, he says. 'Our flood warnings are not making the difference they should. Properly done, warning is a proven means of reducing flood damage.

'This is partly because warning is not given a high priority in the emergency services, partly because governments have not invested in flood intelligence — the warning messages do not always say where the floodwaters will go at the forecast heights, which would help people understand what the flood will do to them.

'Partly it is because people have not been educated about the threat of flooding, and what they can do to minimise its impact at the household level. The nexus between warning, information and education has not been well developed in Australia. This is demonstrated in virtually every significant flood we see.

'Too often people seem not to realise how bad the coming flood will be, and how it will affect them, until it is actually upon them. By this time, it is too late to act.'

Besides, as in the case of fire, most people are reluctant to abandon their homes quickly enough when roads are still safe. During the 2011 floods a large group of people in the Rockhampton suburb of Depot Hill refused to leave, despite days of advance warning.

The police did not use their compulsory evacuation powers there, but negotiators were called in. Rockhampton Mayor Brad Carter warned people they could be on their own and emergency services personnel would not risk their own lives to deliver help. He added: 'If these residents want to stay in their homes, that's their decision, we won't force them out. But we want to remind them that the water level will be high for more than one week after the peak, and we will not be able to resupply them.' Despite this warning a handful of residents refused to leave, and later demanded food drops. 'It's not an uncommon story', according to Chas Keys.

Stories of people who have survived floods and sometimes acted heroically, should help people better understand what floods are all about, how best to deal with them and why they should always be taken seriously.

Chas Keys says that Australians' reaction to flooding is 'flawed to the point of being eccentric and self-defeating.

'After a big flood we focus on sympathy, relief and getting people back to something like "normal" as soon as possible. But we don't heed the lessons or use them to ensure that the inevitable next flood causes less pain to the community.

'Thus we allow development to continue largely unabated on floodplains, ensuring that next time there will be even more damage, and we fail to invest appropriately in flood mitigation initiatives such as levees, house-raising or moving dwellings off the lowest parts of floodplains.

'The Brisbane flood of January 2011 peaked about a metre lower than the well-remembered flood of 1974, but it did much more damage — because there were more dwellings in the flooded areas than there had been earlier.

'We complain that the warnings were not as effective as they might have been, but we do little to develop the flood intelligence or help people to understand how they can manage the occasionally undesirable consequences of living on a floodplain.

'The most easily mitigated natural disaster for those of us who live within Australia is rarely well mitigated. Our thinking is primitive and short-term in nature, and it guarantees that we subject ourselves to more pain every time floods occur.

'Nor am I sure the inevitable after-flood enquiries get to the nub of the problem, which is our continued inappropriate and ill-advised use of floodplain land. There are many vested interests which between them ensure that we go on behaving as we always have, guaranteeing that we set ourselves up for more pain and heart-break. That's why I say, as communities we behave in a way that is self-defeating. We tinker with flood management around the edges, but at the same time we exacerbate the problem which makes the management so much more difficult next time.

'Don't get me started on Maitland, which want to put 1700 new dwellings on the floodplain in and around the CBD in areas which were inundated to depths of nearly 5 metres in 1955. That's insanity.'

When the Rivers Roared
Drensmaine and Charleville, Western
Queensland, April 1990

Helen and Len Sargood own Drensmaine, an 8000-hectare
Santa Gertrudis stud on the Landsborough Highway about
fifty kilometres out of Tambo, 900 kilometres west of Brisbane.
Their nearest neighbour on another cattle property is about ten
kilometres away.

The Sargoods are well-known locals, with a somewhat
surprising international reputation: they make teddy bears. In
1990 Helen Sargood and two other local women, Mary Sutherland
and Charm Ryrie, were looking for ways of supporting their
struggling and drought-stricken community. They came up with
the idea of making and selling woollen teddy bears. Since then,
30,000 Tambo Teddies have been sold aross the world. The
enterprise is now one of the biggest employers in the region, and it
brings an enormous amount of revenue to the tiny town of Tambo.

Helen and Len Sargood live between the Nive River and a dirt
track that leads back to the Landsborough Highway. On one side
of the road are horse yards and a machinery shed. The country
— Australia's famous black-soil plains — looks wonderfully fertile
and prosperous, but as Helen Sargood explains, this is deceptive.
'This black-soil country is always changing,' she says. 'After rain
the country becomes quicksand. It feels and looks dry, but as
soon as you walk on it or drive over it, down you go. You can't get
out of it. It's very dangerous.'

The homestead is about 100 metres from the edge of the Nive
River. Surrounded by big old gum trees, as well as brigalow,
gidgee, bottle trees, box, sandalwood and wilga, it looks serene,
more like a sheep property in the Grampians or the Riverina than
an outback cattle station. Away from the homestead and sheds,

the country settles out into cleared undulating downlands for miles around.

The Nive is usually benign. A tributary of the Warrego and 263 kilometres long, it is mostly a series of billabongs that only run together during the wet or monsoon season. And when water comes, there is usually plenty of warning. 'You know when water is coming down because the frogs start to yell,' says Helen. 'The Nive creeps up, a foot or so at a time, giving the water a chance to soak in deep. We never worry: it's a very steady old river.'

There was a time, she says, when the monsoon season would come every year and dump huge amounts of rain on the land around the Nive and Warrego rivers. It was something landholders expected: they had to endure only a few weeks of isolation, and they never felt threatened.

But in April 1990, however, the area was receiving atypically heavy rain. 'It had rained for a few days, and on that afternoon, the 18 April, it was raining very heavily. The water was coming from the Carnarvon Ranges one hundred kilometres to the east.'

There was no warning at Drensmaine. Water broke so quickly out of the Nive that Helen wondered whether a dam upstream had broken. Over the years many graziers had installed massive unauthorised dams, some 100 or even 200 metres across and wide, to harvest the monsoonal floodwaters. The possibility of bursting dams is often on the minds of people who, like the Sargoods, live downstream.

'It rose very quickly. It was up to the fence of our house yard by about three in the afternoon. But then it stopped so I thought, OK, that's it.'

There seemed no danger: the house is on a slight rise, with six steps leading up to the front door and three to the rear. By the time water reaches the back fence of the house, it will already have flooded out for hundreds of metres all around, and for many kilometres along the riverbed. The amount of water required for this to happen is massive, almost beyond comprehension. So, for a short time the Sargoods assumed it would quietly go away. Instead, it started to rise again.

'I went down to the river and poked a stick into the ground to measure the speed of water rising towards the house,' says Helen. The stick disappeared, indicating that water was rising rapidly. 'When it came another metre in the next forty-five minutes into the yard and more than halfway up to the house, I started to get very worried.'

The steady old river was steady no more. The Sargoods and their friend Greg Blair immediately got to work moving items off the floors. Helen's first thought was for the house. 'I opened all the doors because I thought that if the floodwater did come inside it wouldn't meet any resistance, and it would prevent the house from washing away.'

But the water was rising so fast that they quickly changed their approach. 'Len, Greg and I started moving our belongings up to the sand dune. The fridges, the freezer, small bits of furniture all went into our horse float and we took them up to the top of the sandhill.' The bigger furniture could not fit into the float, so had to stay in the house. The sandhill is about 100 metres away, across the track out the front of the house, and behind the stables. It is the only nearby high ground, but it is neither very high nor very stable. It is also totally unprotected.

Darkness was coming on fast: they worked frantically. Helen's beloved pets needed help. 'We've heard horrendous stories about dogs being tied up because they get frantic around floodwaters. Then they drown when their owners forget to untie them.' They moved the pregnant border collie. 'I was worried about the cats, but we couldn't catch them, so we left some furniture in the house for them to climb onto if they returned,' says Helen.

Moving a house full of belongings is not easy. 'We only had those flimsy black plastic bags. So we flung clothes and linen into those.'

By evening the Nive covered hundreds of metres on both sides of the main channels. The water swirled around the house, completely covering the road between the homestead and the sandhill. The water in the natural gullies around the house and sheds was deep and rising fast.

The Sargoods and Greg Blair drove their station vehicles, a panel van and the horse float up to the top of the dune and left them there. Now everything had to be walked up to the sandhill through the fast-flowing menacing water. It was also freezing, which surprised Helen. With the water level still rising, they realised they would have to decide whether to stay in the house or move up to the dune. In the meantime, they were trying to outrun the rising water, still hoping to retrieve as much from the house as possible. But continuing to work was not a sensible decision.

'We were desperate,' says Helen. She snatched clothes off the washing line, realised she could not carry them and decided to throw them into the bathtub. But mud and dirt and sand started coming into the bath from the outside. She tried to stem the inflow, but the water was now coming into the house, and was unstoppable. Moments after it reached the bathroom, it was flooding in the back door, and then came in through the air vents. It was now quite dark, but the electricity remained on. Leaving the house, a familiar safe haven, would not be easy.

Then a neighbour telephoned. 'Colin Clift of Yarndarlo station, about sixty kilometres north, and upstream, called to say this was the highest he had ever seen the river, and that we'd better get out.

'We realised that if more water came down the river, the road would be an impassable gully of water more than two metres deep. We decided the house would not be a safe place to stay. So we took a bag of clothes to keep us warm and a torch, and headed out the front.'

But in the darkness the water held yet another nasty surprise. Helen, who is small, could not cross the road. 'The water was too deep and running too fast. I was scared witless. I didn't think I could get across, so Len and Greg grabbed me under my shoulders and sort of dragged me across the water while I was trying to hang onto the bags and their arms.'

Len Sargood says the water was up to his neck. 'It kept washing our feet out from under us. I was concentrating on getting across the road without being washed away.'

The three struggled in the water, pushing and steadying, moving one foot at a time, sometimes into mud and often finding big holes that had not existed before. In places the water had washed away the soil, exposing boulders, which were then washed away themselves, or were tumbling round. The roots of the gum trees were exposed. What was once a roadway was now a treacherous path. It was the longest three minutes of Helen's life.

Eventually they were pushed up against the horse yards, where they could cling to the rails. As they guided themselves around the edge and up onto the sandhill they began to feel safer. Each step took them higher out of the water. But they were still not out of trouble. It was still raining: they watched the floodwaters rising up and up. It was going to be a miserable night.

They finally reached Greg Blair's panel van and changed into their warm dry clothes. Now they could do nothing but worry and wait. They did not know how high the water would reach. 'You just never say never,' says Len. 'We know the sandhill was put there by the river in the first place, so it could take it away, or make it higher. History has a habit of repeating itself.'

Trapped on the sandhill all night, they heard the big machinery shed collapse. 'When the shed went, all my tools went with it,' says Len. 'I didn't have a pair of pliers, a hammer or any screws or nails to fix anything.'

But as dawn broke, they realised the water was already receding.

This brought no comfort at all. By mid morning, still in shock, they waded back into the water to see what was left of the house. There were five dead bullocks close by, which led them to wonder how many they had died in the paddocks. The road over which they had struggled the previous night had disappeared. The river had taken all the soil away, exposing the roots of the trees. 'We didn't have a road: we had a fifteen-foot drop,' says Len.

In their home, the water had reached the heights of the bench tops. Fences, tanks, garden equipment had been washed away, never to be seen again. Every attempt to straighten things out ran them into serious problems. The power was off. The roads into town were impassable. Ironically, there was no water for the stock. They would have to clean up by hand: backbreaking work.

'We used a board to scrub the water and soil out of the rugs,' says Helen. 'We jumped up and down on the blankets to get the sand out of them, then we'd wring them out and start again.' It sounds simple, but the largest cloth most of us have had to wring out is a wet beach towel. Wringing out heavy woollen blankets can only be done by the sturdiest of people; the work took hours. 'The new carpets looked like old carpets when we'd finished cleaning up, but they lasted ten more years,' says Helen. She and Len slept on the kitchen floor for the first week.

Drensmaine is a working business and Len needed to get the property going again: to feed the animals and keep them off the roads; and to try to resume earning an income to pay for the damage.

All the benches in the toolsheds had collapsed, so there was no workshop space. The grain for the cattle had been soaked, so went to seed and was ruined. A 1200-litre fuel tank, recently refilled, was found months later downstream. The water destroyed a 30,000-gallon water tank and windmill that stood next to it. They lost eight kilometres of fencing.

While the river had brought new topsoil to places, it had washed away pasture that had taken years to sow and nurture. 'There was no soil to stabilise anything,' says Len. More cattle were lost in the black soil quicksand, as they could not be rescued in time. Len came across dead cattle for months afterwards.

The operation to save towns downstream was completed after a few days and governments made promises about immediate compensation to help property owners. But this did not help the Sargoods, who weren't insured for flood damage. 'Well the house had never been flooded before!' said Helen. 'We're not big property owners, but we didn't get the disaster grant because apparently we were too wealthy,' says Len. Their money was all tied up in land or loans. 'Shearers got $3000 for their personal belongings and we were told we'd get nothing.'

Helen saw red. 'I was in a fair state and I went down to the authorities in Charleville and tore strips off them,' she says with some pride. The Sargoods received a small grant and recovery vouchers, but were told they would have to use them to buy whitegoods, furniture and floor coverings. They could not use the vouchers to buy tools or a new water tank. 'We had no running water, so why would I want a washing machine? People should be allowed to decide for themselves how they spend the small amount of compensation they do get.'

It took the Sargoods a year to fix the obvious damage and three years for the property to be profitable again. They thought of moving the house to higher ground, but gave up the idea when told it would cost $18,000 just to move the electricity wiring.

The Sargoods have endured floods since — in 1997 and 2008 — but they had learned by experience and the river did not threaten. But they will never forget their 1990 experience. 'It was very scary,' says Helen. 'And I'm paranoid about floods now.'

The Grungies

In April 1990, Donna Reynolds was in her house in Charleville with her two children, four-year-old Katrina and six-year-old Nicholas. Situated between Bradleys Gully and the Warrego River, the house was trapped when floodwaters began their inexorable rise. Donna's husband Brian, deputy controller of the SES, was not at home: he was helping with rescues and evacuations. Before he could return, water cut off access to the Reynolds' house. As night closed in on the 21st April, Donna was stranded, watching the water move up the sixteen steps from the ground.

'The boats couldn't get across to our side of the gully because the current was too strong,' she says. 'As the night wore on the water came up another step every hour.

'Our neighbours came to us as their houses started going under. They brought their pets. My mother-in-law was ringing every thirty minutes. She was frantic, particularly when the phone lines went out about midnight. She had been evacuated earlier in the evening as her home was inundated.

'Nicholas looked out the back and saw his little trucks floating out from under the house. I told him not to worry, they would stop at the back fence and we'd pick them up in the morning. Little did I know that by morning we would not have a back fence.'

The electricity went off. The house began to tremble as floodwaters swirled around the pillars on which the house stood. 'Eventually the railing of the front steps was shaken off completely,' says Donna. 'A big square steel tank landed in our front yard. Cars were tumbling over each other. Whole houses were being swept away.'

'The kids were disturbed, we were up all night, there were lots of people in the house, and dogs and cats, and water everywhere. And their father wasn't there.

'I kept saying it would all be fine, but they thought their father had drowned in the flood. They asked if their grandmother had gone too. At the same time, Nick was excited by all the dogs and people. He was running from the front door to the back and I was busy making sure he didn't fall into the water.

'When the sun came up, it was like we were in an ocean. There were people on their roofs screaming for assistance. One woman two doors down had a brand new baby and was absolutely hysterical.

'We couldn't help because the water was flowing too fast and there were more than two metres of water outside the door. We could see that everything outside the house was gone, including the fence. The water kept rising and eventually came right up to the floorboards. Nick was upset about his toys and the birds that were drowned, but was thrilled to find fish in the branches of trees.'

The rescue effort was cobbled together in a desperate hurry, with local helicopter musterers working alongside army helicopters to lift people from their roofs. 'We were taken first by a boat driven by two young brothers who lived a few doors down, to a home with a flat roof, which was the only place the helicopter could safely fly people off,' says Donna. 'There were thirty of us from the neighbourhood, huddled together on the roof.'

Donna, who had been calm for the sake of the kids, started to lose her composure. 'I was trying to stop Nicholas running over to the edge of the roof. He yelled, "Look, Mum, there's a sheep!" and this poor bedraggled ram would be swimming in the water, and as it went past it disappeared.'

Katrina was very quiet. She had picked up the terror of the people screaming on the rooftops. 'When we were lifted off the roof, there was no door on the helicopter. I think that experience was worse than the flood. I'll never forget the view of houses completely submerged to the rooftops. And when we got to the airport they had to prise my arms off Katrina, they had completely locked up.

'Brian was waiting for us, distraught. He had thought we were on our own very steeply pitched roof, and he thought we couldn't keep the kids there for long. We had no mobile phones or any way of contacting him.'

The Charleville recovery took years. Families who had been evacuated were dislocated. Money was tight, but gradually the town started to return to normal. But the children still suffered and were traumatised.

'Katrina became very frightened of the sound of the wind for many years afterwards,' says her mother. 'If she was downstairs and the leaves rustled in the trees she'd take off upstairs, get into bed and pull the doona over her head.

'I encouraged her and Nicholas to draw pictures of things like helicopters and the big flood that wrecked their pre-school,' says Donna. Katrina's flood drawings still take pride of place on her grandmother's lounge-room wall.

After the floods, Donna and her friend Michelle Sheehan thought about the traumatised children. 'I worked in the School of Distance Education library,' says Donna, 'and I thought there are no books addressing natural disasters for children. I had some things on my mind, and Michelle had the same idea.'

'People wanted a book for their grandchildren so the floods would never be forgotten,' says Michelle. 'We had the newsagency, and tourists were coming to the shop asking for things about the flood.'

Both women, deeply affected by the flood's impact on their own young children and knowledgeable about things that helped in their recovery, decided to write their own book, with Michelle doing the text and Donna the illustrations. They called it *The Grungies*. 'It's a lighthearted fun approach to the floods,' says Donna. 'Aimed at four- to eight-year-olds.'

It tells the story of alien beings, the Grungies, who appear in Charleville and bring with them all the dislocation of the floods. The Grungies were creatures who lived in water. 'Because if a flood came you could blame the Grungies, it's their fault, that's why we experienced the floods. The Grungies only come into town when it rains,' says Donna.

'We didn't want the book to be scary. We don't use words like *destroyed* or *damaged* or *trapped* or *devastated*. It does avoid being scary.'

She laughs when she describes how the book ends. First the Grungies are imprisoned in the town's water tower, but then they return seven years later (during the 1997 floods). After a town meeting, it is agreed that something must be done.

The solution is to use one of Charleville's tourist attractions: the Steiger Vortex guns. These were shipped from Italy during the great drought of 1902 in the belief that, if aimed at the sky and fired with sufficient velocity, they would disturb atmospheric pressure sufficiently to create rain. They did not, but they still feature in the museum, and are a well-known oddity in the district. 'So the Vortex guns blasted the Grungies out into space to get rid of them,' says Donna.

Other local features are used. 'One of the mascots of the Augathella football team — Augathella's about a hundred kilometres from Charleville — is a meat ant. He came down on the floods from Augathella, and he's hiding in the pages of the book.' The other illustrations reflect the experiences of people in the 1990 floods. Cars are shown floating in the streets, helicopters come and take kids for flights, families are separated.

'When it rains, we can now say we hope the Grungies don't come tonight,' says Donna.

The Grungies proved an enormously popular book in Charleville. It has sold about 4000 copies and has been shipped to family members and friends all over the world. Unlike most disaster books, this one is read to the town's primary schoolchildren. It has proved to be cathartic for the whole community.

For Donna Reynolds, the book reflects a lifetime of love at Charleville. She has come to understand that floods are part of the landscape. 'My family came to this area in 1880,' she says. 'and they saw many droughts. My father told me stories of the 1902 drought which was broken by floods.

'I went to St Mary's boarding school here and a couple of floods went through. I can remember the clothesline with the nuns' undergarments and habits in the water, slowly turning with the flow.'

Michelle Sheehan has also come to grips with the floods. 'The 1990 flood was exceptional,' she says. 'It rained for thirty-nine days before that flood — almost the Bible's forty days and forty nights — and the flood truly was of Biblical proportions.'

Donna adds: 'The day before the flood I was horrified to find a rat in the house. It had been climbing the curtain to reach the ceiling. I'd never seen a rat before. We caught it and took it to the wildlife park, and found out it was a native water rat. So I thought if I ever see a water rat in my house again, I'm heading somewhere where it is very high and dry.'

And Donna Reynolds will stay there until the Grungies have been despatched again.

A Close Run Thing
Newry, Gippsland, Victoria, June 2007

'It started out as a normal day.'

There were mixed feelings at the Maffra offices of Gippsland's Southern Rural Water Corporation. The region had undergone three years of drought, with little rain and record low water allocations for the past twelve months. Now rain was falling steadily, but there was some nervousness: a really big rain event was predicted. The Bureau of Meteorology forecast for 27 June was: 'Rainfall up to 60 millimetres has fallen in the Macalister Catchment upstream of Lake Glenmaggie since midnight and heavy rainfall is continuing. The rain band will persist during today with rainfall totals up to 70 millimetres possible over the next twelve hours. A second prolonged period of heavy rain will develop later tonight with further rainfall totals up to 50 millimetres possible.'

The Macalister River has its headwaters in the forested alpine mountains of the Great Dividing Range and it becomes a river above the tiny hamlet of Licola. The river runs into Lake Glenmaggie, about forty kilometres from Licola. It then joins the Thompson River, then the Latrobe River near the town of Sale, then flows into the Gippsland Lakes and eventually out to sea.

Lake Glenmaggie was once a huge dam by Australian standards. It was built in 1927 to support the local dairy and agricultural areas and to provide water for neighbouring towns. When built, it was the second largest in Victoria; its size further increased after World War II when returning soldiers took up land in the district. Fourteen 'radial gates' were constructed along the top of the original dam wall and capacity increased to 190,000 megalitres. The gates can be raised to regulate the amount of water flowing out of the dam, but would be damaged if water flowed over the top without restriction. In 1987 the dam wall was strengthened by drilling through the wall into the bedrock and installing seventy steel cables.

Lake Glenmaggie is relatively unusual among large water-storage facilities in Victoria in that it fills and spills on average in nine out of ten years. The catchment is large, long and narrow, and during rainstorms it rises and falls rapidly. The lake's floodplain has a large number of depressions and former watercourses. The towns of Tinamba West and Newry are in the middle of the floodplain. The dam at Lake Glenmaggie is primarily for water storage, though it has a role to play in smoothing out flood peaks.

Floods of varying severity are part of the Gippsland landscape. Lake Glenmaggie recorded its first big spill less than a decade after it was built: in 1935 'disastrous flooding' occurred, water spilling out at the rate of 77,000 megalitres a day. In 1971 came the heaviest flooding then recorded, when 110,600 megalitres a day poured out of the dam, causing flooding of all river systems in the region. As a result many of the homes in the region have been built on piles about eighty centimetres high. There was another flood, though less severe, in 1978.

Most people at Newry who heard the Bureau of Meteorology forecasts for 27 June 2007 were not expecting trouble. The town had survived all floods since 1971 without any problems. They knew the flood warden system was in place and expected both the flood wardens and people at the bureau to keep their eyes on developments.

Only a week or two before the rainstorm, in fact, people's minds had been on the continuing drought. In the summer, massive bushfires had scorched 95 per cent of the catchment area. The ground was rock hard, the soil welded by the fierce heat and denuded of all ground cover, twigs, bushes and logs. It is generally agreed that, after a fierce fire, there is little or no soakage for at least three years, which means that in the case of heavy rain, runoff occurs at a damaging rate. But hydrologists estimated that 40 per cent of all water flows would be retained by the regrowth for forty years or more.

Besides, heavy rain would fill Lake Glenmaggie, which was only half full. And so the best outcome of the rainstorm would be moderate flooding. The bureau issued a 'heads up' on the Monday and Tuesday: not a warning, just an encouragement for people, particularly irrigators, emergency authorities and water agencies to prepare for possible flooding.

Large quantities of water started flowing into Lake Glenmaggie at about 11am on Wednesday 27th. Farmers from high in the catchment area began making anxious calls to the Southern Rural Water office and to the Bureau of Meteorology, reporting that the water was 'like 1971'. And Licola County Fire Authority captain Lindsay 'Ralph' Barrowclough, who lived in a valley just out of Licola, was disturbed by what he was seeing.

The rain seemed to form instant rivers as it fell. Hundreds of thousands of fire-blackened trees were washed into the torrents raging in every waterway and valley. Along with rocks and boulders, the timber tumbled into gullies, churning massive waves that ploughed out new rivers and creeks. Bridges were smashed as debris crashed into supports.

'Two-hundred-year-old trees were brought down,' says Ralph Barrowclough, 'right on top of the water measuring gauges.'

According to Clinton Rodda, general manager of water supply at Southern Rural Water, the final gauge failed just before 7pm. 'We don't know why,' he said. 'The inflows were forty to fifty thousand megalitres per day, which is high but not enormously high.'

The only remaining gauge for Rodda and his team to rely on was alongside the dam wall at Lake Glenmaggie, which measured dam heights and therefore inflow. 'As it got later in the evening our measured inflows showed that volumes of water going into the lake were far greater than we had ever seen before,' says Rodda. 'I began to feel apprehensive, not because I thought any of our facilities would fail, but just because we didn't know how much water would come down the river and what damage it might cause.

'It's a flashy catchment, which means we got a surge of water four to six hours after the rainstorm. We would make a decision every hour about how much water was likely to go into the dam, and if we'd have to let some out, and how much.'

On the morning of 27th, the dam held about 100,000 megalitres of water. By midnight the storage held 145,000 megalitres and water was being released. It was a phenomenal downpour, the likes of which had not been experienced before. Rodda says the people in the control room watched in disbelief.

'There had never been more than 110,000 megalitres a day discharged from Lake Glenmaggie,' says Rodda. 'We saw the rapid rise of the water levels and made a judgment about when the dam would fill and start overflowing. By eleven that evening, we knew we would have a major flood event.'

The timing and volume of water releases from the dam have always been crucial. Care needs to be taken to avoid sudden flooding, usually of rivers and creek banks, and water moving at high speed destroys fences, roads and bridges and washes away stumps under houses very quickly. It is extremely dangerous. 'When we knew we would be releasing water at levels that would cause flooding, we wanted to try not to let the largest quantity of water out in the middle of the night,' says Rodda. 'We think it is very important to avoid a severe night-time flood if we can — it's when people are less likely to respond quickly to the floodwaters.

'Our primary role is to manage the dam. We called the police and the State Emergency Service. We told them what we were seeing — the largest inflows ever. We told them the dam could fill and spill probably in the morning. We had to make everybody understand that we had never seen these flows before, and that we were worried about their size.'

The inflows were going off the scale. As the Southern Rural Water team made their calculations, the hydrographs kept rising. 'We were in awe of what we were seeing,' says Rodda.

Meanwhile, ABC Local Radio regional program manager Gerard Callinan at Sale was on duty all night, breaking into nationally networked overnight programs to keep listeners in touch. He was prepared to broadcast possible flood warnings. He took a phone call from a person claiming to be from the State Emergency Service, advising that water would be released from Lake Glenmaggie at a rate that would cause a 'major flood'. This person declined to be identified, saying he was not an authorised spokesperson for the SES.

Without caller identification or confirmation from authoritative sources, Callinan could not broadcast the information. He called the SES media office, but only got voicemail, so left a message requesting confirmation. The police had no information about the flooding. Callinan continued to search for someone to confirm the report, but until he found such a person he could only continue to give out warnings from the Bureau of Meteorology, which predicted 'moderate to major flooding downstream of Lake Glenmaggie'. It was a warning that gave nothing like the required context. And so it was many hours before ABC Local Radio knew what was going on at Newry.

As planned, the Southern Rural Water team released water in ever increasing quantities: 50,000 megalitres at 4.30am, 73,000 at 5.30am, 140,000 megalitres at 6.30am. For the first time in the dam's history, all gates were fully open. The reservoir was at full supply level, and rising.

As dawn broke the rivers and creeks were already full. Joe Matthews, an engineer and manager of Headwater Assets, had come down from Melbourne to replace a couple of the local engineers who were doing a training course there. He knew how concerned the Southern Rural Water people and others in authority were and, aware that the roads would soon be cut, he drove up to the dam. He could not believe his eyes.

'When I first saw the water coming over the spillway it was a sight to behold,' he said. 'The turbulence was far greater than I had imagined. The water comes down over the sill at angles, and the water flumes crash into each other. At that point near the bottom of the dam wall, waves were leaping six or seven metres into the air.

'The noise was louder than anything I had ever experienced. I could see the roof and walls had been smashed off the power station. It was quite incredible.'

Matthews did an inspection of the structure and found it was performing well. Seepage was coming through old cracks in some areas, but not in great quantities, and this was consistent with normality. He went to inspect the gallery at the bottom of the dam wall that allows operators to walk into the dam and check on seepage and instrumentation. Even inside the gallery, below ground and enclosed by several metres of concrete, he could hear the roar of the water going over the spillway. 'The gallery had flooded five or six metres deep,' he says, 'and there were tiny vibrations I hadn't felt before.'

This was worrying, but the main concern was that one of the pressure relief drains drilled into the foundation was spouting water about one metre into the air — water that was being pushed up from underneath the dam wall. 'Imagine the dam wall is a slab of concrete standing upright on a big rock,' says Matthews. 'The water upstream of the concrete exerts a force on the wall that would push it over or cause it to slide downstream if the concrete block does not have the weight, or the bond with the foundation rock, to resist it.

'But water also seeps under the dam and exerts an upwards pressure on it, and this can cause the dam to become buoyant. Excessive foundation pressure has been known to result in dams collapsing.'

At Glenmaggie Dam, a number of measures had been taken to guard against this, including the grouting of the foundation to reduce seepage, installation of steel cable anchors to hold the dam to its foundation, and the drilling of pressure relief wells, allowing water that seeps into the foundation to escape and be safely discharged. Joe Matthews was convinced that the water coming from the foundation was not a threat to the dam, but he called the dam engineers at Snowy Mountains Engineering and got it confirmed anyway. He was reassured to hear there was no cause for alarm.

But he didn't realise that none of the town residents in Newry had been warned there would be flooding.

Newry is a tidy little dairy town with a population of about a hundred people. The narrow main road runs northeast through the town: most homes and properties on the road are below road level. A small bridge crosses the Newry Creek 200 metres to the north. On the west side of the road is the pub, a butcher's shop and a few homes. Most of the residential blocks are on the south-eastern side of the main road. As is common in Gippsland towns, there is a Country Fire Authority shed, housing one truck. There is no school in the town, no police force. And, crucially in 2007, no State Emergency Service volunteer crew. Even though the town was built in the middle of a floodplain downstream from a lake, present Newry residents had not experienced any particular problems. Consequently there was no planning or community activity around possible flooding.

A dry gully or lagoon, once part of the river itself, runs through the eastern side of the town: it became the site of a car park and a children's playground. Nobody was precious about property boundaries: homes backed onto the lagoon, separated from it only by a few rusty sheets of tin or straggling timber paling or wire fences. There were other gullies and lagoons, which were known to fill up to two or three metres in heavy rainfall, but were mostly dry and dusty.

Brian Weatherly, born in Newry in 1934, has been watching the movements and changes in the river and lagoons after every flood for many years. 'Once people wouldn't settle on the flats for fear of flooding,' he says. 'In the early days people lived in the hills, but they got burned out by bushfires and gradually they came into town.

'There are hundreds of little gullies in and around the town now. There have always been floods, some more serious than others. My father used to talk about the big flood of 1935, when haystacks floated down the main road with chooks on top. The river changed its pathway that year. There was another big flood in the 1950s when the Macalister River and Newry Creek both filled and the water came into the town.'

The severity of the floods decreased as time passed, and people in Newry became a little complacent. The dam was seen as a mitigation device; and most homes were set up on small piles anyway. 'I can't recall the shire ever setting any flood levels for building codes,' says Weatherly. 'And in 2006 the shire cleared thousands of willow trees from the banks of the creeks and gullies. I always thought they used to stop the water flowing quickly.'

Dairy farmers Wayne and Leah Brunt, who live about four kilometres west of town, have a property of 440 acres with a herd of around 360. 'We live and earn our money on a floodplain,' says Wayne Brunt. 'That's what makes Newry so good. The water improves the pasture.

'When we came to this house the owner showed us where the water had gone in the most recent flood. They explained we needed to understand what heights the water would reach if a certain amount of water was released from the dam. We knew that a 35,000-megalitre release would cause a fair bit of inundation on the property; the house would be surrounded by water if they ever got a flood anywhere near the biggest — which we thought was about 75,000 megalitres.'

At 2am the flood warden, Peter Gault, warned the Brunts that there would be some flooding. Leah Brunt says: 'We put some tools and equipment on a higher level in the shed and though it was dark, we could see the river rising fast. The roar of the water told us that something big was happening.

'By dawn we could see water everywhere, covering every paddock.'

At 7am they decided to get their two children, Hayden, 13 and Lachlan, 11, off the property. Leah took them to the home of friends Jacquie and Mick Thorn, who lived between their farm and Newry. 'I was better off out of it,' she says. 'I could hear the calves calling to each other, they were separated by the floodwaters and had found some higher ground. I was hoping they wouldn't try to get back to each other … they would have drowned.' As they drove away, Leah heard the relentless and menacing hum of fast-moving water all around. The sea of water had not only flooded the paddocks but, she said, 'seemed to be following us up the road'. Wayne stayed in the house and was quickly marooned.

The first sign of real trouble came at about 8am, when two young men in a car were washed off a small bridge into the Newry Creek. The water quickly filled the car, and the young men were stranded on the roof. They called the Country Fire Authority for help.

Clearly floodwaters were on the rise and, not having a local police or SES crew, alarmed Newry residents called the Country Fire Authority volunteers. Karen Whitehurst and her husband Mark were the CFA brigade leaders. They live out of town in the nearby hills and back then knew little about Newry or its residents. Mark was on his way to Sale, so Karen called him and asked him to get the truck. He picked her up and they headed into town. Mark dropped Karen off in town and drove off to pick up the crew. He called Bull Linaker, a reliable longtime member of the CFA and a man with a forthright view of the world.

Bull and his wife Kay, were aware of the possibility that the region could get continuing heavy rain, estimated on the radio as 'up to 200 millimetres'. They had also heard reports that water would be released from the dam. 'I was expecting some sort of minor to moderate flood,' says Bull, 'maybe something affecting paddocks, maybe the back and front yards, blocking off a few roads for a short time.'

There were no reports of overnight flooding on the radio and, after breakfast, Kay went outside to check the state of the paddocks. 'I couldn't believe it,' she says. 'I thought, hell that's wide, and full on. There was a roar, like the ocean. Then I realised that timber was crashing and smashing full-grown gum trees, fences. Everything was being ripped apart in the creek.'

Bull said: 'You get used to seeing floods after a while in Gippsland, but the Newry Creek overflow was something special. It was like a wall of water, and it was coming down fast, smashing full-grown trees in its path.

'I realised that water was now out of the creek and coming up towards the house.'

Kay moved the goats from the front yard to higher ground, but the water kept coming. A few minutes later she had to shift them again. Sensing danger, the goats broke free and jumped into the small stock trailer in the front yard. Kay was not able to help the calves in the rear paddock: they would have to fend for themselves.

At that stage Bull did not think the water would cause too many problems within the house, but as a precaution he lifted some of the furniture onto tables. When he received a call from the CFA to ask for help in rescuing the young men stranded in Newry Creek, he had no hesitation in leaving Kay behind.

She calmly turned the power off and waited. 'I wasn't worried about the water or our possessions,' she says. 'You can replace those things as long as everybody's still alive.' She was quickly marooned in the house with her two cats, Jamieson and Bubbles. 'They didn't like the water much!' she says. 'They were yelling, jumping on chairs then on the kitchen table.'

The cats knew something the Linakers didn't: the water was continuing to rise. Within a few minutes of Bull's departure, water twenty-five to thirty centimetres deep was flowing through their house. 'It was carrying a lot of sticks and leaves and gumnuts from the trees,' says Kay. 'I thought I might as well open the back door to let it go straight through.

'I wasn't too worried. I had gumboots on. It was clear that I wouldn't be able to stop the water, so I read a book, because I couldn't do anything else. It was *The Stockman* by Rachael Treasure.'

Kay didn't think of calling friends and neighbours: she lived on the edge of the river and didn't for a moment think the water would spread throughout the rest of the town.

'I was now very fearful of what would happen next.'

In her low-set home in Newry's main street, Lisa Reeves climbed out of bed after a good night's sleep. That day she intended to go shopping in Sale 32 kilometres away.

She heard men's voices in the street, but apart from that all was quiet. Then she went to the window to see what was happening. She says: 'I saw some utes out the front, first of all, and when I looked to the right I saw the water across the road near the bridge, about a 100 metres away. The road was already covered in brown water and it was coming towards the house very quickly. I started to get a bit worried.'

Lisa's home sits on stumps 60 centimetres above the ground. There are three steps down to ground level in the front, but the rear faces a steeply declining block that runs into the billabong behind neighbouring houses.

'My first thought was that the dam wall had broken,' says Lisa. 'I tried to call people, but there was no phone reception. I went to the car to get it out of the way, but the water was above the wheels and I didn't think it would move. By now the front yard was rapidly filling with water.'

Lisa thought the water would enter her property from the street out the front and so became quite disoriented when she saw more water out the *back* of her house. Newry Creek had flooded around the back of the town and had filled the lagoons and low-lying areas at the rear of Lisa's block. Water was coming at her from all directions.

She started to panic, confused by the direction of the water, its relentlessness, and the cold. Floodwater is rarely warm: most people are surprised by how cold it is and how strongly it can flow. 'Ten minutes after I first saw water in the street out the front, it was coming into the house. The whole backyard was completely covered in water'. Lisa did not have a plan.

'I just wanted to find a way to get out,' she says. 'I stepped off the verandah out the back and tried walking across the yard, but the water flow was too strong. I got back onto the verandah just as the water started coming inside the back door.' The river water was filthy, carrying stumps, grasses, trees and rubbish.

The house represented Lisa's best hope of staying safe. She went to the bedroom to put on some day clothes and, as she hurried out water was starting to rise through the toilet and shower in her en suite. 'I knew it was rising in the whole house, there was too much water for me to try and stop it,' she says. 'I decided I'd have to swim to the neighbour's house. I'm a good swimmer, but it looked really difficult. There was nothing I could have done. And now I could smell the sewage.'

At that moment Bull Linaker and Mark Whitehurst arrived in the CFA truck to find Lisa staring out the front window.

'They yelled, "Do you want to come out?" So I picked up my Jack Russell terrier, Woof — he can say his own name! — and headed for the front door.

'The water was across the front verandah and at least sixty or seventy centimetres deep. They drove right up to the front window and I climbed onto the truck from there.' As she did so, there was a massive cracking sound and a big tree in the front yard broke off and smashed across Lisa's fence. It had been there for more that one hundred years.

The CFA fire-truck set off to rescue the young men on the car washed into the creek. But they were unable to get through the water at the other end of town, so they called on a couple of farmers who agreed to use their tractor as a flood rescue vehicle. 'We had no training in flood rescue,' says Bull Linaker. 'We tried a few things that seemed to work, though.'

Other local residents were in a similar situation, including Anne and Keith Bartlett.

The Bartletts lived in the lowest house on the main street, backing right onto the gully. They had been dairy and cattle farmers in the district all their lives and now, in retirement, Anne was still busy. Keith was frail, suffering from Parkinson's disease, and Anne was his carer. Her brother Bill Napier and his wife Pauline were visiting from Mornington Peninsula, staying in their caravan parked behind the house.

On the Wednesday morning, they were all having breakfast as normal. Anne says: 'We saw a couple of cars go down the street rapidly, so we looked out the front of the house to see what was going on. There it was, all this water heading towards us. The lad next door had a goat tied up and I saw someone wading through waist-deep water towing a goat behind them. But nobody said anything to us.'

Bill Napier received a call from a mate in another town who had heard on ABC Radio that minor to moderate flooding was forecast for Newry. He asked Anne whether he should get the car and his caravan out of the paddock. Because water had never affected their house in the past, Anne said no.

But then they saw water coming towards them in a wave. Bill rushed to hook up the caravan. 'I had just put the van on the tow ball,' he recalls. 'Didn't worry about the shackles or wiring or the towing hitches. And drove out the gate. The car got just past the gate but then the water hit the van, and it was pushed sideways onto the gate post. The bumper on the van was stuck, and the Ford's wheels were just spinning.'

Bill watched in disbelief as the water immediately rose up higher than the handles on the doors. 'I remembered that our cat Chloe was in the van, and I wanted to get my phone and camera,' he says. He hopped on top of the van, broke a hole in the canvas pop top, climbed inside and rescued the cat and his electrical items.

Bill realised that the water was deep everywhere. He reasoned that he would be best off if he stayed on the roof of the van. However, he did not know whether he would be able to be rescued. He tried to call out to Anne and Pauline in the house, but they were unable to hear him; his mobile phone did not work. Bill sat for a while taking pictures, capturing the image of the 60- to 70-centimetre-high wave of water as it advanced across the paddocks.

Inside the house there was real worry. 'I came to warn Keith that we were in trouble,' says Anne, 'and I saw a river of dirty water coming down the front verandah. It was a real shock to see that. I realised there was absolutely nothing we could do.

'The water came around the front door and immediately through the windows, which were open. The water was up to our knees in a matter of minutes.

'I came in to put drawers up on the table and to get some antique things out of the cupboard and put them up high. I wanted to save a pansy jug, handed down over generations, and cake plates, and I grabbed books from the entry hall.' Anne is a stoic woman who is not given to panic.

'I tried to move things for about five minutes but it was pretty futile. Then I realised I had to organise Keith. He was sitting at the kitchen table in the water and couldn't move.' Pauline stayed with the now bewildered Keith, holding him for comfort.

Anne considered trying to get him on top of the pool table, but decided that was a bad idea. 'It was in front of a huge window, and I was frightened the water would break through and wash us all out.' The water was now above their knees and it was difficult for Anne and Pauline to move — and Keith could not walk unaided.

Anne thought she heard Bill calling and went out to the back door to find out what he was doing. The moment she opened the door a surge of water rushed inside: 'To this day I don't know how I shut it,' she says. She did not see Bill.

Anne waded to the phone and managed to call triple zero. But when she asked to be rescued she was horrified to hear the operator say they probably couldn't send anyone immediately. 'I told them I had a very sick husband, but they said they couldn't get in,' says Anne. 'We thought, well, they can't get to us, we'll just have to wait. I thought we'd need a helicopter to winch us out.

'The water was still rising, and roaring so hard we couldn't hear ourselves talk. We decided we would have to get onto the roof somehow: the back verandah seemed the best place to do that. I tried wading through the water in the backyard to get a ladder from the shed, but it was flowing too fast and was dangerous.'

Anne and Pauline dragged tables onto the back verandah, put one on top of another and tried to work out how they would get Keith onto them and then up on the roof. To prevent Keith from being washed away, they tied him to the back verandah post.

They saw the car and van perched on the gatepost, but Bill was nowhere to be seen. Cold, frightened and desperately worried, they breathed a sigh of relief when they saw a dinghy apparently heading their way. 'There were two fellows in the boat,' says Anne, 'but they were looking for livestock, not us.' Anne, Keith and Pauline were stranded on the back verandah; Bill had disappeared and no help was coming. They called and called. People heard them, but nobody could help. Everybody was dealing with their own problems.

Pictures taken by Bill with time stamps on them, show Anne's ordeal had taken just 20 minutes to unfold.

Don and Christa Dwyer, both in their mid-forties, lived with their two young sons at the other end of town opposite the other main billabong or gully. When dry it was about two metres deep and more than 50 metres long. A neighbour had fenced it off and planted fruit trees in it.

Don, a pump mechanic who works on irrigation equipment, has lived and worked on properties most of his life. He knew that the rain would create fast flows in the river, but when he went outside that morning, he was astonished. 'Water was running through the gully at the bottom of the property,' he said. 'It was a thirty or forty-megalitre flow, the sort you see running through a big irrigation channel. I called my son Jim and told him to get his mother so she could look at this! It was amazing.'

Christa went running out in her dressing gown. 'I saw what looked like a big wave. I've heard of not camping in a riverbed because it could flood overnight and suddenly I could see why. This water came from nowhere. It filled up the gully in an instant.'

Don's first thoughts were for other people. The water was still 50 metres away in the gully, and he was worried about his neighbour's pump. 'I saw the gully fill up and his pump was sitting on the edge of the bank and all I could do was think that I should go over and tell the neighbours they might lose their pump,' he said. But the water was coming closer and faster and it was headed for the Dwyers' home. Don started to feel they were in danger. 'It occurred to me that once the gully filled up, the water had nowhere to go.'

Christa was also sensing danger. 'From the other side of our property, the lower side, I saw the neighbour's little above-ground pool get washed away like a beach toy. And their shed was half under water.' Christa is a nurse educator who knows how to deal with emergencies and she reacted quickly. 'When I saw the pool move I yelled to our boys to get onto the verandah so they wouldn't get washed away. It was coming as fast as that.'

The Dwyer verandah is more than a metre above the level of the backyard on a sloping block. It looked safe but the water was appearing in places nobody could ever have imagined, and it was difficult to think ahead.

Christa ran inside and unplugged the electric fence, telling her sons not to leave the house. The water was still coming up very fast and the chairs in the barbecue area began to float away.

Don and Christa saw a neighbour, Clare Shingles, on the main street, watching as the water went past her house, and they waved. As they did so, the water flow turned and headed for their home.

Christa asked Don what he thought was likely to happen. 'He said he didn't know and I thought, this is how people die,' said Christa. 'They hesitate.

'So I told the boys to get their bags and school bags and pack their gear and to get on the carport roof. Sammy grabbed jocks, I grabbed tracky dacks. Jim grabbed his teddy, a scout blanket and other little treasures.

'I went into ambulance mode, danger response. I thought, I need a tent, water, food, essential papers. I got our photo albums and went through a small checklist ... ticked off food, water, accommodation, documents.'

Only a few minutes before, Christa had seen water flowing across the main street, a few centimetres deep. Now, as she looked, a bigger wave arrived and suddenly there was enough water to float a medium-sized rainwater tank. Water was knee deep at the front of their home, much deeper in the backyard, and rising fast.

Christa headed for the roof of the carport. 'We couldn't go anywhere else,' she said. Getting up there was something of a trial in itself. The two boys were lifted easily enough, but the ladder wasn't quite long enough for Christa, and she could not get enough momentum to clamber up by herself. 'So I got Sammy to put his arms around Jim's waist, and told him to just sit back. I grabbed Jim and told him to hang on. Don was on the ladder below. On the count of three Sam pulled on Jim, Jim pulled on me and Don pushed from below.'

Don laughed. 'It was a wonder she didn't end up over the other side. It sounds funny now; it sure wasn't at the time. But it worked.'

Don decided not to join them on the roof straight away. 'I thought I'd try to stop the water with rolled towels under the doors, and was trying to seal the whole place up. But the water started coming up through the floorboards on the corner of the house. For a while I was a very busy man. First I tried to move the bottom drawers. Then all the shoes from the bottoms of wardrobes, and I folded up the bedding on all the beds.

'I had a job to save the piano and organ. It was hard to know what to put things on. I put chairs face to face and stacked lounge chairs on them, and stuff on the lounge chairs. And then I put the couch on a coffee table and the pouffe upside down on top.'

On the roof, Christa was very worried. 'I was constantly calling Don on the mobile. As soon as I got onto the roof I asked myself, Is it appropriate to call triple zero? Is it really that much of an emergency? It was weird. I couldn't tell if we were really in danger. I could hear screaming down the gully, and felt really distressed because I couldn't help these people. I could hear the Bartletts calling for help from their verandah. They were under much deeper water than us, but there was nothing I could do.

'Jim was upset because he thought he was going to lose his dad. I told him, "You know how much he hates water, and he can climb through the manhole like a monkey if he has to. He'll be all right." But I wasn't sure.'

She decided that, yes, the flooding was an emergency. Triple zero operators said they would get the SES out to them in a boat, and she could do nothing but wait. 'The kids were getting cold, and I remember thinking I could put the tent up and manage here for several days if I had to. But I thought it would be better for the kids if we got off the roof ...'

In the house, with water 30 centimetres deep, Don was wondering what had happened. He thought the wall of the dam might have been broken. 'With no warning, and water coming in like that with just two inches of rain in the town, I wondered if the wall at the dam was broken.'

His efforts to save furniture and to reassure Christa were interrupted by a call from Adrian Smits, his neighbour from across the road, who needed help to get his boat going. He intended to rescue people. Don waded through the floodwaters up to his waist to see what he could do and found Adrian frantically trying to start the little outboard. Don admits that at the time his relationship with his neighbour could have been better, but he put the past to one side as he saw what was needed. 'I pulled the choke out — I didn't do much — and the boat started. He invited me to jump in.'

But Don's calf, which had been forced to swim, had become entangled in the top wires of the fence. Don was worried about it and so he stayed behind. Adrian took off up the back lanes in his small boat, the only rescue vessel in town.

In the main street the Dwyers' neighbour Clare Shingles was home with her young son. Her husband Brad, a waste carter and general goods transport driver had gone to work collecting rubbish in Maffra at about five that morning. She said: 'We always get a bit of floodwater in the backyard when it rains very heavily here. Mum called and asked if we got any extra flooding. I went out the back to check on the rear of the house and only saw a little puddle.

'I was still talking to Mum when our son interrupted my conversation and asked if I had seen the water out the back. He sounded insistent so I told Mum to hang on and went out to investigate. Water was up to the top of the fence!

'I said to Mum, "There goes our pool," and she said, "I told you not to put it there!"'

Clare, still unperturbed by the water, wandered out to see what was happening in the main street. She saw the first trickle of water come out of the river 200 metres away. 'The boys from the pub across the road were watching what was going on,' she said 'I told them I'd give them fifty dollars and a kiss if they drove our two cars to higher ground for me. They didn't take up the offer, but asked if I was sure I'd be all right. I said we'd be fine.'

But water had rapidly swirled into the house and Clare was soon walking in water up to her thighs. 'After about fifteen minutes I couldn't feel my legs, the water was so cold,' she says. 'My calves were cramping, I thought I was in the first stages of hypothermia.'

Her husband Brad heard what was happening in Newry, realised he should be home, swapped trucks at the depot and came back in a tray top with an empty shipping container on the rear. He was stopped at the bridge on the edge of town by a road block manned by a policeman who was talking to the driver of a fire truck. 'I said I had to go and rescue my family and he said he didn't know whether the bridge was safe,' recalls Brad. 'The bridge was underwater by that stage. But I had a seventeen-tonne truck with a big container on the back, and I thought I would be OK.'

The policeman waved the fire truck through; and Brad thought that his own vehicle had more clearance than the truck and was probably not much heavier. But still he hesitated as he watched the truck plough through the water. He was contemplating his options when he had a call from Clare. 'She shouted! "Bloody come and get me!" she was saying.'

Brad drove home as fast as he could. He soon discovered that the road he had lived on for years was not as flat as it looked. 'As I drove up the main street I realised that I didn't know where all the dips in the road were. Sometimes the water was very deep.

'I got to the house and realised how dangerous it was. Two young blokes were trying to get across the road. They started to cross and stepped into the gutters: the water was above their shoulders.'

Inside the Shingles' house, darkened without electricity, the scene was appalling. 'The steel wood heater was floating!' says

Brad. 'The beanbags had floated across the room and were touching the heater, and had started to melt. All the furniture was wet. We grabbed the TV, our photo and wedding albums, the kids' kindergarten work and their school reports, and all four got on the back of the truck.'

They left two cars parked alongside the house, picked up the men at the pub and drove through metre-deep floodwaters to the high part of town, where everyone got off — relieved, wet, exhausted and alarmed by what they had just experienced.

Another bewildered couple, Keith Towns and his wife Lila, were having breakfast and getting ready for the day. They had planned to spend the day at home: low to moderate flooding had been forecast and the roads around town might be cut, so if they left Newry they might not be able to return.

As Lila was washing up the breakfast dishes a neighbour called. He asked Keith to move the irrigation pump in his paddock before it was damaged by low-level floodwater. Keith agreed, got into the car and had reversed out of the driveway when his neighbour Mike asked him what he was doing.

'I told him I was going to move the neighbour's pump before the water got too deep,' says Keith. 'Mike said he thought it was too late, the flood had already arrived.

'We could see the water rising, then the water started coming out of my shed, under the roller door. It wasn't raining, there was no noise, just this water rushing out of the shed,' he says. 'I tried to move the equipment in the shed. I had a compressor but the water was rushing so fast I was battling to keep it upright. I didn't have time to move all the freezers and fridges or other tools. It would have been less than fifteen minutes from the moment I walked outside to when the water was thirty centimetres deep all round us.'

Keith and Lila hitched their car and caravan up and drove to a nearby hill on the edge of town. They had to drive across a gully and Keith said, 'I could hear and feel the water under the car. We ended up getting water on the floor of the caravan.' They had been away for only a few minutes and when they returned to switch off the electricity they were just in time to see water enter their home.

'The fence out the back was flattened. I came inside and grabbed some towels to place under the doors, but they immediately got soaking wet,' says Lila. 'Keith suggested opening the doors to all the cupboards to prevent them breaking if they expanded as they soaked up the water. We opened all the other doors to let the water go straight through.

'I threw the bedding on top of the beds, then I had to get out.' Keith and Lila went to a neighbour's home — Joan Robinson — and waited for about three hours while the water took over their town. 'We were all in shock,' says Lila. 'I remembered that we'd been through it all before, thirty years ago, and couldn't believe we'd copped it again.'

'We thought the dam had gone.'

Every home in the centre of Newry had to be evacuated and so did many dairy farms. The SES, police and CFA did not have boats, equipment or staff trained to do the job. They could not make a plan: water was still rising in consecutive waves, each deeper than the last, and nobody in the town had any warning or understanding of what might happen next.

Eventually the SES found two flood boats, which they brought to the bridge on Newry Creek. However, the volunteers said the situation was too dangerous for them to be used. Outboard motors could snag on submerged fences and there was a danger that they would be capsized by trees and other debris. In some places the water was too turbulent for the outboards to hold direction. And so the boats remained on the road and were not used; the SES volunteers were therefore trapped outside Newry.

The CFA truck was more effective. It collected about sixty people, including Bill Napier, marooned on the roof of his caravan. He grabbed Chloe the cat, jumped off the caravan roof and battled through waist-deep fast-flowing water to reach the truck. The house with Anne, Keith and Bill's wife Pauline, was only about 20 metres away, but he was unable to reach them, and the truck had to back out quickly or risk being stuck and useless. 'The water had reached the windowsills, but the house looked sound and I thought the family inside would be safe,' says Bill. He looked back at the car and caravan wedged solidly on the gate post and thought they wouldn't move.

Bull Linaker, on the CFA truck, remembers the frustration of knowing people were in their homes and there was no way he could help them. 'We weren't trained and we didn't have the equipment,' he says.

'The water was belting the truck and we lost a couple of jerrycans off the back. Water was up to the back of the tray, about a metre and a half off the ground; and often when we drove into a dip the headlights would be flooded. We were lucky this happened during the day and not at night, or we would have lost lots of people for sure.'

Bull and Mark Whitehurst dropped everybody off at the CFA shed, which was higher than the rest of the buildings in town, and therefore became the first flood evacuation centre. Mark's wife Karen was in charge at the shed as they dropped people there, although she had never done anything like this before. But the water kept rising and there were fears that it would flood the CFA shed, so then everyone moved to an empty block beside the local shop. 'It didn't have any shelter or phone, and no water and no toilets.' says Karen, 'I thought we should stay in the CFA shed which gave a bit of protection from the elements and was warm. But the bosses on the radio said there was nowhere for the helicopters to land near the CFA shed, and they told us to find another place.'

RAAF and police helicopters were now responding to frantic calls from dozens of people stranded on farms and in their homes. Of those on high ground, few were in immediate danger of drowning provided they stayed where they were. But the water had risen extremely quickly and was still rising, so most people who asked to be rescued judged that the water would eventually overrun them.

In floods, older and weaker structures begin giving way; trees with waterlogged roots start toppling over. The tonnes of debris washing up on fences, walls and other barriers eventually smashes them. Escape routes seem impassable. This is a dangerous time in a flood-affected community, the time when panic can take over. Mass panic does occur when people realise that escape routes are blocked.

Emergency agencies fear this panic point because people start to take matters into their own hands. Their need to do something often leads them to take appalling risks. It is for this reason that flood experts try to evacuate people who live behind levees or who will be isolated by floodwaters well before the emergency peaks.

But people have a strong attachment to their homes. Clare and Brad Shingles abandoned their home, leaving in a truck with a small quantity of furniture. 'We thought we should help people,' says Clare, 'but there was no way of getting back in, once we left.' It is a regret she still carries with her, a case of 'survivor guilt' that affects many people in disasters of various kinds.

Panic was setting in, frustrating every effort to organise an orderly evacuation. And reliable information was hard to come by. Then suddenly the word went around that the dam wall was about to collapse.

Everyone in town heard some version of this story. At the dairy farm down the end of Factory Lane, Wayne Brunt, who had decided to stay in his house, suspected that all could be lost. He called triple zero and asked for help. 'They said they would send a helicopter, and I saw it fly over three times, but it kept going every time. Eventually I realised they weren't going to pick me up.' Wayne watched as the helicopters winched people from their homes nearby. 'I started to wonder if I'd made the right decision to stay.'

He became increasingly anxious. He knew he was safe and, unless he did something reckless, he was not really in danger of being injured. But doubt began to gnaw away at common sense and sap resilience. Had he done the right thing by staying? He had tied his Hungarian Vizsla dogs Remy and Kirby in a boat and put some tools in there as well. He thought about the cows that would need to be milked in the afternoon and how they would suffer mastitis and other physical damage if not milked. He watched cows stranded along the fences hunt for dry ground, saw massive logs in the water and was sad to see one of his bulls float past, dead.

Meanwhile, people at the Newry evacuation zone were shouting and making demands that Karen 'the evacuation officer' couldn't answer. At one stage there was a danger that anxiety would turn to panic and there would be violence.

Karen Whitehurst was doing her best. It was hard, because she knew few of the residents. She and her husband Mark had been drafted into the situation because there was nobody else, but they did not understand what was happening. They were 'command and control', but were unable to give reassuring information and advice because they had none.

The extent and severity of the floodwaters continued to fuel speculation and disbelief. 'At three in the afternoon the CFA came to where we were staying with our friends on Factory Lane,' says Leah Brunt. 'They told us we had to evacuate because the dam wall was going to break.' Leah recalls going up to the helicopter loading zone in tears, worried about Wayne, who was still at the farm. 'Someone called the water authority and they told us the dam would be fine. I calmed down after that.'

It would have been useful had that information been given to other people in Newry.

Helicopters were being used to ferry people from their homes to the high ground and, if necessary, to the hospitals in Sale or Maffra about 20 minutes away. The helicopters kept disappearing and Karen had little idea where they had gone or for how long.

Lisa Reeves stayed in town for most of the day, not wanting to be evacuated before the elderly or the children. 'We sat down beside the shop until seven-thirty that night,' she says. 'It was cold, actually freezing.' They lit a fire for warmth.

'People were panicking. Late in the afternoon some started to get really annoyed. A couple had to be told to wait their turn, like the rest of us.'

Concern turned to disbelief when the RAAF announced that they would not allow pets on their helicopters. The police helicopter crew made no such order, so many opted to stay with their animals, despite the cold and threat from rising water: two young girls arrived in the shelter with two boxer dogs and a bag full of newborn puppies.

'People say we didn't do enough,' says Bull Linaker. 'Mark, me and young Josh Clarke were in the truck when we got a call about some people stuck in Factory Lane. We knew we would have to get through a fair bit of water to get to them, and we couldn't take the risk. People in Factory Lane needed to get out but the chopper never came. It was a communications failure: the chopper saw people standing outside the factory on the corner there and realised they were all right, but they didn't go further down the lane.

'We went to help some people on the Maffra Road. They had tried to get through the water in a four-wheel-drive ute, but got stuck in a low spot that washed them off the road and they were sitting on the bonnet. We didn't know how much higher the water was going to rise, but we were getting pager messages and radio reports saying the worst was still to come.

'Anyway, we turned the truck around and reversed through the water, not knowing if there was road underneath. They jumped on. We had to leave their vehicles there.'

The CFA had to set up its own priorities, says Linaker. 'We were getting messages that people were stuck everywhere. Elderly people and kids were our priority and we got them out first. We had one person in a wheelchair; and we got him into the truck and put him into a chopper. It is very difficult to get a person in a wheelchair into a fire truck.

'Our oldest rescued person was Mrs Nielson, who was ninety-three. Getting her into the fire truck was a bit of an effort. She apologised that she didn't have a bikini, which would have been useful in the water!'

The Newry Hotel on the main street was washed out. Publican John Gray told the ABC how bad the situation was. 'We're being told it's going to come back twice as bad, and we've already had water up to our pool table, we've got sewerage and water floating around everywhere,' he said.

Gradually it became clear that some areas in town looked far safer than others. One of those was Joan Robinson's house at the southern end of town and on a small rise. Neighbours converged there, while Joan made pumpkin soup and tea and coffee. The neighbours didn't dry their feet when they walked inside, but Joan didn't mind.

It's not that people in Newry did not help each other: it was just that the water came up so fast that everybody's first thought was for their own safety. Only after they had organised themselves a little did their thoughts turn to helping others.

Two people who everybody agreed saved lives were Adrian Smits and Ryan Hanley. Adrian realised that all round him were people who needed immediate help. He picked up Ryan and headed straight for the Bartlett house, taking the dinghy down the back of the town where the water was a little deeper because of the gullies and billabongs. Knowing the layout of the blocks, he was able to take his little boat to places the SES volunteers could not.

Marooned in her house Anne Bartlett watched, her heart in her mouth, as the boat approached. Debris — huge logs, gas bottles, wheelie bins — were everywhere. The current was strong. Adrian was finding difficulty in making headway and it became apparent very quickly that there were some places that even his boat could not reach.

'We saw that boat down the back towards the creek where it was very turbulent; and it was driving along under the treeline,' says Anne. 'It seemed to be heading towards us, but then it stopped and turned away. Pauline was screaming and I was yelling out, "Help!" They didn't even look at us.'

The boat had snagged on a fence line and was trapped by the current. For a moment it was in danger of being tipped over. Adrian worked frantically to free the propeller before turning the boat and heading towards Anne. 'We were so relieved,' she said.

The boat pulled up nose first onto the verandah, with the rear end swirling around and kicking away with each new wash from the current. 'Adrian and Ryan had to get out of the boat to lift Keith in, while Anne held the dinghy,' says Pauline. 'It was all very precarious and, once Keith was in, we just wanted to get out of the house as fast as we could. But next in went Rosie, Anne and Keith's much loved Cavoodle.'We got pulled in,' says Anne. 'Our clothes were heavy with water, it was very hard to get in but we weren't letting go for anything. I remember I had shoes on, normally I don't wear them. I wore those lace-up shoes for three days. Keith was soaked from his slippers up.'

Their situation was perilous: five adults and a dog in a tiny dingy, heading across the swirling current, being buffeted by logs, wheelie bins and things under the water they couldn't see. They reached Joan Robinson's house, but before they could make it to dry land, Ryan and Adrian had to smash down the backyard fence to get near the steps. Even then, for Keith the ordeal was not over. The CFA crew thought it was best if Keith could be immediately airlifted to hospital.

'They said they'd get Keith out immediately on the RAAF helicopter,' says Anne. 'I was very disturbed at the idea, but it seemed best at the time.' Anne packed Keith off in the front of the fire truck and sat down for a cup of tea.

A few hours later, in the afternoon, Anne was convinced she should leave town too and she headed to the evacuation point. 'When I got there I found Keith sitting in a vehicle by himself. They hadn't got the ambulance out to take him to hospital, so he was sitting there, shivering and alone.'

Keith was eventually evacuated by helicopter. Anne, suffering hypothermia and some distress, left town shortly afterwards by ambulance. It was a longtime before they saw their home again.

'The whole thing was a shambles,' says Anne. 'There was nothing malicious in it, it was just that we weren't prepared. Everybody was doing their best, but it wasn't enough.'

Christa Dwyer and her two sons waited to be rescued. 'After I didn't hear anything I wolf-whistled really loudly,' says Christa.

'But everybody was so busy with their own disasters they didn't realise we were in the middle of town, totally isolated.

'I was talking to Don on the mobile and he said someone had told him the dam wall had burst. But I looked around and I could see that the water had started to go down. 'I said, "Where is it coming from?" What Don was told over the phone just seemed ridiculous, impossible. They said the water was coming from the Thompson River, but if that was so, it would be halfway up the water tower in Maffra! I said it couldn't happen.'

Bull Linaker was not so sure. He had heard reports that the wall had burst and he arranged for a helicopter to lift his wife Kay out. At first Kay said she would rather stay in the house. 'It was actually quite peaceful,' she says, 'although I could hear the crash and bang of water outside. The water had damaged all the carpets and cupboards.'

But she changed her mind when the chopper arrived. 'The police helicopter came and I went out the front. We've got an electricity pole close to the house, and they dropped a policewoman down to the ground a bit further away. I had put my gumboots on to walk to the helicopter, and as soon as I stepped off the verandah I could see they wouldn't help much — they filled up immediately!

'I was out the front and the policewoman was hanging by the rope yelling out to me, she said she'd come to get me and slipped a strap around my waist, and it sat under my boobs and I grabbed and the rope pulled tighter. She said, "Don't hang onto me, don't touch me, put your hands down beside you and you'll be fine. I'll hang onto you."

'As we were going up I looked down and saw my boobs right under my chin!' Kay felt unsafe. 'It was like I was climbing a ladder without hanging onto the sides.'

Kay was winched up. She looked down at the flooded town and isolated buildings and felt other people seemed to be in more trouble than she was. These fleeting thoughts were interrupted when she reached the lip of the helicopter. 'A bloke grabbed me by the back and told me to sit down and turn around. The gumboots emptied and there was water all through the helicopter. We all had to sit in it. I apologised, but they told me not to worry.' For Kay the rescue seemed to last forever, but it was only a couple of minutes before they dropped her down at the evacuation point and flew off.

Adrian Smits rescued Christa Dwyer and her two boys. He dropped them off at Joan Robinson's house. Don stayed home, even though the water came up 30 centimetres over the floorboards. Christa says, 'He has no concept of danger.'

By mid-afternoon the water had peaked and most of the evacuations had been completed. By nine that evening the water in the streets and houses had drained away. Newry had escaped disaster by the narrowest of margins, certainly more by good luck than good management. The frantic period was over but the townspeople had a great deal more work to do.

It was possible to take stock. The Macalister River catchment underwent major flooding upstream as well as downstream of Lake Glenmaggie. The flood peaks recorded along the Macalister were the largest on record. Inflows to the Glenmaggie Dam were in excess of a one-in-two-hundred-year event, while the releases of water were more like one-in-a-hundred-year events. The outflow was lower because the dam was only half full when the flooding began and because Southern Rural Water prudently released water early.

Because the gauges on the Macalister River were washed away, it is difficult to know how much rain caused the near catastrophe. Rainfall totals were generally between 50 and 300 millimetres over the four-day period that the system moved slowly out to the east and eventually to Bass Strait. Mt Wellington, slightly east of the Macalister catchment, recorded 319 millimetres of rain on 28th, setting a Victorian state record for June and being the second highest rainfall for any month.

A few hours of havoc left the residents of Newry with twelve to eighteen months of cleaning up. Some never fully recovered.

Those who watched television that night would have seen footage of the dam wall, where water was pouring out at a phenomenal rate. They would have been surprised to see what appeared to be an entire weatherboard building floating downstream from Newry: perhaps this would have helped the bewildered folk of Newry understand what they had been through. There is no footage of the evacuation, because there was neither warning nor organised recovery for hours, by which time the water and the media had moved on.

That night, Don Dwyer stayed the night in his wet house alone. He slept little, worrying about his family, the house, the neighbours. 'A couple of old friends told me about their experiences in 1971,' he says. 'They thought they had cleaned up really well, but three days later the furniture doors and timber swelled up and everything had to be dismantled and thrown out. I wanted to get the water out of the house as soon as I could so that wouldn't happen to us.'

Don started mopping and sweeping, and apart from finding frogs in the spare room, he quickly discovered just how hard it is to get water out of a house. If the floor is flat or concave, water is inclined to rush away from the sides of the broom or mop and come back inside. Starting in a corner, he realised, was futile. He was like everybody else in town: at a time when they were exhausted, dirty and distressed, they had to clean up, often the hardest part of the whole ordeal.

Don decided to do what he does best. 'I'm a pump mechanic,' he says. 'That's my job. I pull pumps apart and fix them. And so I got my pumps from the backyard, dried them out and got them going to hose off the verandah. I emptied all the contents of the kitchen table onto the verandah — the table, the chairs, the food and everything in the cupboards, which were all in good condition.

'By the time Christa got home the next day, we could walk on the lino. The carpets were a different story: they were filled by sludge.' But soon an exhausted Don and Christa discovered more trouble. 'By the end of the day the edges of the lino started curling up. We realised they were useless and had to be thrown out. So we had no floor coverings.' It was heartbreaking.

Christa also worried about their sons. 'I felt we needed to be a family very urgently, or they would be traumatised. My mission was to get the boys back into the house. I told people who came to help that I needed to get the boys' room ready for them to sleep in safely. While they were away they were more and more isolated from the reality of what had happened. I really felt strongly about that.

'They came back within two nights. It was distressing for them. Sam would wake up in the night, crying, and I had to put him on the floor and let him feel that it was dry. Getting floor coverings was an important step for him, to prove that we were returning to normality.

'Many of the older kids who were involved in the flood said they felt they couldn't do anything to help, and that added to their feelings of distress and trauma. They needed to be able to live it to see that it was ok. That's what I wanted for my boys. In the end I feel they coped all right.'

Bull Linaker went through the day in the CFA truck without anything to eat. 'By half past nine that night the main street was dry, but there were still people milling around who couldn't go home and who didn't want to be evacuated. I said, "Why don't we open the football sheds, where there are showers, warmth, water, a bar and a place to sleep?" So we did and a few people stayed there that night.'

The next day Bull helped the town clean up. The CFA volunteer crews from throughout the region came to help everyone in town for the next three days, hosing out and shovelling mud and dealing with the ruined furniture. 'We chucked furniture into a skip. Maffra Sewerage sucked out all the sewerage tanks for nothing,' said Linaker.

'Cleaning was difficult because we didn't know where to start. We were dealing with people's possessions and we felt we didn't have the right to get rid of them. A lot of people thought they had to wait for insurance assessors to detail their losses. But in the end people chucked everything out.

'The insurance assessors arrived on the Friday, so that meant we could work really hard on the weekend. It was great when

Melbourne members of the Four Wheel Drive Club came to help. They use a paddock here for driving and camping and they said that because they always come up here for a good time, it was time to give something back.'

Bull and Kay Linaker were quick to help others, but it was three days before they and the CFA got around to cleaning up their own place. The usually laconic couple were angry for a longtime about many aspects of the event.

'We lost everything that was in the yard outside — kids' toys, outdoor settings, rubbish bins and fences. We were insured by CGU who told us initially that we would get some money for the fences. But in the end they paid nothing.

'We lost all our inside furniture. The Red Cross gave us a hamper of food; the Lions Club replaced our freezer.

'It wasn't just us. The CFA blokes busted their arses and got no recognition for what they did.'

Lisa and Keith Towns returned to their home the next day, expecting to be faced with a wrecked house, as they had been in 1971. 'It was quite funny,' says Lila. 'The place was a complete mess, and our four-year-old granddaughter said, "Grandma, I think you'd better do some housework!"

'We hosed out the mud and debris and it never even marked the walls. The cupboards, although made of chipboard, didn't soak up the water. The door jambs expanded but it all dried out fine afterwards. Nothing in the house was damaged.'

Keith believes that if he had closed the doors between the rooms, and the cupboard doors, they would have expanded, buckled and broken. But he left them all ajar. 'We were very lucky,' he says.

Lisa Reeves, who had been among the first to be lifted out of her home by the CFA, was among the first to return the following morning.

'We had heard there was water around,' she says, 'but by nine in the morning we came to have a look and there wasn't a drop.

'The house was covered in sewerage and mud across all the floors and furniture; and the marks on the walls showed that water was more than a metre deep inside. We lost everything: TV, computer, brand-new lounge suite, washing machine, all electrical appliances, dishwasher, beds, clothes, everything stored in the shed. The council said that for health reasons everything inside had to be thrown out.

'Our insurers, CGU, knocked us back on contents coverage. They said we weren't covered for contents, as it was a flood. As far as we are aware, every other company paid. I was a bit annoyed; it cost me $50,000 to replace it all.

'I was lucky that I could rent the place over the road. It was flooded too and as the owners were with CGU they didn't get covered either. The owners were able to move to their farmhouse, and they let me rent there for three months. I had to work to get the money to replace all the goods first, so I moved back in with my parents for seven months. I didn't go back home for nearly a year.'

What did Lisa learn from the flood? Would she have done anything differently?

'There was nothing I could have done,' she says. 'If we'd been warned I would have put stuff higher up. We changed insurance companies and chose one with a clause for floods. Surprisingly there was not much difference between the premiums.'

The Shingles returned at midnight. 'We found the cat asleep on the bed,' says Clare.

'We had a metre of water through the house. All the cupboards were hardwood timber and panels, but after a short while they all went mouldy and cracked. We dried out the fridge and washing machine, but a month or so later they packed it in. Our two cars were write-offs.'

Out at their dairy farm, Wayne and Leah Brunt captured the devastation on video. 'The farm is a couple of kilometres wide, and we saw water cover every paddock. As far as I could film, even with the zoom full on, there was water,' says Leah. The video shows the flood overtopping the irrigation channels, forming rivulets of fast-flowing water at every fence post, tree and shrub, and around pieces of equipment in the paddocks.

'We had lost all our fences and had stock wandering around everywhere. We couldn't hold the cows in until we got the fencing back up, and then some bulls got in with the calves for a short while.' A dairy farming disaster, in other words. 'We lost a four-year-old bull which weighed a good tonne. It was found way up by the church.

'A good Samaritan, Paul Bourke, came with his family and asked if we had anywhere to take the calves. We didn't and he offered to look after them for us. They drove the lot on foot up the road. It was such a relief, and a wonderful gesture.'

Leah and her friend and neighbour Jacquie Thorn milked the cows while Wayne and his mates set off to try to repair the damaged fences. Things were just starting to return to normal when Leah had a huge shock.

'Water started flowing down the channels and across the paddocks again. The kids were in the house. Outside Jacquie and I were moving the cows into a safe paddock when suddenly, water was coming up to the bonnet of her car. Lucky her four-wheel-drive had a snorkel ...

'I was running around, completely nuts, like, a complete breakdown. I rang emergency and screamed at them to warn the residents of Newry that the water was coming back. They said more water was being released from the dam and not to worry.

'This was a more normal water release, light to moderate, and the paddocks were covered but that's to be expected on this floodplain.

'I could see that not much was happening and calmed down, but for a while it was terrifying.

'The flood improved the pasture. That's why Newry is so good. But the rubbish stayed in the paddocks for a longtime. Sticks and rocks and debris smashed the mower blades for months afterwards. When we bought the stock, we asked our insurance agent to cover us for flood and fire. CGU is our insurer. We got most damage fixed, but we didn't get the full value of everything back.'

Bill Napier stayed with friends the night of the flood and returned the next day, expecting to find his car still hitched to the caravan and leaning up on the fencepost at Anne Bartlett's home. Car and caravan were gone, as was the fence. The vehicles had been pushed more than 60 metres away, until they smashed against some trees in a small gully. The caravan appeared to be resting in the tree, with neither wheel on the ground. Both were write-offs.

Anne Bartlett returned to Newry to find the house devastated and everything she owned, including her car, personal possessions, even golf clubs, destroyed. Her insurer APIA, covered everything. As Anne said, 'You feel a bit guilty that you get insurance and others don't.

'Everything was lost in the house. All the furniture, except an oak hardwood table. We lost photos and all the items stored here by my daughter when she went interstate.

'We decided to abandon the house while we cleaned up and we moved to my daughter's home at Briagolong, twenty kilometres away.' Eventually it was too much for Anne, who left the cleaning up and rebuilding to her son Colin and daughter, Miffy and her husband, Bernard, and 'an enormous amount of help from the locals'.

Anne says: 'I moved out to my daughter's and didn't come back to town for ten months. I think I am happy here, and I had to make the decision to get on with my life. I don't want to sound like a victim, but I had some issues with stress. A bit of a meltdown, really. I had counselling because I'd go outside and get down the road a little way and turn around and think about personal security issues — had I locked the gate, checked the heater? I felt that I had lost all my personal security. I dealt with the anger, then the security issues, then I started having panic attacks.

'I'm a bit isolated down this end of town,' she says. 'The older people are up the other end.' Anne expected the local government authorities or welfare staff would find her and keep in touch. But nobody came. 'In the end I thought to myself, well, bugger them. I'll be fine. I'll look after myself and we'll be fine on our own.'

At Christmas, Anne realised what social damage the flood had done. 'I was a member of the golf club, but hadn't been there in months. I had a handicap of 17, which is not bad for a woman my age.

'I walked into the Newry Hotel and saw all these golf club members sitting there with a freebie Christmas lunch. I knew nothing about it.' The golf club had moved on without Anne.

Anne's house in the main street at Newry was for sale for many months after the flood. There were no buyers, but Anne didn't mind too much. 'I wasn't sure I wanted to sell up anyway,' she says.

Keith died three months later. 'It shortened his life by a good twelve months. I felt so sad for him and he felt sad for what it had done to me. I lost fifteen kilos. We did know that Keith was going downhill before, but it really did shorten his time.'

Official records show that the Newry floods of June 2007 resulted in 'no deaths'. The State Emergency Service apologised to the community for failing to issue adequate warnings. The Wellington Shire Council put in new flood plans and warning systems, and community education about floods and flood prevention is progressing. But Newry is still coming to terms with what the flood washed away: possessions, homes, equipment and friendships.

A Desperate Race
Charleville, Southwestern Queensland, January 2008

'We have a problem on our hands.'

In the minds of many Australians, outback Queensland is a dry place. But as those who live in the towns of Charleville and Augathella will tell you, their part of the world is anything but. In 1990, for example, the Warrego River burst its banks at Charleville and the water reached to the top of verandahs in the shops and pubs: 1180 homes out of the total of 1470 were flooded.

Mark O'Brien was elected mayor of Murweh Shire partly because he promised to build a levee to prevent the flooding occurring again.

It was a long and heated political battle. O'Brien was given consensual agreement to build the levees in the towns of Charleville and Augathella only after there was further flooding in 1995 and 1997. Agreement was finally reached in 2006 to build a 6.3-kilometre-long earth embankment-style levee that would direct the water from the Warrego River around Charleville. It was agreed that in two places a concrete wall of 260 panels would be built, each panel 5 metres long and 2 metres tall, attached to piles driven 6 to 8 metres into the ground.

When the embankment was finished, it would be 9.5 metres, fully one metre above the record level the river had reached in 1990. In January 2008, the concrete wall had two big gaps yet to be filled: one of 375 metres and the other of 150 metres. The levee, without the concrete walls was only high enough to hold back water at about 5.5 metres. Work was on schedule to be completed by March 2008.

The Augathella earth embankment had been completed, but levees take time to settle down, and this had not yet happened, largely because grass, an important element in binding the earth levee together, was sparse after years of drought.

For much of the year the Warrego lives up to the meaning of its Aboriginal name: 'river of sand'. It is a typical inland river — a series of permanent waterholes dotting a sandy riverbed. Around Charleville numerous tracks through the waterholes, reeds and sand dunes made by motorbike, car and feet reveal how important it is to the leisure activities of residents.

The Charleville catchment is complex and water movement is difficult to predict. Five river systems are crucial. The Ward and Langlo intersect the Warrego below Charleville and, if they are full, they can back up the Warrego and increase river levels at Charleville. North of the town, the Nive flows into the Warrego and increases the catchment area far to the north and west.

There is also Bradleys Creek. This rises in pastoral country about twenty-three kilometres northeast of Charleville and flows through town — where it is known as Bradleys Gully — before it too flows back into the Warrego a few kilometres below the town. If the Warrego is high, waters do not escape easily, and Bradley's Gully can create havoc all on its own.

These are not well defined intersections. As is typical with inland waterways, each previous flood can move the sandy riverbeds, creating new watercourses. The country is flat and floods often spread out for many kilometres. Installing a levee simply means that the water will move elsewhere, changing the riverbed yet again. Many people in Charleville were fearful that the levee would stop Bradleys Gully from emptying, causing more serious flooding on that side of town.

At the beginning of January, rains from ex-tropical cyclone Helen drenched the Carnarvon Ranges, 200 kilometres northeast of Charleville, home of the headwaters of the Warrego River. Because most residents understand the complexity of the local river systems, it is not surprising that many began to move their belongings away before any warnings were issued.

Making things difficult was the nature of Charleville houses. Like many towns in Queensland, Charleville has high-set homes, with a lot of space underneath. Residents do not waste this area, often turning it into outside living quarters, complete with electrical items, television sets, lounges, kitchens and laundries. It is against council bylaws to live in these areas, but many residents have made substantial renovations, even including air conditioning. The possibility of flooding means that a great deal of time and work is necessary to prepare houses. But many residents of Charleville and Augathella 100 kilometres away were taking no chances.

In the low-lying area of Charleville shop owners, who had been hit by floods in Bradleys Gully in 1990, 1995 and again in 1997, were quick to move stock and equipment. In the offices of the council and the State Emergency Services, work began to protect a handful of homes and businesses. Shire work gangs set to clearing out drains and culverts, ensuring that water could escape from Charleville's most vulnerable places. People started measuring the height of the water at the Mitchell Highway bridge that crosses the Warrego in the centre of town.

Over three days, the remnants of Cyclone Helen had brought nearly 150 millimetres of rain, accompanied by winds that sometimes reached 90 kilometres per hour. Lawns were soaked and drains ran freely, but there was no sign that this would be anything more than a monsoonal downpour to be welcomed by pastoralists and horticulturalists.

The first sign of trouble came on Thursday 17 January.

Council supervisor and controller of the SES at Charleville, Allan Pemberton, was on his way to work at seven in the morning. 'I was quite close to the gully and could see the water was higher than normal, so I went down to the flood gauges to take a reading. I took two readings half an hour apart and I thought to myself: We have a problem on our hands here.

'Water was rising a hundred millimetres every half hour. At seven am it was already at 1.8 metres and by the time I looked later it was two metres. We'd had rain of thirty, forty and seventy millimetres over a few days, which brought the gully up to the two-metre level, but the level always fell again in a couple of hours.

'A few people had seen water coming into their businesses in the low part of Edwards Street where the flood gauge is and they were already starting to move gear out.

'Then on Thursday afternoon we had 105 millimetres of rain in a couple of hours. It was really hammering down.

'A lot of people keep their roofing gutters clean, but there is only so much rain a gutter can hold, so the SES started getting calls. There are a lot of places where stormwater does back up in town and people who lived there were getting worried that water would come into their ground-level laundries. They called us to sandbag them. Generally a few sandbags will hold that sort of water out.'

In charge of the sandbagging operation was works supervisor Allen Johnstone. He was hoping to prepare 1000 sandbags. However, it had been a decade since the last serious flooding in the town and flood mitigation had generally concentrated on the new levee. Allen discovered that many bags at the depot were old and frayed. Getting supplies from the coast would take time, and the request went immediately to Toowoomba for 6000 more bags. 'Businesses were desperate for them, and the supply couldn't keep up,' says Allen. 'We started at two in the afternoon, in pouring rain on the Thursday, using a post hole shovel to fill the bags.'

They discovered straightaway that the apparently simple task of filling a wheat bag with sand is not easy. 'The sand was damp and heavy and initially we didn't know how much to put in. We thought we wanted the bags about five hundred millimetres high, with enough room to tie the ends down. A very strong man could lift one in one hand, but they quickly got tired.

'We put too much soil in them initially and tied the string too tightly; and when the string broke we would lose the soil. The rain belted down all afternoon and it was stinking hot and humid. We realised we wouldn't get the job finished in daylight and a few people started wondering what the bloody hell we were going to do.'

The operation was moved to the council depot, where a concrete agitator was brought in to fill the bags. Volunteers were recruited from the usual places — the SES, service clubs, family and friends — and gradually work practices improved. Two people would hold a bag while dirt poured out of the agitator. It was effective but very tiring: the bags pulled on arms and bodies not used to this kind of work. It was also wet and dirty going. The ground was muddy and slippery; the atmosphere was itchy and tropical. The supply of sandbags ran out at nine that evening and the operation ground to a halt.

The water in the gully had receded and it appeared the worst was over, but the SES kept their office open overnight anyway. It was just as well they did.

Allan Pemberton says: 'I'd been in bed an hour and I got a phone call at 2am from Geoff Whitehead, the deputy controller, saying "We need all hands." The big storm had travelled along the catchment of Bradleys Creek, which was already full. And so we copped it again. The water in Bradleys Gully was rising two hundred millimetres every half hour. Geoff said the water had risen to 2.5 metres and was still rising.

'I got straight back into my overalls and got to the depot with my eyes hanging out of my head. The water was a lot higher than I had expected and very fast-moving. I came across a couple of people trying to move a trailer which had been pushed into a fence by the flood waters. They looked like they were going to be trapped between the fence and the trailer, which was bobbing around and very difficult to handle.

'The water was chest deep at the gutter, but by the time I walked to the crown of the road the water level was back to my thighs. It was moving so fast I had to hold on to the door of the car as we made our way over to the people. I was a bit lucky as I knew where the edges of the footpaths and gutters were, but the water was very cold. I didn't expect that.

'It was also very choppy and I could see branches and logs floating along. I was worried: in floodwaters you do not know what is going to come down the channel. I could stand up but it was hard work to walk and I was buggered by the time I got to them.'

'Every time you go into the water to rescue somebody, you put yourself at risk. Of course, with all that tension, once you get them out you give them a right shouting to let them know they put you in danger.'

The three pushed the trailer away and Allan waded back into the water. He crossed over to the homes on the high side of the road, to warn the inhabitants about the impending threat.

The police were using a loud-hailer to alert people. But people in large towns are used to hearing police and ambulance sirens and most of them slept through the announcement.

'The fire service has an air-raid siren and I asked them to let that go to wake people up,' says Pemberton. 'People in Charleville know that the firies have a big job on if that goes off. It worked. People woke up and thought, "Oh my God, look at the water." Word of mouth began, people started calling each other.

'We wanted them up so they could make their own decisions. We didn't have to evacuate anyone. We wanted them to know the river was rising.

'The people I spoke to in Edwards Street were pleased that someone was letting them know what was happening. They had plenty of time to react — at least an hour.'

Allan Pemberton could hear the low roar of what was a massive torrent of water in Bradleys Gully and he was worried the town was going to get a lot more water. 'The previous highest flood I had experienced in the gully was just over two metres, and here we were, well and truly over that.'

The water reached 3.1 metres at 9am. Fifteen homes were evacuated, the historic Corones Hotel bottle shop was flooded; some motel units had to be abandoned. About forty people found accommodation with family or friends.

Allan Pemberton did not yet know that the rainfall had been widespread and intense across three of the five rivers in the catchment area. Station owners 100 kilometres or more to the north knew that the water rivalled the 1990 event. This meant that stock losses would be high and pastures wiped out. Many owners began leaving.

By dawn people started to realise that the rising floodwaters might breach the Warrego's levee and attention turned to the two gaps in the concrete wall. Mark O'Brien was exasperated. It had been a long, wearisome struggle to get the support of the town for the levee's construction and an even longer battle to persuade the Queensland and federal governments to stump up the $6 million necessary. 'A lot of people had put their heart and soul into building this levee,' he said, 'and now, at the eleventh and a half hour, it looked like it was all going to go pear-shaped.'

Matters were clearly urgent. Mayor O'Brien made a call to Emergency Management Queensland headquarters in Brisbane at about 6.30am. He said he doubted the town could handle the Warrego on its own and he reminded EMQ directors that there were still two gaps in the levee. EMQ Operations Director Mike Shapland picked up the call on his car phone on the way to work. 'I was a bit gloomy because we couldn't find any solutions,' he said, with a certain amount of understatement.

EMQ's emergency operations had been activated for three weeks at this point. Cyclone Helen had cut a swathe through coastal and central Queensland on its way to the Carnarvon Ranges; EMQ had been actively saving lives and properties. The management team was exhausted, but they could not relax yet.

During the phone call, Mike Shapland remembered that he had heard a mobile flood barrier was being tested by the NSW SES. If they could get access to it, disaster in Charleville might yet be averted.

Mark O'Brien felt great relief. 'It was the most enlightening moment of any meeting I have ever had in my working and community life,' he says. Being an optimist, he was confident that the solution was at hand from that moment.

But Mike Shapland did not share O'Brien's enthusiasm. 'We didn't know anything about the flood barriers, where they were or how they worked. But we had to find out,' he says.

'We realised we had about twelve hours to make some plans. We also had to deal with about five other towns in Queensland that were facing serious flooding at the same time as Charleville.' Shapland describes this as 'wet finger planning': trying to find a quick solution to every new problem as it arises.

Allan Pemberton says: 'The conversation focussed on how we were going to close the gaps. They were too long to fill with dump trucks and the gap was too high and too long for sandbags.' He called for SES volunteers to use the remaining sandbags to help businesses and to start planning for evacuation. It was not easy to find people to help, he says. 'A lot of our members have their daily jobs and responsibility to their employers first, especially if their employer looked like being affected. But we managed to get eight or nine people who could respond early and start preparations.'

Pemberton, who lives with his wife Leisa and his family in the middle of town, had already decided not to evacuate. 'We were informed that a dead cow was fished out of the swimming pool in the backyard in 1990,' says Allan. 'Now we only had one hundred millimetres to go before the water went into our house and I had to make a decision about evacuating. But I got calls from upstream in Bradleys Gully that the water had started to fall, so I decided it would be safe for the family to stay for a while longer,' he says.

Never ignore human nature.

People were putting a lot of faith in the untested, portable flood wall from the NSW SES; and everybody suddenly became familiar with the idea of a 'pallet barrier'. The day before the floods nobody had ever heard of such a thing, yet it was now regarded as the instrument of salvation. First deployed in Britain in 2003 and in widespread use overseas, especially in New Zealand, the pallet barrier consists of a series of foldable aluminium struts that stand upright and on which standard-sized wooden pallets can be rested at a sixty-degree angle. Black plastic from long rolls is stretched over the pallets horizontally to the ground. Sandbags hold the plastic in place against the floodwaters. This way of holding back floods had never been tried in Australia and the New South Wales SES was only evaluating it for local conditions.

It was estimated that about 880 wooden pallets and 2000 sandbags would be required to hold the plastic in place. The barrier, which was intended to mend the gaps in the wall, would have to be installed before the water in the Warrego reached the top of the earth embankment. The equipment was stored in Wollongong south of Sydney and it would have to be in place by lunchtime on Saturday: only twenty-eight hours away. The logistics were immensely complex, and everything had to go right.

But almost immediately everything went wrong. The weather in Wollongong was as bad as it was in Charleville, so the RAAF were unable to fly from there. Everything had to be moved by road to the Richmond air base 100 kilometres north of Wollongong. Because there were not enough pallets in Charleville, the Brisbane-based company Chep arranged three road trains to deliver nearly 880 pallets to the town. In these weather conditions, several outback roads would certainly be cut, meaning detours of 100 kilometres or more.

The race to get the flood barriers up meant that all other bureaucratic barriers had to come down. Mark O'Brien had some experience in dealing with different jurisdictions — local, state and federal governments — who do not work smoothly together and who indeed sometimes appear to be actively working against each other's interests.

However, he had two important allies. Holidaying in town was Neil Roberts, the local state MP and Queensland minister for police and emergencies. Roberts had grown up in Charleville and worked alongside the disaster committee. He told O'Brien to call the Queensland premier, Anna Bligh. 'I told Anna what we were trying to do and what was needed, and she just said simply: "If that's what you need, it will be done." The role she played was critical.'

Mark O'Brien could now tell his residents that there was a plan. He went on the local commercial station, 4VL, and the community station, 4RR, to explain what was happening. Nobody breathed easily. The pallet barrier was untried, the odds against it arriving and being installed before the water reached its peak were long. And who knew how high the river would rise, in any case? Augathella and Charleville, 100 kilometres apart, as well as pastoral properties in between, were put on flood alert.

The announcements galvanised the towns and a remarkable effort of co-operation and goodwill began to unfold. Offers of help started coming in: most were gladly accepted.

Michael Schneider, the owner of Charleville pharmacy, flew up to inspect the flooded rivers with local pilot Cracker McDonald. They reported back to the council mid-morning that water had flooded out across the pastoral plains and in places had broken the banks of the Ward River, but the Langlo and the Nive were not affected. This information was crucial to Mark O'Brien and his team. 'You can use all the measuring gauges you like, and we did, but we never had enough information, ever. There is nothing like a photograph and description from people who know this country from the air to put the situation in perspective,' says O'Brien. 'Cracker baits wild dogs and Michael flies regularly, so they knew the country really well.

'A day and a half before the water reached Charleville, Michael and Cracker estimated that it would arrive in eighteen hours and reach 6.1 metres. We trusted their advice and made decisions based on it.' The pallet barrier would hold the waters back, up to 6.5 metres — if it worked.

Former drover and town historian George Balsillie was wary about the whole proceeding. 'We've created our own problems with this river,' he says. 'The Aborigines, the Bidjara and Cooma tribes, they nursed this area. Fifty years ago the Warrego was like a big waterhole. We could catch plenty of fish, and the waterhole stretched from the bridge in town to Gowries Crossing two kilometres away. Now it's all sand, and silted up, so of course the river's going to flood the town at times.'

He worried that the new levee had changed many things in Charleville. 'Look across the river to the high side,' he says. 'In the 1970s and 1980s people started building there. All our pioneers lived on the other side, out of harm's way. Before the levee went in, people would say that if the river flooded you had to get out of town. At least you'd be safe. Now people are building on the levee side of the river.

'I've seen umpteen floods in my fifty years here,' he adds. 'I felt downhearted when they put the levee in. I could see all the water being trapped in Bradleys Gully and all the businesses there, which are often flooded, would have no chance.'

Because the Langlo and the Nive had not flooded, Balsillie listened to people's reports of the rising floods with scepticism. 'Mark told us on the radio that we were in for a flood, but there was no need to worry because the levee would hold the water back. I didn't think it would get to the same height as the 1990 floods.'

For Betty Wyman, who lives behind the new levee on Riverview Street, there was no advice. She does not listen to the radio and lives mostly alone on the outskirts of town. An elder of the Bidjara tribe, she spends much of her time underneath her high-set house. Kids come and go from her place, where they clearly feel welcome. 'In the good times the river is a clear green colour and the kids have a good time. When I was a kid it was way too deep and we weren't ever game to swim in it. We still see brolgas, pelicans and ducks.'

She went to bed on the Thursday without any warning of danger. 'I heard a bit of noise from the river, but I didn't take much notice,' she says. 'The next day, though, it was roaring like I'd never heard before.'

By 11am on the Friday, water in the Warrego had reached the same level as it had in 1997, when the low-lying areas of the town had been flooded. The caravan park, with only a handful of residents, was hastily evacuated and many people in low-lying homes were surrounded by waterlogged yards. A few could see ankle-deep water rushing through parkland and along streets. So far there was no damage. But there was a rush to stock up and some supplies — baby food, batteries, nappies, milk and bread — quickly sold out of the town's main grocery store. Elderly and frail patients at the hospital were moved out of town, though the hospital itself, a two-storey structure, was never evacuated.

The atmosphere in Charleville varied from mild concern to what one longtime local, Pete McRae, describes as 'near hysteria'.

Pete has worked for the Department of the Environment in Charleville for more than twenty years. He's best known for creating a reserve to protect the endangered environment of the bilby. Thanks largely to his efforts, the population of this rabbit-sized, long-eared and pink-snouted mammal increased from nine to almost a hundred.

He lives in a low-level timber home that seems oddly out of place in the street. 'It's a railway hut from the Quilpie line,' he explains. 'It's made of timber and hardwood so if I get flooded there won't be too much damage. But I wasn't ready for these floods.

'Nature isn't accountable to human beings. It's quite disappointing that we have this amazing computer in our heads, better than anything anyone can build, and it doesn't need virus protection or Telstra to prop it up ... and we only use 50 per cent of it.

'Before we were here, with all our radios and telecommunications and libraries and banks, there were natural systems. If something couldn't get out of the way of those systems — when there was flooding, for example — it wouldn't survive.

'We can learn, like any species of tree or beetle, that we have to survive to breed. But we continue to build settlements on flood plains and riverbanks.

'Anyway, the town was frantic. A lot of people were panicking because they had been in big floods and knew the impact on their families. There was real fear and hysteria from some people who were thinking about what another flood could do. One of the problems when that happens is gossip. The whole town gets involved, and there's so-called expert opinion throughout the community.

'Mark O'Brien was great, giving regular radio updates to let people know what was going on.'

George Donohoe was the chairman of the Charleville welfare support service known as the Neighbourhood Centre, looking after the elderly, homeless, unemployed and anyone else who needed help. He was in charge of the SES during the 1990 floods in Charleville, so he knows a thing or two about the Warrego and about human nature.

'The 1893 flood was the same size as the one we had in 1990,' he says, 'and I remember in 1990 when I was trying to warn people, they wouldn't believe me. Everybody said floodwaters would never be that big in Charleville. Well, ever since then everybody's attitude has been totally different.

'Now, with only a bit of rain, people panic. They mishear information and that causes utter chaos. People called us wanting furniture moved straight away, including some people who were not affected, and they screamed at us. They were driving us mad.'

Judy Wilson works with George. She helped with evacuations to the showground, and she agrees with him. 'People were upset. Many were complaining they couldn't get help and a small number had very unrealistic expectations. Others were just too lazy to help themselves. If people don't deal with everyday life terribly well, things get a lot worse for them when a crisis comes.'

George Donohoe had been the hero of the 1990 flood evacuation and recovery, but he had long since retired. Many managers are naturally reluctant to seek advice of long-retired former managers; overcoming that attitude takes humility and focus on the outcome, not on the personalities involved. The disaster committee at Charleville were facing a situation they had never experienced before and needed as much information as possible. Advice was coming in from everywhere. In these circumstances it is easy for managers to choose a plan and base their hopes on one idea, ignoring other options.

Donohoe contacted the disaster team to give them his view of the floods. With the benefit of hindsight, he admits his advice might not have been helpful. 'At nine o'clock in the morning, I called the council to talk about the Ward River backing up the Warrego and reaching 1997 levels. That time the Ward had stayed up longer than any other river, which was unusual, and I was worried that it might happen again.

'The council was planning for a river height of 6.3 to 6.5 metres and I said they should go closer to seven metres. They listened to me and I think that caused some problems.

'I mentioned that again at a town meeting on the Saturday night. Some people were saying eight or nine metres and that caused big panic.'

Meanwhile, the plan to get the pallet barrier to Charleville was in jeopardy. 'The RAAF told us they couldn't get a plane until midday,' says Mike Shapland. 'And because of the weather at Charleville, which had no control tower or ground facilities, they told us there was serious danger of the planes not flying at all.

'We started preparing to get trucks to take the pallet barrier to Charleville from another airfield, but the nearest was hundreds of miles away.

'We also realised that nobody in Australia knew enough about the pallet barrier system to install it. So we got onto the New Zealand manufacturers, who agreed to fly some specialists in to Queensland. We asked some people from New Zealand Civil Defence to assist as well.'

Chep loaded three two-trailer road trains in Toowoomba, 600 kilometres away, with 880 pallets. The trucks were due to arrive at about nine on the Friday night, if the Warrego Highway remained open. But water had already flooded across the road in many places. The trucks could go north via Augathella, but that would add four hours to the journey. 'The drivers got on their radios and started to talk to other truckies and they agreed they would risk driving the flooded Warrego Highway,' says Shapland.

If the RAAF planes flew, they would land in the early evening, and the barrier had to be in place by dawn the next day. The flood peak was still estimated to arrive after lunch on Saturday. A small number of pregnant women were evacuated on the last commercial flights and the relief centres were opened.

Now, however, there was some good news: the sandbags arrived on Friday at midday and so began a second, bigger sandbag operation. 'We worked in two teams of about thirty people,' says Allen Johnstone. 'There was a great sense of urgency. Ten-year-old kids were running water to the baggers and, as people got tired and stopped, others took their places. When we needed more people, we asked over the radio, and they came running.

'We realised we only needed to half fill the bags, so when they were dropped down they would be slightly pliable and would spread out nicely. And if they are half full it is easier to bend the edge over and do them up.

'It was physically difficult work. There were two teams working on two trucks, females against males, and the girls were doing better than the boys.'

The road bridge on the Mitchell Highway, which spans the Warrego and joins the halves of Charleville, had to be closed so the floodgates could be installed. These gates are placed in slots on the upright posts located at the end of the bridge. The town was now effectively cut in half, and the people on the northern bank, most of whom live on 2.5-hectare blocks, were isolated, away from shops, schools, the hospital and the only route out of town.

The weather closed in. Rain pelted down all day and the barrier delivery flight departure times kept being postponed. The RAAF also had to find new aircrews who had flying time on their rosters. Eventually the planes were scheduled to arrive at 9.30pm.

At the same time, Charleville had to find the workforce to erect the barrier. 'Every carpenter, builder, plumber and electrician — anyone who could handle an electric drill and hammer — was asked to help,' says Mark O'Brien.

George Donohoe says that residents have to understand what role volunteers play in a floodprone community. 'People should make certain they have families and friends who can assist with personal preparations, because sometimes volunteers are overwhelmed. Having family and friends around saves phone calls for help and doesn't drain manpower. Some people won't ask their families for help, which takes manpower away from emergency tasks. And of course some people just think others should be helping, not them ...'

Judy Wilson said many people hadn't worked out what to do with their pets: 'a very emotional thing.'

The Queensland government jet arrived at 8pm with the men and one woman from New Zealand who knew how to install the flood barriers. At 9.30pm the first of the air force planes carrying the aluminium supports touched down and dozens of people arrived to help unload. The New Zealand crew took over and, with the assistance of the council staff and Charleville residents, began transporting the barrier to the two sites. The semi-trailers with the pallets arrived shortly afterwards and the exercise to erect the first of the barriers began in earnest.

Then the RAAF advised they might not be able to fly the second plane, a Hercules, to Charleville. A new weather system was approaching the town, and the plane might not be able to land. And if that plane could not arrive, the whole exercise would be wasted.

The pilots were responsible for the final decision and, as they approached Charleville, a small window of clear weather fortunately opened up. The pilots agreed to land, but said unloading would have to take place very quickly indeed, for a storm was coming. They might be forced to fly out again with some of the equipment on board.

The Hercules skidded onto Charleville airport at 11.15pm. The SES, council staff and volunteers started to manhandle the equipment off the plane, but they were unfamiliar with it and too many people were helping. 'It was spectacular to watch the way the defence forces operated,' says Mark O'Brien. 'The pilots said to everyone, get out of the way and let us get on with it. The way those guys worked was magnificent to watch.'

The planes flew out a few minutes after midnight. The effort to fill the gaps in the levee was now in full swing, led by the New Zealanders. 'They don't have flood warnings of a few days in New Zealand,' says O'Brien. 'They've only got a matter of hours and they know exactly what is needed and how to do it.'

'We had two teams of sixty to seventy people working in shifts on the two sites,' says Allan Pemberton. 'At any time there would be twenty or thirty people working on a single task. Any more than that and they'd get in each other's way.'

Pete McRae joined the sandbagging teams. 'It's a primitive response, building temporary levees like that,' he says. 'We had a team of about five or six, filling bags, hauling them over our shoulders and then climbing up the levee bank. It was exhausting. The bags are quite heavy, but eventually you get to a point where you stop noticing how heavy they are.

'It's dangerous to do this in an emergency situation, especially for people who aren't used to this kind of work. One small girl was trying to help and I just thought she'd get hurt. I reckon I've got lower-back problems from the carrying.'

'The position of the bags was the key,' says Allan Pemberton. 'The pallets had to be in a straight line. The pallets are heavy. It was slow, difficult work and there was a reasonable amount of scepticism from those building the barrier that it was no good anyway.'

Pemberton, the SES volunteers and Allen Johnstone, Mark O'Brien and the shire staff had now been working for more than twenty-four hours. They had helped their own families to move furniture, assisted others when called upon, they had made quick decisions, kept morale up, and were frequently beset by panicky residents. They were tired almost beyond exhaustion. And at the back of all their minds was the same thought: would the Warrego stop rising before it reached the top of the pallet barrier?

At 4am on the Saturday morning, the final sandbags were placed on the plastic. As the levee builders stood back, they could see the water in the Warrego rising, rising, until it stopped just 30 centimetres below the top of the sand levee. So far so good, but nobody knew whether the levee would hold. All they could do was see what would happen next.

The river had isolated the town by cutting the Warrego Highway to the coast and the Mitchell Highway to Augathella. Nobody could leave. If the Warrego flooded over the new levee, everybody would be evacuated to the showground and the airport. It would be 1990 all over again.

The water kept rising all day Saturday and Sunday and now the pallet barrier was being tested, as water over-topped the levee and started rising up the wall. The frantic hard work, had so far, shown its value — but it would all be futile if the barrier gave way.

'We couldn't work out where the water was coming from.'

The water continued to rise slowly and final preparations and evacuations were continuing in Charleville. On the Saturday morning a call, which shocked everyone, came from council staff at Augathella, 90 kilometres upstream. The levee there was starting to collapse. They needed sandbags to repair a breach.

Council works supervisor in Augathella, Howard Edwards, was told that the levee was letting water into the town and would collapse within 15 minutes.

He quickly went to look, and decided that although water was seeping in quickly, the levee was safe for the moment. He moved some council pumps to the site where the water was coming in — Dead Dogs Gully opposite the shops in the middle of town. After a couple of hours he could see the pumps were not having much effect, so something else had to be done to stop the leaking.

'We couldn't work out where the water was coming from,' he says. 'Eventually we realised it was seeping in around the outlet pipes.

'Those pipes were packed in by rocks and sand. The action of the water from the river had washed the sand away. Water was threatening to wreck the whole structure and take the entire levee away with it. We knew we had to do something to block the outlet.

'We had recently closed Augathella's swimming pool, and the big water membrane was available. We thought we could build a metal frame and use that to stretch the membrane over, and hold the lot down with heavy weights, like sandbags.

'We attached the membrane to some box steel and some full petrol drums that were stationed on top of the levee. A couple of blokes volunteered to jump into the water and try to get the structure in place at the bottom.

'It was very dangerous. We had them tied in harnesses. Mostly the water was over their heads. I was hoping they wouldn't get sucked down and into the pipes that were letting water through.'

This heroic action virtually stopped the leak. But floodwaters are not safe until they are gone. They are relentless. When one hole is plugged, it seems there is always another somewhere else. Floods are battles of attrition.

'We noticed that the top of the levee bank seemed to be giving way,' says Edwards. 'It seemed to be wearing away slowly, then a couple of metres fell away altogether.

'We asked people to help fill sandbags to fill the gap. A hundred and fifty people — in a town of six hundred — arrived and started to work shoulder to shoulder to fill the bags and drop them into the gap. The bags probably weighed thirty kilograms and young kids, girls and boys, all did their bit and lifted them as part of the human chain. We had a line of people who were handing these big bags to each other, when those on top of the levee started to feel it move.

'It was a very tense time. We all knew that if a wall of water had knocked out the levee, there would be people downstream who would be flooded and in real trouble.'

The sandbagging went on into the evening: Edwards began to despair that it didn't seem to be having any impact. 'We just couldn't seem to put the sandbags in the right place,' he says.

Eventually night fell and, without any form of industrial lighting, the human conveyers had to stop. Exhausted, the people of Augathella pulled back and watched the river. They went home to put their belongings as high as they could. The levee bank stopped crumbling, but the river continued to rise.

Howard Edwards called Allen Johnstone in Charleville. Johnstone recalls his feeling that the team at Augathella were desperate. 'We thought we could try to fix the breach in the levee by placing big blue tarpaulins over the earth wall and holding them in place with sandbags,' he says. 'But Augathella had run out of sandbags.'

Johnstone asked council driver Mark Singleton if he would take a load of sandbags up to Augathella. 'We told him there would be water over the road at the 27 Mile, and made it clear that taking the trip was entirely up to him.'

Singleton had two options: the direct route to Augathella or the longer trip via the small settlement of Morven. He didn't hesitate. 'They were in real trouble up there,' he says, 'and if I'd gone via Morven that would have been another two or three hours. So I decided to go direct.'

Singleton drove off up the Mitchell Highway with a semi-trailer and two dog trailers loaded with sandbags. At the 27 Mile, as expected, he came to floodwaters surging across the highway. They were much higher than he had thought they would be. He tentatively drove the semi into the water, which grew deeper and deeper. Eventually he could not see the road beneath his wheels, and was following the top of the guide posts, which stood a metre tall. They were barely visible at times and in addition Singleton had no idea whether the road was damaged. From time to time, too, the semi was being buffeted by water, and hit by debris and tree branches.

'I was really sweating,' he says. 'I kept thinking, what would I do if the truck got stopped in the middle? I didn't have a plan. And I can't swim.'

Eventually the floodway grew shallower and Mark could drive on. He delivered the sandbags to Augathella.

Edwards and the townspeople of Augathella went to work again, this time sandbagging from the town side. They used about forty cubic metres of sand, two semi-trailers full, and the levee held.

'The blue tarps saved Augathella,' says Howard Edwards, laconically refusing to acknowledge his own role in organising the people of the town to hold back the river. They never gave up and in the end only two houses were affected by flooding.

In Charleville there was another new threat. The water had not overtopped the pallet barrier, but a great deal was seeping through the levees. Some seepage is always expected in levees — some would come under the temporary bridge gates or through in places where the earth was not compacted. Pumps were installed to deal with this problem. However the water in the town's gutters, roads and low-lying areas was rising.

Eventually the work crews realised that water was leaking through all sixteen outlet pipes along the levee bank. The pipes, about thirty centimetres wide, were designed to allow stormwater to flow out of the town through the levee and back into the river after rain. Each pipe had a cap that should have shut automatically by the action of the water pushing on it from the river side.

'We worked out that when the river last went down, silt must have gathered in the drainage pipes,' says Allen Johnstone. 'The one-way flaps were being held open and water was pouring back through them. We didn't know the bloody things would leak, but we knew we would have to clean them out.

'And we would have to do that by hand. Someone had to jump into the water and prise the gate open, scrape away the silt, then close the flap properly. Sixteen times.'

Billy Juniper and Les Baker volunteered and worked tirelessly to fix the faulty plumbing. Holding their breath under the freezing water, they were buffeted and smashed around. 'Those guys were under water for long periods,' says Allan Pemberton. The pipes were closed, the seepage stopped. The pumps were holding the water.

Then came another report which caused even greater consternation. A dam upstream had given way.

Many Queensland property owners have installed dams that can hold many megalitres of water. Not all are registered, engineered and authorised. It is sometimes difficult to tell whether water is lying in a hollow or in a shallow dam. The argument about dams has long divided the community. Many people believe the water should be used for environmental purposes downstream.

And so the reports about the dam erupted around town like noise from a startled flock of cockatoos! 'We were told that a massive dam had burst and a ten-metre wall of water was headed for the towns,' says Mark O'Brien. 'It was Armageddon, we were told. But it was odd that this was a dam that the people at the council had never heard of. Our pilots did see one small dam give way, but they told us it was far too small to make any impact on water levels. We had to chase the rumour down and it turned out that the big dam never existed at all.'

Mark O'Brien was advised by Pete McRae and George Donohue, among others, that he needed to go on the radio frequently to negate these sorts of problems.

'People put their own speculations on things,' says Donohue. 'It was all getting out of hand. We pressured Mark to go on radio, because too many people were abusing us. We felt the person in charge should let the public know all information available, and be upfront. And he did. It alleviated the anxiety and stopped a lot of stories.'

The levee was holding, but there was plenty of water coming through Charleville. The levee would only protect homes in the main part of town. At either end, it was always expected that there would be water in the streets, sometimes quite deep. People living between the levee and the river would be flooded.

Agricultural consultant Dominic Devine had a lot to lose. His modern, big two-storey, glass and concrete home overlooked the tops of the trees that line the Warrego, one of the most spectacular views in town. His rear fence was the new pallet barrier. If it did not hold, his house would be swamped.

Not only did his house back onto the Warrego, but water would also flow out of Bradleys Gully down the streets at the northern end of town and would have to pass through Dominic's property to escape to the river. The blocked pipes held the water inside the levee, and the property started to flood.

Dominic felt a weary sense of déjà vu. He had been in Charleville during the 1997 flood, living in a high-set house. 'We had sixteen people sheltering there with us,' he recalls. 'We emptied every home between the gully and the river in twenty hours, working in crews with trailers, vehicles and eight men. Then we spent the best part of a week working in gangs again to help clean up.

'In 1997 we had just four hours' notice. This time we were pretty well prepared.'

Devine was in touch with his clients in the upper reaches of the Warrego. 'I was getting information from Tambo, north of Augathella, where one of my clients said water was at the gate in the horse yard. It was higher than 1990.'

Some of the property owners outside Charleville were having a bad time. 'A mate, Michael Flynne, who lives fifty kilometres from the junction of the Warrego and Nive rivers, was cut off and couldn't get away. He lost fifteen kilometres of new fencing and some stock.' Downstream another property owner was isolated, and called for help when thousands of snakes invaded. In outback Queensland, there are no such things as harmless snakes.

Devine had to make preparations of his own. 'I shifted all the furniture out of downstairs. We sandbagged the doors and windows downstairs and kept out most of the water that came from the rain and Bradleys Gully. I was concerned the temporary levee wouldn't withstand all the water, but I just had to wait to see how much water would come down.'

In town SES controller Allan Pemberton's wife Leisa needed help. 'I didn't expect a flood at all,' she says. 'The day before, when Allan was heading off, we put all the electrical items above the floor — the washing machine, fridges, freezer, computers. Allan said to me the water wouldn't flood, but when it reached an agreed level, I should call him and he would get a truck.'

The water kept rising and the backyard had more than a metre of water in it.

Leisa was worried, but she did not want to show her children — sixteen-year-old Teegan, fourteen-year-old Cody and Alex, eleven — any sign of panic. 'They were playing in the yard and didn't even see their toys float out of the shed and away downstream. The water was a murky brown colour and started to flow much faster.

'The toilet backed up. We hadn't thought of that. Then the power went off. The floors started getting wet, so I thought water was coming in the back door.'

Leisa realised that water was coming in the air vents at the lowest brick level, even though their house was on small piles.

She and the children covered the vents. 'It was rushing past the back door really fast, so I started to pack our "panic boxes".' These are fishing boxes with essential items.

'I didn't want to face this by myself, so I called Allan and told him water was coming in the back door. It was very close to the doors and quite choppy. Water was flowing off the cars in the street and heading for our house.'

The relentless pressure from the river started to take its toll. The neighbours, thinking that because Allan was in the SES he would have special understanding of the floods, called Leisa and said they would not leave until she did. 'I was close to tears,' Leisa says. 'I was thinking all the time that we wouldn't be able to get flood insurance cover because we're in a floodprone area.'

Teegan and the others started to worry too, despite their mother's attempts to hold everything together. Their priorities were slightly different, however. 'The most important thing to me was to get my computer and speakers off the ground and somewhere safe,' says Teegan. There were boxes of pictures, books and schoolwork too. But where was safe?

Allan came home and reassured Leisa that even if the levee did breach, they would have four or five hours to remove all their belongings and evacuate to the relief centres. 'I thought she was a bit of a wreck, but she was still very strong in her thinking and quite focussed.'

At the other end of town Mark Galletly had an altogether different approach. When the water reached the doorstep of their two-storey home, he and his kids hopped on airbeds and raced downstream to the eddies. The property had been through floods before: in 1990 water went almost thirty centimetres over the floorboards.

Mark Galletly is a market gardener, one of the region's last. 'We were told there are only two vegetable growers between Toowoomba and here,' he says. 'I think there are a couple of Chinese families, one up at the 27 Mile and another at Augathella. We're still learning what will grow out here.'

Even though Charleville is in semi-arid country, it has a history of smallholders trying to use the ready supply of water and the black soil for high-value produce. A 1947 souvenir booklet in the museum calls Charleville 'The Queen City of the West' and 'Sovereign of Queensland's endless plains'. The water supply was an attraction, with reports that 'the quality of the citrus is unparalleled'.

Mark Galletly's market garden, on the river side of the levee, was ready to harvest zucchini, squash, beans, tomatoes, grapes and pumpkins. They decided to abandon their house on the Saturday night.

'The water covered the property for four and a half days,' says Galletly. 'When it went down, there was twenty centimetres of mud covering everything. The flood killed everything we had growing. We had a whole field full of pumpkins and the water got in, which collapsed them, and they turned to mush.

'But the water left the seeds in the ground and the next lot started shooting all over the place. Out of that we got lots of crossbred pumpkins, some of which were wild and wonderful. We got four tonnes. We would normally expect one and a half. We didn't have any trouble selling them.' Which was fine, except that the floodwaters brought another serious problem: weeds. They smothered the property for many seasons afterwards, defying all efforts to kill them.

Outside the levee at the other end of town, perched in a paddock close to the river, is Shane Carr's home. 'When the floods came in 1990 our timber home was washed away,' says Shane. 'This new one is built thirty-five centimetres higher, so I was surprised the floor nearly got wet.' However, safety was not an issue: he says that if the water levels had risen even higher, he would have felt safe.

Another family surrounded by floodwaters was in a residential area. Steven Maher and his wife Noie bought a house in Kennedy Street in 2005, knowing that water had covered their property to a depth of about forty centimetres in 1990. They found silt in the wall cavities during renovations.

'Our compensation for the floodwaters was the view of the river,' says Steven Maher, as he looks out onto the river on one side of his house, with parkland settings of gums, cypress and other massive trees all around. Echidnas and wallabies live in their yard.

'I was excited because I had never seen the river in flood before,' says Maher. 'I stared at it for ages. All I had ever seen up to then were the muddy holes. It makes a lovely noise in flood. But eventually we started to get apprehensive, because we didn't know how high the water would rise. We listened to the radio and thought the council knew how much water was coming down the river.

'We also listened to some of the old timers, people who had lived here all their lives, and talked to our neighbours. They said our house was in a good spot.' Maher's wife Noie adds that if there is a flood at their home, they know that in town things are a lot worse.

The Mahers' yard flooded to a depth of about 30 centimetres, but the water remained outside the house. They could watch as water swirled around their property, coming from all directions, and then settling. 'When the water went down, it was horrible,' says Maher. 'The sandflies hang around for months and they are vicious.'

The Warrego peaked on Tuesday at 6.02 metres. Water had risen about 30 centimetres up the pallet barrier, and the temporary levee held. This was extremely fortunate: that amount of water coming over the levee would have caused serious damage to Charleville.

Allan Pemberton had watched the water for three days and eventually realised that it wasn't rising any further. In some parts of town the clean-up began next day. Pemberton succinctly describes the fate of the unfortunate few who had water come into their homes: 'Stink, silt, sandflies and debris.

'The clean-up at each property took twenty-four to forty-eight hours before people could return home, but many yards were covered in silt and rubbish and the roads were not safe.

'The bridges had to be checked for damage before people could use them, so the council kept them closed. That angered a lot of people.'

Pete McRae's beloved bilbies, he says, were OK. 'They don't burrow when there is a flood; they move on when they get wet feet.'

There has been much soul-searching in Charleville since the flood. The levee was finished before the next wet season. But Bradleys Gully flash flooded again in 2010, a dozen homes were hastily evacuated and there was some damage. Allan Pemberton was not surprised. 'After the 2008 flood we found the previous highest level was actually in 1963, at 3.2 or 3.3 metres, so in 2008 we were close to the 1963 record.'

Mark O'Brien has not stopped trying to find an engineering solution to the problem of the Warrego and Bradleys Gully. In 2010 he reported to the Charleville residents that a solution had been suggested. It involves a 'retarding basin' which will capture water before it flows into town, the water being contained by a wall 10 metres high and 3 kilometres long, with a spillway into the river if it ever filled. The engineer quoted that the retarding basin, with a two-metre-high gully flood, would have taken twenty days to empty. O'Brien continued: 'The option would have successfully controlled the 2008 floods. The estimated cost for these works is $23 million. This is far beyond the resources of council. Our general rate revenue for Charleville residences and businesses is currently $1.1 million a year.'

O'Brien, however, remains an optimist. He says: 'The floods bring out the best in people. There are some fantastic people in every community and a crisis brings out their best. They belong to groups like the SES and other volunteer societies and when you need them, they just show up.'

He believes that the 1990 floods were responsible for townspeople starting to take greater responsibility for their future and to build resilience. 'It took about a year to recover and people were exhausted, but after that they started to build a stronger community.' That spirit was evident in the next three floods, including 2008.

'We've got a heap of work to do, not just building levees, but also building resilience,' says O'Brien, 'For example, we need people to meet their elderly neighbours and say to them,

"Now, what do you want me to do for you next time there is an emergency?" and offer to work out a plan.

'The council will also get people practising their response to a range of disasters, to help build confidence.

'There is a fantastic camaraderie in this town. People do what's needed for the sake of the whole town, no matter how hard it is.'

Never Enough Time
Emerald, Central Queensland, January 2008

'They thought I was joking.'

Hastings Donaldson, a third-generation cattle grazier at Medway Station, 100 kilometres west of Emerald, looked out from his homestead at a brown, murky sea. Metre-deep water covered hundreds of hectares of his paddocks. Shrubs and bushes, grasses, fences and tracks disappeared beneath the swirling currents. He couldn't see much more than the tops of the trees along the watercourses and the steel rails on top of the house paddock cattle yard.

Donaldson had previously witnessed great flooding, but on Thursday 17 January 2008 he saw water where it had never been before. Members of his family further north and grazier neighbours had already been in contact, confirming that a massive rainstorm was flooding every dam, watercourse, creek, melon hole and river as far as the eye could see. They knew fences would be smashed, crops and pastures destroyed, cattle drowned or swept away, roads damaged and homesteads isolated for weeks. Hastings Donaldson was also pretty sure the town of Emerald would be flooded.

'I could remember the '83 flood in Emerald and I thought I should tell some bugger,' he says. He rang the Emerald Council and told the engineer that Theresa Creek was rising very fast and would affect roads to the north of town. He added that when water reached the drought-stricken Lake Maraboon, 20 kilometres south of Emerald, it would fill in about three days. Emerald would be flooded.

'They thought I was joking,' he says. The engineer knew that sometimes cattle graziers in this part of the country, echoing the size of their properties and responsibilities, can be a bit larger than life. Lake Maraboon, the second biggest in Queensland and one of Australia's biggest inland freshwater storages, was only about one-third full after three years of drought. It hadn't overflowed since 1990.

And so they hesitated. But Hastings Donaldson was right.

Emerald, named after a verdant local pastoral property, lies on the Nogoa River 270 kilometres west of Rockhampton. It is on the main train line and road to Longreach. It's a pretty green town that has grown significantly since World War II. The Nogoa is joined by Retreat Creek and Theresa Creek downstream of the town.

The Fairbairn Dam on Lake Maraboon, built in 1972, holds back the Nogoa River. It regulates water flow and feeds the large irrigation industry downstream of the dam and centred around Emerald. Irrigation channels transport water to cotton; broad-acre crops like sunflowers and soybeans; and aquaculture and horticulture. The region also grew rapidly with the discovery of coal, and the development of the mines. The first mine in 1979 was at Gregory followed by Gordonstone in 1991, then Ensham and Crinum in 1994. Many of the mines need massive levee banks to divert water away from the underground or open-cut mines back into the rivers.

Emerald has been subject to flooding throughout its history. A 1906 photograph shows a steam train standing on the flooded Emerald bridge which then disappears into the Nogoa River. After that the bridge was rebuilt on massive stone pillars standing 51 feet and 6 inches above the water level — 15.7 metres. It is a key landmark and a gateway to the town.

A 'very big' flood occurred in 1918; and the Emerald and District Historical Association reports that floods 'occurred twice a year in the 1970s'. The Fairbairn Dam spilled for the first time in 1990. Most residents can remember when the dam overflowed, but it caused little inconvenience and only minor low-level flooding.

The flood that loomed largest in Emerald's history occurred in 1950. Almost every house was submerged or surrounded by floodwaters, many with water up to their windows. There were dramatic rescues throughout the district and, unfortunately, one of the rescuers died. There are memorials in Emerald to these events.

Floods can prevent road access to Emerald. The Gregory Highway, which runs north and south, is frequently cut by flash flooding at Theresa Creek. The main east–west Route 66, the Capricorn Highway, runs to Rockhampton and eventually to Longreach. The Capricorn Highway runs across the Vince Lester bridge, below but parallel to the train bridge, at the town entrance. People know that this, the last road out of town, will be closed when the water level is at 14.4 metres.

But few people are aware of other critical measurements: when the town's electricity is cut off; when the sewerage and water supplies are disabled how long before domestic portable phones fail and most mobile-telephone towers go down; and water will flood the main business district? These are significant statistics for the Local Disaster Management Committee, chaired by the council, and emergency agencies.

Emerald is on a floodplain so it is inevitable that flooding will occur. Residents should prepare thoughout the summer wet season for flooding in low-lying areas.

The dilemma in 2008 was that the region had experienced a relatively dry period for the previous 30 years, including seeing the enormous Fairbairn Dam at times reduced to 16 per cent capacity. Floods were not something the community were tuned in to. People had forgotton about them. No flood had exceeded the minor flood level of 14 metres at Emerald since the Dam was completed in 1972.

Emerald didn't have a plan; and during floods people do stupid things.

Tropical cyclone Helen began as a tropical low near Groote Eylandt in the Gulf of Carpentaria during the Christmas period of 2007, then moved slowly southeast. By New Year's Day 2008, however, it had changed direction and begun to move west, arriving in the Joseph Bonaparte Gulf off the northern coast of Western Australia, where it settled long enough to begin sucking up energy from the warm tropical waters.

The Tropical Cyclone Warning Centre at Darwin named it Cyclone Helen on 4 January. By that afternoon it was tracking steadily east and was intensifying. It reached Category Two with destructive winds of more than 125 kilometres per hour that damaged road signs, caravans and homes and stripped trees as it moved across the Top End, just out of Darwin.

Helen was downgraded to a 'tropical low' the next day, when the system was about 100 kilometres southeast of Darwin. It headed east for three days and crossed the coast of Cape York in the early hours of the morning on 7 January. The low slowly tracked eastwards across Cape York Peninsula and on 14 January was off the far north Queensland coast near Cardwell. It intensified and drifted slowly over the coast. Northeast of Townsville the Palm Island Indigenous community was hit, houses damaged and roads and bridges affected.

The system passed over Townsville, which received 100 millimetres of rain in one day; there were eighty calls to the SES for help. There was more significant flooding when the system reached Charters Towers, inland, on 15 and 16 January. Fifty homes were affected; four people had to be rescued from floodwaters and fifteen businesses were damaged.

The system travelled on, bulging with water and generating strong winds. Widespread intense rainfall was recorded across many catchments along the central Queensland coast as the low continued its slow drift southwards towards the headwaters of the Thomson and Barcoo rivers and Cooper Creek. On 16 and 17 January the system produced very intense rainfall over the Belyando and Nogoa rivers and Theresa Creek near Emerald for twenty-four hours.

The town of Bogantungan, 100 kilometres west of Emerald and the epicentre of the storm, received 700 millimetres of rain in five days.[*] This massive storm is what Hastings Donaldson saw when he looked across his property at the Drummond Ranges.

---

[*] Thanks to Peter Baddiley at the Bureau of Meteorology for these details.

Apart from the remote cattle stations, the first populated areas to come under siege from the floodwaters were Sapphire and Rubyvale, 40 kilometres west of Emerald. 'There was so much rain, it scared me,' says Tess Batts, the State Emergency Service Gemfields group leader, who has lived in Sapphire for thirty-seven years. 'The rain was heavy, really heavy, and came in waves for four days. Normally our rain comes from the Bowen area and approaches from the east. This came the other way, so we were in a blind spot and we had no idea it was coming.'

Tess Batts's description of the rain coming in waves is reminiscent of the way people describe the intensity of a cyclone. In these circumstances many find it difficult to tell the difference between flash flooding from rainfall and flooding as waters break the banks of creeks. One thing was certain — Sapphire was flooded.

'Theresa Creek rose really quickly and was running five kilometres wide between Anakie and Sapphire,' Tess recalled. 'We tried to get to people to find out how they were. People were trapped in their homes, but it felt like we'd had thirty inches of rain, and the place was saturated.

'More than a dozen homes were flooded with water to bench-top height. People didn't know it was going to happen and they had no way of getting out.

'At least one of the homes was undermined by the floodwater and slowly subsided into a nearby disused shaft. A four-wheel-drive vehicle parked at the Bullock Holes was pushed over by the waves of water washing across the ground.' Eventually helicopters were needed to rescue a dozen people from their homes. The little creeks were flooded, so there was no road access. Phones didn't work very well during storms in normal times, and it was hard for people to get messages out.

The Gemfields towns are not cohesive communities, with meetings held by flood-wise disaster committees and resources of a big town. They are informal places with laconic people not used to asking for help. In fact many people live in the Gemfields to avoid authority. Flash flooding is not unusual in the region, so initial reports of problems did not galvanise emergency agencies outside the town. Their plight was not immediately recognised by their local disaster committee, which was based at district council headquarters in Emerald.

On Thursday night Councillor Col Brunker, the chairman of the Emerald District Council Disaster Committee, was calling bingo when he received a phone call from Anakie police, describing widespread flooding in the Gemfields. Brunker contacted Emerald Councillor Kerry Hayes. Hayes, a real-estate and pastoral agent and a water trader, had been talking to his contacts in the region and knew there had been heavy and widespread rain that had probably caused damage to the stations and pastoral country. But he didn't get any idea of what was happening only forty kilometres away.

'In a normal summer season flooding at the Gemfields happens all the time. It doesn't cause a lot of damage,' he says. 'What we didn't understand was how much water, where it was going, how many people it was affecting. We didn't get told it had covered mines and filled in holes. The response to Anakie and the Gemfields was predicated on the fact that in the past flooding had been very minor.'

Kerry Hayes has lived in the Emerald region all his life. His grandfather arrived in the district to work on the rail lines in the 1890s. The family won a block of land in the irrigation ballots of the 1970s. Kerry was elected to the council in 1977.

Like everyone he'd heard stories about the floods of the 1950s. 'My dad rescued a man out of a tree,' he recalls. 'They needed a little fella, a bit lightweight, to climb the tree with ropes.

On Friday Emergency Management Queensland district disaster officer Shane Wood, based in Rockhampton, contacted the Emerald District Council and advised they set a local disaster management committee to coordinate flood response and recovery.

Kerry Hayes was genuinely surprised. He had a very good knowledge of the region, but had never participated in a flood or disaster exercise. 'I had no training and no awareness of how the recovery agencies would work together,' he says.

In Queensland, local government co-ordinates disaster response, with help and support from the professional agencies such as the police and Emergency Management Queensland and the volunteer agencies such as the SES and rural fire services. Mayor Peter Maguire was on holidays in Fiji, from whence ironically a cyclone prevented him returning in a hurry. However, he had no experience of floods either. In his absence, Kerry Hayes was named acting mayor. The Local Disaster Committee was activated.

Col Brunker and Jim Chan chaired the group. Each worked at the Council Chambers for twelve-hour stretches throughout the 2008 floods. Acting Council CEO Phil Brumley advised them of possible actions and coordinated council teams to respond.

Hayes watched with interest as those around him went about their business in a low-key way, setting up the coordination room. Shane Wood from Emergency Management Queensland, travelled out from Rockhampton.

'EMQ suggested we set up the LDMC and a response room and a coordination centre,' says Kerry Hayes. 'Phil Brumley said the Bureau of Meteorology had predicted that in the next week or so, there would be a large rainfall event to the north and northwest of us.'

Kerry Hayes quickly came to realise he was in charge. But of what? There was no emergency. Certainly Lake Maraboon was filling quickly and it looked as if it would spill water into the Nogoa River. This did not happen often, but it had occurred at least twice before with little drama. Pastoralists were also talking about rain damage to their crops and properties, but again, this was not unknown during the monsoon season. Besides, it had been dry: the rain was welcome.

'At that stage in my mind, the Local Disaster Management Committee existed in minutes only on Council charts. I had an awareness that the committee existed for local disaster management, but I think everyone thought it was an SES group and they had yellow overalls, a boat and a four-wheel-drive and attended road accidents.'

But on the Friday, there were stirrings of concern from some people. The road to the BHP-owned Gregory Mine, north of town, was cut by the flooded Theresa Creek and management had advised mine staff to have the day off.

David Butler, an employee at Gregory, lives with his wife Julianne and their family in Whitchurch Road in a higher part of Emerald. Although this section of town backs onto the northern side of the river, no one who lived there thought for a moment they were at risk. The Butler property is about three hundred metres from the river.

Butler, a cautious man, watched the Nogoa River rise and read Bureau of Meteorology forecasts online. The water was rising steadily, but he wasn't concerned. He says, 'The worst case in my head was that it might get to the pool in the backyard, but the house is a metre above that level.

'Even so, we have always had flood insurance. Even after the floods in the 1990s when the water didn't reach our property, we kept that.'

Butler's mother-in-law lived in a lower part of town that, he says, 'always floods', so he went down, put her furniture up on the benches, collected some valuables and brought her back to his home.

Retired grazier Gerald Mayne also prepared his home in Emerald, even though it appears to be built high above the Nogoa River. He lives adjacent to the botanic garden and, after eight years of toil, his own garden appears to be an extension of that. It consists of a beautiful array of dense thick green plants, carefully manicured lawn and hedges, wonderful shade trees and flowers.

Mayne installed a floodproofing system around his home. The windows on the brick house are all a metre above the ground. Water below this height can get in only via the doorways where he has installed vertical metal brackets, so when a flood comes he can slide boards into them and they keep water out of the house. It's an elegant solution. Mayne has painted the boards and he keeps them in his garage. In effect he has built a levee all the way around his home.

'I've been in floods plenty of times before, with cattle,' he says. 'You were always trying to make sure stock were out of flood reach and you had to make sure the gates were opened so cattle didn't get caught on the corners of the fences.

'In the 1950 flood after a big cyclone, it was common to see bullocks hanging in the forks of trees fifteen to twenty feet up. They'd be swimming around and, to get a breath, they'd head for the fork of a tree: when the water went down they couldn't get down and they died.

'This time, a lot of the creeks and gilgais* were empty. The first two hundred millimetres of rain filled them up.'

Gerald's home looked impregnable up to the height of the windows, but he was taking no chances. 'No one can tell you where the peak will be and how safe it is. You can see people living on the edge of the river and they thought it would never flood. Every flood is different.

'The water was rising one foot an hour, so we had to think about getting out. I got bags off the Wheat Board and a ute load of sand; and when I got back home there were about a dozen mine employees in the street, asking people if they needed a hand. They couldn't get to work so the company told them to help anybody who was going to be flooded.

'They hopped in and put plastic around the doorways and sandbags three feet high to protect us.

'I thought the water might get into the house. We put everything in the house on trestles. We didn't want to shift at night.

'One of our neighbours came down to help and saw a furniture van parked in the street with the keys still in it. He drove it down and we put all the furniture we could into it and took it up to my daughter's place and, after a couple of trips, put the truck back. To this day we don't think the owner knows we borrowed it!'

---

* Gilgai (pro: gill-guy): a depression or hole in the ground, especially one which drains off surface water, forming a natural reservoir; crabhole; dead man's grave; melon hole; runaway hole. [Australian Aboriginal (Wiradjuri and Kamilaroi): *gilgaay*, waterhole.]

Gerald's front yard opens onto the path which leads down under tropical shrubbery and established trees to the Nogoa River. He tied different coloured pieces of tape on various trees so he could watch as the water rose up the path.

'This is pretty serious.'

The rural community was also watching developments with some concern. They needed as much time as possible to get their irrigation and farm equipment off their paddocks. Those on Theresa and Retreat creeks were becoming worried.

It continued to rain up in the catchment, although for the most part Emerald received only minor showers. On the Thursday night and Friday morning Theresa Creek flooded and cut off the northern route out of town. But people could drive east to Rockhampton, so long as the Vince Lester bridge remained open.

Lake Maraboon filled. Hundreds of people went out to witness and photograph the first trickle coming over the dam. Those who stayed there long enough believed they could actually see the water rising up the dam wall, an amazing event at such a big lake.

Councillor Hayes called friends at a company called 4T Land Water and Resource Intelligence to find out what they knew. 'Geoff Kavanagh and Ian Rankine know more about the region and the catchment than anyone,' explained Kerry. 'Geoff told me: "This is pretty serious." That, quite frankly, got my attention big time.'

The hydrographers at the Department of Environment and Resource Management (DERM) also made predictions of large inflows, with water likely to rise to up to 4 metres over the spillway. 'He was predicting inflows would fill the Fairbairn Dam and the level of the water spilling out would be quite substantial.'

But the Bureau of Meteorology was only forecasting moderate flooding on low-lying areas and EMQ was comfortable with that advice. Kerry Hayes did not know what to believe: would there be enough rainfall to cause serious flooding in Emerald?

Peter Baddiley at the BoM's Queensland Flood Warning Centre, a man with enormous experience of Queensland weather systems, was also battling uncertainty. 'The very high rainfalls overnight on Friday 18th and Saturday 19th made a significant difference to the eventual size of the flood,' he says. 'Unfortunately nobody could get this critical rainfall information from most of the automatic and manual rainfall stations because the telephone network and equipment had failed.'

The DERM staff advised the council of what they knew, but the information flow at the Local Disaster Management Committee wasn't creating a useful picture of the threat, yet Kerry Hayes was worried. 'The bureau was making calculations on the rainfall events but 4T couldn't correlate them with water flows past significant points.

'I was really surprised that there had been a significant amount of water in that area and yet it seemed that not many people knew about it, including people who could do something about it.

'I felt embarrassed. Why didn't we know more about what was happening? The reality was we had never done this before. But I felt my role as a community leader was to get on top of the information. So I brought 4T into the mix.'

Hayes started referring to information provided by his friends at 4T. This was unprecedented: to some it also suggested that the inexperienced council wasn't following standard operating procedure. Hayes admits this caused considerable tension at the disaster headquarters.

'The mindset of people who deal with situations like this tends to be quite military. Very lateral views on things seemed incongruous. The discussion on Friday and Saturday became about the level the dam would overspill. BoM said two to two and half metres, at an extreme, but our guys were saying four metres plus.

'Two and a half metres is not a problem, but four metres plus is a significant threat.

'The EMQ District Disaster Committee in Rockhampton were saying, "We get information from BoM and we treat that as gospel."' Kerry Hayes disagreed and continued to take advice from the local water specialists. He thought he was being 'prudent and diligent'.

'There were people at EMQ saying we needed to be consistent. Being very naive I said: "Why? We are getting good information from these people."' But the conflict was preventing the agencies and council issuing useful advice to the public; and no plans were being put in place to prepare Emerald.

Hayes realised that an 'offline' conversation between both bodies was necessary to eliminate confusion. On Saturday he arranged a phone hook-up between Peter Baddiley at the Bureau and 4T. 'We had a long conversation and Geoff and Ian and Peter kind of came to an agreement. BoM accepted these guys were making correct predictions.'

For the first time those in charge of the flood response agreed: the dam would probably spill enough water to flood Emerald.

In fact between Thursday 17 and Saturday 19 January, Fairbairn Dam rose about seven metres and began spilling at about 11am on Saturday. The level at the spillway, which is 250 metres wide, continued rising to a peak of 4.44 metres at 2pm on Tuesday 22 January, its highest point since construction of the dam in the 1970s. The outflow over those four or five days was 200 gigalitres of water, enough to provide all of Adelaide's water needs for more than eight months.

When the water spilled over the dam just before lunch on Saturday, ABC Local Radio News quoted Glen Pfluger of Sunwater (the operators of the dam) as saying, 'The current overflow was not expected to cause any problems.'

What would happen if the overflow continued at the same rate was clear. The water would first fill the irrigation channels and ditches, then it would hit the Nogoa River, which would quickly break its banks. Low-lying farmland all around Emerald would flood; and then water would enter houses and shops. The council engineers believed homes along the irrigation channels to the north of the town would be affected first; then the low-lying areas where the highway and train line crossed the bridges; and later some parts of the central business area.

As is usual in these circumstances, Queensland Emergency Services Minister Neil Roberts declared a 'disaster' to allow people to be forcibly evacuated by emergency authorities if necessary. The Emergency Services Department put out a news release to that effect. But it only added to the confusion in Emerald, where residents still did not believe there would be a disaster.

Understanding how the water flow at Fairbairn Dam would relate to water heights along the river and into town required considerable flood mapping, which was expensive. It might also have required substantial interference with town planning regulations. Flood mapping had been under discussion in Emerald for years, but the Council and water authorities had done nothing about it.

Bill Wilkinson, a highly respected natural resource management officer at the Department of Natural Resources and Management and a longtime Emerald resident, had had an interest in flood mapping for many years. 'There was no flood inundation mapping available. Any knowledge people had of previous flood behaviour had been altered.' The landscape had changed greatly — the new dam irrigation, coal mines and laser-levelled crops all surrounded the town.

Wilkinson later estimated that the Gemfields town of Rubyvale has only 30 minutes to an hour warning of flooding in its catchment; Sapphire 6 hours maximum; and that only 12 hours later Theresa Creek will flood the Gregory Highway, just north of Emerald. That cuts off one of the town's two road exits.

Theresa Creek skirts the Ensham open-cut coal mine. 'It blew out first,' says Wilkinson. The massive floodwaters of Theresa Creek breached the levies and all but collapsed the open cut. 'It hit it hard,' he says in something of an understatement. Damage was estimated at hundreds of millions of dollars and part of the mine was out of action for months.

The Emerald Shire Council would be responsible for residents in town, but those along the rivers out of town were overlooked. There were no warnings issued for these rural landholders. The residents along Theresa Creek suffered massive stock and crop losses.

Kerry Hayes says people were more inclined to watch the Nogoa River and its catchment. 'Theresa Creek affects a number of large, rural properties which border the riparian area. Historically people say if there is a high rainfall event along that creek, it will flood some farmland but people won't be threatened. It will cut some roads.

'But the rain at Theresa Creek fell at such a rate and with such velocity that when it came through the Gemfields it didn't just flood a road. It pushed out into areas that, quite frankly, we would not have known could possibly be affected.'

No one knew either what would happen to the water coming from the Fairbairn Dam when it met floodwaters from Theresa Creek. All Saturday afternoon the disaster team conducted scenario planning.

'By Saturday night,' says Kerry Hayes, 'we still didn't know how the height of water at the dam translated to levels in town. That was frustrating and the most frightening thing of this whole event.

'I was thinking: If it keeps raining, how high can the water level go? Can the impoundment hold it at all? We started go through scenarios. We became hydrographers all of a sudden.

'We knew problems were going to occur when the water reached about 14.5 metres at the Vince Lester bridge. The road would be cut and we'd have no road exit from town.

'At about 15.4 metres we believed we would have no sewer and water and we would effectively be on an island, and the only way to get out would be over the train bridge.

'There was talk that the water would reach sixteen metres, so we also did a scenario plan for seventeen metres, although the reality was at almost sixteen metres the rail bridge goes out and ends completely any chance of evacuation via a conventional route.

'If the water got to seventeen metres, we needed to be gone.'

The council started to advise residents late on Saturday that flooding was likely in the town. Kerry Hayes told ABC Radio at 10pm on Saturday widespread flooding was possible. He said they would make a decision at six the following morning, so that if necessary an evacuation plan could be put in place. 'Depending on the calculations we can gauge overnight and the rate of increase of flow over the dam, anything up to twenty-five per cent of the population could be affected.'

He adds, 'We were very conscious of the fact that residents knew we had two days of inaccurate information; and they would question our statements and ask themselves, "What if it keeps raining?" We didn't want people to be panicking.'

Unfortunately, few people were listening to ABC Local Radio at 10pm on Saturday, so the warnings were not widely distributed.

The LDMC duly met at 6am on Sunday. As a precaution they set up evacuation centres at the town hall and the local pastoral college, capable of caring for about five hundred people. It was important to set up an evacuation registry so emergency agencies knew what people were doing. Residents who felt uncomfortable about the water levels were asked to register and then go and stay with family or friends.

The plan being shaped at the council was to deal with the town section by section. 'As problems arose, they would be fixed,' says Hayes. 'There was no way known we could warn everybody about everything.' Council also started planning for a mass evacuation centre at the cotton mill on the high side of town, which would hold four or five thousand people. Pets would be impounded at a location in Emerald and someone would have to stay behind to water and feed them.

In the early stages, Hayes was not sure that the evacuation centres would be needed. 'We felt it was prudent for us to open them up for people who didn't feel comfortable, or for people from outlying areas who were caught in town without being able to get home.'

When a dam spills, people usually expect the outflow to level off quickly, as though a plug has been pulled. They tend to forget that, if water is still running into the dam somewhere else, and inflow exceeds outflow, the water level will continue to rise.

The new 'measuring gauge' consisted of the pylons that held the road 20 metres above the dam wall. Now the water level was judged by how far it rose up the pylons at the roadway. In 1998, the highest outfall recorded at the dam, water levels reached just under 2.7 metres. But now the volume of water tumbling into the Nogoa River was fantastic: at the dam wall the river is about 250 metres wide and the turbulence as water crashed into the river below — where it would affect hundreds of river properties before heading towards Emerald — was awe-inspiring. Even so, most people did not realise how the water would affect them.

In town, the LDMC decided to rely on community groups to provide the support residents would need. 'We already had community group organisers in the building asking whether they could help,' says Hayes. 'These people are generally the caregivers, the people in the community who can provide reassurance to older people and those who are sick. We got them talking to people to find out what they needed.'

The committee sat down with engineer Ken Bickhoff on the Saturday night. Given the rate of water rise, they wanted him to tell them what areas of town would be inundated first. 'We identified the northeast and the northern part of town affected by water backed up by Theresa Creek,' says Hayes, 'and we nominated some of the low-lying drainage areas that always back up when there is significant rain.' They did not nominate the higher areas that run along the river in the middle of town.

Kerry Hayes authorised public announcements on Sunday morning news bulletins, to be delivered by the SES, police and other volunteers. They all said there was a chance of flooding. 'We said to people that water might enter their property and they might like to evacuate. They should register at the town hall and make sure that people knew where they were. They didn't have to stay there, but just register and maybe go back to their property. We also asked the SES to visit the properties we felt would be flooded and to ask people to be prepared, have a bag and a toothbrush handy.'

By Sunday morning, a few people in low-lying areas had packed up and left. However, not many. It had stopped raining and in the beautiful sunshine most of the population were celebrating what appeared to be the breaking of a three-year drought. Queensland premier Anna Bligh flew in to look at the water at the dam and to talk to officials to ensure that flood planning was proceeding smoothly. 'We told her that we didn't know how high the water would rise when it got to Emerald,' says Hayes.

'The town, quite frankly, was rolling along. We were just standing here celebrating the break from the rain, watching the brown water just coming and coming. People kept wondering where it was coming from.'

But there had been massive flooding in many parts of the region and some helicopter evacuations at the Gemfields, as well as the damage to Ensham mine. Messages were now being passed around town that families and friends who lived along the Nogoa River would be inundated and many rushed to help. Farmers were reporting that their crops had been wiped out, pastoralists to the north and west were already counting the cost of losing thousands of head of cattle, smashed fencing and infrastructure and destroyed pasture.

The water kept rising at the Fairbairn Dam; and that meant it would keep rising in Emerald. By lunchtime on Sunday, the atmosphere in the town had started to change.

The premier, ignoring trading hours legislation, asked local supermarkets to reopen so people could stock up on essentials. 'People started to grow sombre. That was when people made sure they went shopping, bought water and nappies and all that. Still, eighty per cent of people, about six thousand, remained in town.'

Peter Baddiley from the Bureau of Meteorology says that the flood at Emerald built more slowly than those at the Gemfields because the dam levels had been so low.

On Sunday afternoon Kerry Hayes received a call that worried him. 'Riverview Street was starting to flood. That wasn't expected.' In fact, the street was not in a particularly low-lying part of town and was supposed to be the third area that flooded, not the first. What had gone wrong?

Riverview Street has one row of homes across the road from the river reserve. At one end the river runs past the beautiful tropical botanic gardens. But down in the residential area, the dusty, rocky bank is lined with stumps and logs and is largely obscured by bushes and thorny shrubs. It is a place where the water is always a murky brown. Roy Druwitt, who had lived in Riverview Street for twelve years, reckons there was a time when he could pick up the occasional redclaw, the Queensland freshwater crayfish.

Roy Druwitt watched the river rise up the bank across the road from his home. 'On Saturday night it came through with a roaring sound, about two in the morning, and started coming over its banks. But it was only travelling up slowly.

'On the Sunday the SES told us they thought we should get ready to evacuate. We thought they were joking. But we moved all the heavy furniture, the TV, fridges and stoves, into a mate's removal truck anyway. We left everything in drawers and cupboards because we couldn't see it rising that high.'

Druwitt and his family gathered on the front verandah as the water rose. 'It came up slowly, but by midnight it had crossed the road; and we knew it was still rising in the dam.' They knew they would be trapped there if they didn't move and so, reluctantly, they went to a friend's house.

'It was coming up slowly ...'

As night fell on Sunday 20 January, Emerald went to bed wondering when it would finally stop raining out west and how high the water was likely to rise. On Monday morning, they were at last preparing for flooding. Shops closed so they could be evacuated. Many tried sandbagging. People in low-lying areas were moving furniture higher and packing their important belongings. Everybody knew that once the Vince Lester bridge closed, they would not be able to get out of town. And Kerry Hayes knew that other community connections, like the rail and telephones, would fail and people would be more likely to panic.

'We were telling people, "You might be safe in your house but you will have no water and your street could be cut off from the rest of the town. If you get into trouble we can't come and get you.

'"We need you to be either with friends in a part of town that isn't inundated, or somewhere safe, because we don't want to send personnel back into risky areas."' Council staff worked frantically to set up the evacuation centre at the cotton gin, to prepare sandbags and clear drains.

Meanwhile, the water continued to rise at the Fairbairn Dam. It had now reached the 4-metre mark, the highest level recorded. Evacuation plans went up a notch.

'We could cater for four and a half to five thousand people at the cotton ginnery,' says Hayes. 'We got emergency supplies from the Salvation Army in Brisbane. We thought, the sooner these emergency supplies got moving the better, because if the rainfall situation elsewhere in Queensland changed, the supplies might get held up somewhere else.'

At the time, the Spirit of the Outback, the passenger train servicing central Queensland and the coast, was fortunately parked at the Emerald train siding. As a last resort it could take a few hundred people with their pets and some personal effects 500 metres or so to the cotton mill on the high ground where the council had set up a relief centre. Given enough time it could evacuate every resident, but the turnaround would have to be done quickly. There would no time for errors or unforeseen problems.

'You could take your defibrillator or your toothbrush, your pets and one bag,' said Kerry Hayes. 'But not much else.'

At the very moment Kerry was discussing the plan and how to get the message to the community, Queensland Rail was about to take the Spirit back to Rockhampton, 250 kilometres away on the coast, to resume normal duties!

There was every chance it would leave town quietly with no fanfare and would be gone before Kerry Hayes even realised.

Losing the train would be a disaster. Kerry Hayes knew he had to stop it leaving, but he had no idea how.

At the northern end of town the streets were awash, with water just above the gutters, as if there had just been a tropical downpour. People were unable to drive or walk in the streets and gardens were damaged, but there was little impact on the houses.

At seven on the Monday morning, Roy Druwitt and Tony Grimley went back to their homes in Riverview Street to see what had happened overnight. By now the street was blocked by rising water, so they drove into a street behind and jumped the fence. The water was well up Druwitt's drive by now, though not in his house. He put more items up on benches and shelves and left. 'I was there for about twenty to thirty minutes and in that time the water advanced and completely covered my yard. I needed to move the car out of the street behind, and quickly, or we'd have been blocked in.' This might have been the time at which the Nogoa River was rising fastest. The water in the yard had risen about ten centimetres in half an hour.

Druwitt returned in the afternoon when he realised what the water could do. He was distressed to find that there was 600 millimetres of water through his home. 'I wanted to knock the fence down to let the water run through the property, rather than bank up against it and smash things,' he says. 'I was upset, but not panicking. There was nothing I could do about the water, and I didn't think about damage at that stage.'

There is also the story about Col Brunker and Goldie.

For much of his life Col Brunker worked on exploration parties with BHP, including at Groote Eylandt. He was the first development officer with the Gregory coal mine in 1977. But he had also wanted to do some droving and had always kept horses. His favourite stockhorse, Goldie, was a twelve-year-old mare he kept in a paddock behind the golf course. Goldie was in trouble, caught by the swirling floodwaters rising from the Nogoa. Brunker and a mate raced down to get her out, but the current was too strong and they couldn't get anywhere near the horse. It was dark and dangerous and they had to leave her.

The next morning Col Brunker came back to try and rescue Goldie. He found her waiting patiently at the gate where she was usually fed, with water up to her belly.

'We tried to walk in the current, where the water was up to my waist, but we just couldn't do it,' says Brunker. 'I was worried that if we reached Goldie and the water knocked us down, the horse would smash into us and we wouldn't get out alive.' He had to abandon Goldie for the second time.

Some time later Goldie was rescued by a jet-ski rider. Col saw that excellent news that night on a TV news bulletin.

Out in the rural areas, there was devastation.

Ian Burnett, Emerald resident and vice-president of the rural lobby group Agforce, says the levee system built by many farmers worked well, but was not extended far enough. 'The farms along the Theresa Creek and Nogoa River floodplains all had crops in production,' he says. 'Hundreds of hectares of sorghum and cotton were destroyed. Many tractors and other machinery were caught in the paddocks and couldn't be moved.

'The water lay in the paddocks eighty centimetres deep, and sometimes one and a half metres deep. The structural damage to houses and farm infrastructure was substantial.

'The water came out of the channels and washed away topsoil. It deposited tanks and debris all over the place; and fencing was gone.'

Up in the Belyando district 180 kilometres northwest of Emerald, where the rain had filled the catchment, the damage was extraordinary. In some places cattle yards had a metre or more of topsoil washed away and the stumps were visible, including the concrete that held them to the ground.

'There were thousands of head of stock lost: cattle, sheep and horses,' says Burnett. 'Some cattle were washed sixty kilometres or more away. But it was all overshadowed by the human impact here in town.'

Burnett's own family was affected. 'When it started we had no real concerns, although my son stayed up all night keeping vigil to see if the water would rise and affect the house. When it did come out of the river it covered the whole property in a matter of hours. We lost forty head of cattle and a bulldozer went under, but the boys salvaged a tractor. We didn't save our irrigation engines. The house wasn't damaged.

'Most farmers have very little insurance except for fencing and housing. You can get hail insurance for a cotton crop, but not flood insurance.'

Terry Donohoe has been in the district for twenty-seven years. He owns 320 hectares on the edge of Emerald. 'The flood took out nearly a hundred hectares of sorghum, six of watermelon, seven of pumpkins, all just about to be harvested. And the roadways, a shed and our irrigation pumps were all destroyed.'

In town, all eyes were on the Vince Lester bridge, the traffic bridge that was slated to close when the water reached 14.5 metres. This happened at 1.30 on Monday afternoon; and the water was still rising.

'The closing of the traffic bridge was very symbolic,' says Kerry Hayes. 'People always thought that no matter how bad the situation gets, as long as the yellow brick road was still open they could drive away. When it closed they realised they were in the trenches and they had to stay and fight.' Flooding was apparent on the entire western side of the river through town and on the eastern side out of town to the north. All homes in those areas were affected.

At this bleak moment, there was a little good news: the rate of water rise at the bridge began to slow. More importantly, there had been no more significant rainfall in the catchment. Premier Anna Bligh made a few phone calls and the decision was made to leave the train at Emerald — and it was.

The train was brought into use immediately, ferrying supplies between the evacuation centre and bringing in emergency operations people to the tiny historic railway station. It was a slow process and one that frustrated Kerry Hayes and his disaster team. How many people could the train take out in a short period of time? How much time did they need to evacuate the remaining residents? And when do you tell people they have to leave?

The water continued to rise in town throughout Monday and Tuesday. One of the first buildings in the central business district to flood was the Coles shopping centre: it was on the lowest ground. Devastated shopkeepers lost stock and shop fittings. The government offices nearby had 30 to 50 centimetres of water through them, affecting floor coverings, filing cabinets, electricity and phone connections, Gyprock walls and furniture.

Then the Capricorn Highway shopfronts were affected, though they were many metres up from the road bridge. People watched with disbelief as their town was cut in two. Autopro, the carparts retailer with its distinctive yellow and red walls and garish signage, had a metre of water in it.

Moston Park was a metre deep in water. Someone towed kids across it in a ski boat. It was fun, but very dangerous. The water hid small rises, new debris and stumps, fences and drums. It was typical of the stupid things that emergency agencies fear people will do in times of flood.

Throughout Tuesday the LDMC prepared for the next crisis: when the water height reached 15.4 metres, they would have to switch off the water and sewerage systems. That would mark the end of voluntary evacuation, according to Kerry Hayes. 'We were dangerously close to having to make a decision to say to the rest of the people in town, "You need to report to the railway station with a bag and maybe a pillow." We needed to get people over to the ginnery, and the train turned around in a hurry.

'That was the worst moment,' he says. 'A very, very, very tough decision had to be made. We were faced with asking everybody to leave their homes. The whole town. And if you move most people out, then the management needs to move with them. We would have to arrange new operations centres and new roles and responsibilities for the operational staff like the SES, police and council staff.

'It seemed to be very manageable while everybody was at home, with familiar things all around, and we weren't being threatened. But to move everyone like this would really ram home the message that something serious was happening.

'Even though we knew it had stopped raining, we had to plan. You can't have fifty cents each way. But I was thinking, I am going to move six thousand people and tomorrow morning they will say the river didn't reach the height you said it would and we didn't need to move.

'I thought, well, they'll all be safe. Isn't that the most important thing? That's my role. But it wasn't a war and it wasn't really life-threatening. It was going to involve a helluva lot of people and kids and all their pets. It would be chaos.

'But somebody had to make the decision to evacuate the town, so I focussed on ensuring that nobody would be put in danger, and got on with the plan.

'Our contingency plan was the train. With just an hour's notice we were going to move people to the cotton ginnery. It was set up ready to go. People were going to be standing up in goods wagons and on flat tops.' Fortunately, the evacuation centres at the town hall and pastoral college were coping; and the LDMC felt they could cope, too, if there were no more nasty surprises.

Those watching the dam water levels were told that they had reached 4.4 metres and were still rising. The dam peaked at 4.44 metres at 4pm on the Tuesday.

And then, without warning, at about 5pm on Tuesday, Ergon Energy started turning the power off to whole sections of Emerald.

'That shocked me,' says Kerry Hayes. 'They don't just flick power off house by house; they remove whole streets from the grid and suddenly everyone's off. And the grid doesn't follow the contour of the land. They just switch off block by block, including homes that don't expect to be affected. That means evacuation is a no-brainer: you must move out of your home. If you have no power, you can't see [at night], of course. It became critical.'

A hasty decision was made to see if the elderly and frail could be quickly checked.

And so at 7pm in Waldby Circuit over near Riverview Street, ninety-five-year-old Beryl McLachlan and her husband Neal suddenly found a couple of men from a local church at their door, telling them they had an hour to leave. Beryl was confined to a wheelchair. Neal, or 'Big Mac', was well known throughout Emerald community service clubs. The McLachlans were completely taken by surprise, but they didn't argue. While they filled an overnight bag, the men put their furniture up on tables and bench tops: there was no time for anything to be moved.

'Even as we were leaving we didn't believe the water would get up to our house,' says Beryl. 'We estimated it would have to rise nearly twenty feet [six metres] and we couldn't see that happening at all.'

The McLachlans were moved to an empty home owned by a generous parishioner, but the electricity to the street had been turned off. They patiently waited as the church found another empty home and they were moved again.

Facing the worst

With the water rising, the power going off and night falling, people started to panic. 'The phones were going mad,' says Kerry Hayes.

'We drew the town into eight or nine sections so we could advise people when we wanted them to move. We had to try to describe to people what sector they were in. It seemed perfectly logical at the time. But if you give that to four thousand people with twelve hours' notice, it doesn't work.

'It didn't go smoothly. Even on Monday night, many people were not convinced the water would come up. They felt that historically Emerald is not a floodprone place. They knew we are on a floodplain and they were saying, "We are impressed by what you are doing, but the water won't come up to us."

'We briefed council staff to use the phrase: "We expect" because we hadn't faced this situation before and there were real uncertainties about what would happen. But "we expect" wasn't good enough. People started telling us they wanted to know exactly what would happen and when.' There were some confrontations and the disaster organisation staff had to respond to each issue as it came up.

'Fortunately we still had plenty of volunteers from the community groups, so there was always a group of people if someone needed help.'

The water continued to rise. And as darkness fell on the Tuesday night, the signs were becoming more and more ominous. By 9pm the water was at 15.36 metres on the Vince Lester bridge, making it the second highest flood on record. More than half the town was without electricity, 2000 people had self-evacuated and 500 were at emergency shelters. And the engineers still did not know what would happen when the Nogoa floodwaters met those of Theresa Creek downstream.

Col Brunker was acutely concerned, thinking that if the floodwaters met they might back up into town, sending levels even higher. 'I saw the water at Campbell Street flowing away from town during the 1998 floods, but this time it seemed to be flowing back into town,' he says. 'If that continued, Emerald could be flooded by two rivers, the Theresa and the Nogoa.'

The council received a call that there was new flooding near the racing track. With great foreboding, a works team was sent out to investigate. Was water already coming from both rivers? The team reported that flume gates — hinged covers on water pipes designed to automatically stop water from flowing both ways — had stuck and needed cleaning out. It was a tense time. Kerry Hayes knew that if the water in the Nogoa rose just nine centimetres higher, the sewerage- and water-pumping stations would be turned off. Council staff tasked with keeping the river and dam heights updated were writing up every centimetre of increase.

All was in readiness for large-scale evacuations.

David and Julianne Butler in Whitchurch Road, which had never flooded, were told by police that they should consider evacuating. A metre or so behind his rear fence the river was a maelstrom, a constant roar, very choppy with a brown scungy foam. 'But I thought it would take an incredible amount of water to get to this height,' says David. 'I thought that would basically be impossible.

'I was surprised by how fast the water was moving. It formed a bit of an eddy near our fence and swirling around in the floodwaters were huge chairs, fridges, garbage, logs. And snakes, a lot of snakes.

'There were brown and eastern snakes and green tree snakes. Most were three or four feet long. My oldest son loves snakes so he was watching those and my other son tried fishing!'

The water would eventually rise to the fence. The Butlers' house is about a metre off the ground. 'I never thought the house was at risk, but I thought maybe the pool would get flooded.'

Properties in a new housing development near the Butlers' home were flooded to a depth of 70 centimetres, taking the residents completely by surprise. 'We were told by the real-estate agents the area would never flood,' was the constant refrain from the new homeowners.

On Tuesday night Emerald was tense, tired and wet. Many people had suffered significant damage to their homes, lost possessions and been forced to bed down with family and friends for a second night.

The emergency responders Kerry Hayes, Col Brunker, Shane Wood and others were exhausted and emotionally drained. They had no way of knowing what would happen next or whether their plans would be adequate. The eyes of the sceptical media were trained upon them, adding to the tension and pressure.

It now looked as though the evacuation would occur in the early hours of the morning, in the darkness, with a tired and wrung-out community that did not have good communications and had never practised an evacuation.

But now the council whiteboards were showing something new. The water levels at the Vince Lester bridge had stopped rising at 9pm. The question on everyone's minds was, what would happen when the water reached the Theresa Creek junction? Would it start to rise again?

But 4T and other water experts had some good news. Theresa Creek was already falling. It had not rained in the catchment for two days. On Wednesday the water levels at the dam fell slowly all day.

The disaster, which would have necessitated evacuation of all of Emerald's residents, was averted by just nine centimetres.

2500 people had moved out of their homes; 200 homes were damaged, 60 seriously; dozens of shops were affected. The economic cost to many was debilitating.

The Vince Lester bridge didn't reopen until 2pm on Friday 25 January. Water had receded earlier, but engineers needed to check the bridge for damage, which Kerry Hayes says brought a range of new problems.

'The water dropped off the bridge and everyone breathed a sight of relief, but Main Roads took a long time to open the bridge; and that was one of the biggest frustrations of the whole event. People were really annoyed and they were some of the worst phone calls we got.' People can tolerate a measured holdup until they perceive things 'should' be back to normal.

Recovery teams and inspectors from all over Queensland descended on the town to assist with the clean-up. Insurance assessors were able to get access to damaged properties and start to assist residents with their recovery. They didn't always bring good news, though.

Roy Druwitt returned home to find water still in the house, and three distinct water marks at different levels on his walls. He doesn't know if that shows the water had settled on the way up, or down. He couldn't get the water over the floor seals, so drilled holes in his wooden floors to let it out.

The house was extensively damaged. Roy and his family could not live there again until the end of April. They decided to take no more chances and a year later they raised the entire house two metres above ground level on stumps. There is a much bigger verandah to watch the Nogoa River across the road. 'The reminder of the flood was in your face the whole time,' he recalls, suggesting there was no sense of recovery for many, many months. 'We thought we were covered for floods, but the assessor said we weren't.' They did not receive an insurance payment.

The McLachlans, who hadn't thought they needed to be evacuated, returned home to discover 66 centimetres of water had been in their house for days. Beryl and Neil McLachlan were distraught. 'We lost everything except an old 1898 carved wooden table. We lost mattresses and beds, lino and carpets. A new computer was washed right off the table.'

Beryl's oil and watercolour paintings were destroyed; all chipboard cupboards including the bathroom vanity units were unusable. 'We needed nine new doors; and the water even smashed the windows,' says Beryl.

'The fences were made of wire mesh and steel rails and yet the water pushed them down; and there was a lot of damage in the yard. The lawns took a longtime to recover. It was so sad. Our old cane chairs just fell apart.

'It was classed as an act of God, and the insurers didn't pay.

'It was a pity to lose the whitegoods — at our age they would have seen us out.'

The impact of the floods left Beryl and Neal extremely agitated, but what surprised them most was how long it took to get their lives back in order. 'It was shocking. For months we had hardly any furniture.'

Beryl has nothing but praise for the community groups and fire brigade members who washed out her house and provided basic necessities immediately after the floods. 'They spent two weeks cleaning the walls. They were wonderful.

'Who would have thought about floods like that? At our age, you expect you've seen it all.'

Gerald Mayne left his property and returned twice a day to check it. He was fearful of 'rascals', or looters. 'How low can people get to thieve from flooded homes when there is nobody looking after assets?'

This did not prove a problem, though. There were only one or two reports of what police called 'opportunistic stealing.'

His levee system worked. 'We were fortunate,' he says. The water rose up to the level of the carport out the front and flooded his entire garden. Gerald was surprised that in the heavily forested botanic garden area near his house there was surprisingly little damage.

'The water was travelling at swimming pace and making a noise like a wornout car. The trees in the botanic gardens were well established although some were falling over but it's incredible how nature's looked after them. '

The news was not so good for Gerald's own beautiful garden. 'All our little plants died later on, mainly from root rot. The nurseries did very well because we had to restock.'

Terry Donohoe was hoping the flood might bring some new nutrient-rich topsoil. Instead it brought useless, weed-infested silt. 'There were some new sandbars of silt, which were quite substantial. It took five months for some of the roads on the property to dry out to a point where we could use them again.

'We got weeds from elsewhere, particularly parthenium, which we'd never seen here before and was everywhere.'

Parthenium is on the federal government's list of 'Weeds of National Significance', being 'regarded as one of the worst weeds in Australia because of its invasiveness, potential for spread, and economic and environmental impacts'.

It took three years for Terry Donohoe's finances to recover. 'We got about $25,000 from the primary producers' disaster grant, but that doesn't even fill the diesel tanks. The grants have been at the same level for nearly fourteen years. They should be reviewed.'

Kerry Hayes believes that given the circumstances a lot of people did fantastic work to prepare the community. The town is on a floodplain, but he doesn't believe it should be built elsewhere or that the CBD in particular should be shifted. Nor does he believe the planning laws should be used to guide development away from the river.

'We accept as human beings that a one-in-a-hundred-year flood is an acceptable risk, but if we went to one-in-two-hundred risk assessment, there would no buildings at all in Emerald. We'd all live on the top of the hill. It means every so often someone's going to get flooded.

'Riverview Street, though, is a conundrum. In the 1950s there were all high-set homes there; now there are homes and units at ground level.

'People's properties were affected and many felt a big loss, but the flood was never an emergency. There was always time to make a plan. That's what the dam does in fact: it provides the lead-in time.

'I think both bridges need to be higher, so we always have connectivity if another flood comes. If the linkage is more permanent, we would always have a conduit out of the place.

'This flood was an exercise in understanding limitations, understanding what you must consider in your community plan. It highlighted the quantum leap that needed to happen when the town grew from 3000 people in the 1970s to 16,000 in this decade.'

A week after the big flood, a massive rainstorm dumped 100 millimetres of rain and caused flash flooding throughout the town. Drains were saturated or full from the big flood, so the stormwater couldn't get away. It caused damage to homes and roads on the other side of town which were not affected by the initial flood.

And then, before the town had recovered, before the court cases over insurance claims were over, Emerald flooded again. Much, much worse.

Queensland suffered under heavy rain for all of 2010. By the time the official wet season came, the earth was soaked. The El Niño weather pattern which brought drought had swung wildly towards the La Niña weather system that usually bring widespread flooding rains. The Fitzroy catchment flooded and Emerald went under again.

On New Year's Eve the Nogoa River peaked at the Vince Lester bridge at 16.05 metres, 35 centimetres higher than the previous record flood in 1950 and 69 centimetres higher than 2008.

It remained above 15 metres for two days and above minor flood level for a week. 1060 of the 5000 homes in the town were flooded and 95 per cent of the businesses in the CBD.

This time the planning and preparation were much better and, although the town was seriously affected, the community remained resilient. It had learned a great deal. More than twenty-three cities and towns — including Brisbane — and about two thirds of Queensland were affected by the floods, which resulted in a massive outpouring of volunteer effort for every affected home owner.

The ABC reported on the clean-up:

People from the flood-hit town of Emerald, west of Rockhampton in central Queensland, have been helping each other clean their damaged homes and remove debris.

Businessman Stephen Pyle said at the time that the whole community rallied behind those in need.

'More and more people have been coming along and helping out, so it's just been fantastic, the amount of help and support that people have been giving,' he said.

'I know one day there we were cleaning and, come lunchtime, a ute came round with sausages being delivered out the back of it, hot sausages, and people putting sauce on for you.

'It was just something that they were doing — their houses weren't affected, but they helped out in that way.'

A Week from Hell
Nogoa River Valley, Central Queensland,
January 2008

Many people were awed to see the water flooding over the Fairbairn Dam into the Nogoa River below on 20 January 2008. The dam, among Australia's biggest, had dropped to less than one-third full after years of prolonged drought. But now, after just one rainstorm high up in the catchment, it was officially at 115 per cent capacity and rising.

A wall of water three metres high had crested the 167-metre dam spillway. Hundreds of people from Emerald had driven the 30 kilometres to see this once-in-a-generation event and to listen to the water as it roared over the spillway. The waves created as the water crashed into the channel below were many metres high. Onlookers could literally feel the earth shaking. The sight was so impressive that the Queensland premier Anna Bligh came to watch and celebrate the ending of a three-year drought.

In the middle of the Nogoa River valley, about 9 kilometres downstream and halfway to Emerald, there are dozens of 40-hectare blocks owned by horticulturists and hobby farmers who love the beautiful green countryside and good irrigation.

Jodi and Rod Pike had owned a rural property of 40 hectares since 1991. They had lived in a kit home on the property since 1994, while they built the house they wanted. They moved into it in 2007, despite its being incomplete. For years they had worked hard to create something special for their children, thirteen-year-old Daniel, Chelsea and Hayley aged twelve and seven, and six-year-old Casey.

'We had to work hard to afford this house,' says Jodi. 'We've never had a brand-new car in our lives. We lived with secondhand furniture. It was always about the dream home.

'This is our last bastion. We weren't moving to the coast or selling this for profit. This was going to be the home that the kids could come back to.'

The Pikes had armed themselves with advice from the local council about previous and likely flooding; and a surveyor marked out their home footprint away from known watercourses. Nobody could recall the river flooding in the area.

The home was built into the edge of the wide valley, at least five hundred metres from the river. Between the river and the house was a dam of beautiful clear water, ringed by lily pads and reeds and home to wading birds, small fish and frogs.

The house had a wide verandah with views across the dam to the valley beyond. It was a typical rural property — surrounding the home were a number of farm sheds and mechanical workshops, including two steel shipping containers used for storage, and motor vehicles. There were their own cars, as well as two vintage vehicles that Rod had restored, and parts for more. Farm equipment and toys were scattered around. There was irrigation equipment, boats, trailers and pets. The Pikes owned Shetland ponies and some cattle.

Jodi and Rod had been in Emerald when a previous flood occurred in 1991. 'It was always interesting because when the water was up, people would water-ski and picnic there,' said Jodi. 'We never talked about flooding.' The Pikes knew that sometimes water might travel along different channels between the river and their house and some would enter the dam from tributaries flowing into the Nogoa. They also knew that to flood it would have to be 3 or 4 metres higher and then extend across the valley at least a kilometre or more before it reached the height of their home. It was unimaginable.

As the rain came that January, there was plenty of excited chatter throughout the community about whether the water would spill over the dam wall and, if it did, how high it would reach. People measured the height of the dam by the height of the water under the roadway. It rarely spilled and had never exceeded 3 metres.

The Pikes were in a better position than most to monitor the water levels. There are two roads into Emerald from the Pikes' property — Selma Road, a 13-kilometre journey, or the main road, which goes across the road bridge, built 20 metres above the massive dam wall and resting on six huge piles. This route adds 30 kilometres to the trip.

Jodi described the weather at the time as unusual. 'There was a weather pattern that sat between us and Longreach and we weren't getting inundated with rain here at the time. We didn't pay much attention to it, to be honest.

'There was only one really big downpour here on the Wednesday. It woke us up and we thought, gee, that's heavy.' Jodi and Rod were surprised next morning to see how much water was left lying around and in their dam.

On Friday Jodi experienced the first of a series of unsettling events. 'Rodney had gone into town for a funeral and at about 4.30pm the boys, Daniel and my seventeen-year-old nephew Corey, took a little tinny out into the lagoons at the bottom of the house paddock. Rod had told them not to take the boat into the river itself because there was some debris from the rain and the river might get some floodwaters, which makes it a bit unpredictable.

'About an hour later I couldn't hear or see them any more. I got a bit worried and rang Rodney, who said they'll be in the reeds or something.' He was coming home but was delayed when the people he was with started to talk about coming to see the dam, which might be overflowing. Jodi needed him home, not taking happy snaps of the dam.

Jodi said, 'It was getting dark and I started to panic. I hadn't seen the boys for an hour and a half. I started picturing them in the Nogoa River stuck in a tree or something. I'd started ringing Rodney and panicking and saying, "Get home now, I need you."'

Rodney arrived home an hour later with a group of people from the funeral, all of whom were quickly drafted into the search. One, Anne, had a powerful tool.

'She had a coo-ee like we'd never heard before. It was amazing,' says Jodi, who becomes emotional retelling this story even a long time later.

'We turned off all the electricity in the house so the air conditioning noise didn't interrupt us. At one point we thought we heard Daniel's voice but when we stopped to listen, we didn't hear it again. There are no town or street lights here. When it's dark out here, it's pitch black.

'I was a complete mess by this time.'

Rodney was panicking too and about to call the SES when the boys wandered in from the scrub. They had been helping their neighbour dismantle irrigation equipment to take out of the river and lost track of time. When they heard the coo-ees, they realised Jodi would be really worried and they hurried home.

On Saturday massive amounts of water from the catchments 40 to 100 kilometres west of the region were pouring into Lake Maraboon. There was no suggestion that this might cause a problem. But elsewhere in the Selma Road community concern, at first slight, was growing.

Maurie Iddles, a farmer on Selma Road whose low-set double-brick home is one hundred metres from the Nogoa River, heard from a number of his friends that the river would be in for a big soaking. One call made an impact. 'A mate, an irrigator who'd been involved in water for years, said there was a pretty good chance I'd be flooded,' says Maurie.

Maurie assumed that his property would be flooded and water would rise as far as the back door of his house. In the previous year his family citrus farm had been wiped out when citrus canker blighted the region and he had been ordered to burn his entire crop. It had been heartbreaking. The prospect of a flood on top of that was enough to break a lesser man's spirit, but Maurie didn't hesitate. He decided to evacuate immediately. He packed as much stuff as he could on benches and table tops, and put other items into storage on a nearby property.

He told friends and neighbours of his plans, including Karen Bray, a neighbour of Jodi and Rod Pike's. 'He's an old-time local and he was flustered,' said Karen. 'That was enough for me. I started calling family and friends immediately to get them to come and help get the stuff out of our house.' Karen and Peter Bray lived in a Queenslander on stumps nearly two metres off the ground, and higher up the valley than Jodi and Rod Pike.

Karen's husband drove down to the dam to have a look at what was going on. Even after looking to see what was happening, he remained a little sceptical.

Karen called Allianz Insurance to check on the state of her cover to see whether it included floods. She was referred to the underwriters, Commbank, but they referred her back to Allianz. They told her that she should call on the following Monday to get insurance details and she did not want to wait. 'Someone told me that Suncorp was agreeing to give people flood insurance over the weekend, so I called them, explained that I thought there was a very good chance that we would get flooded, and asked for insurance cover.

'They said there was a forty-eight-hour waiting period, but they'd be happy to sell me a policy under those circumstances. Our first payment wouldn't be until the next Wednesday at the earliest.' The insurance would come into effect at 5pm on Monday.

Karen had great difficulty packing family belongings. 'We had no packing boxes. Everything had to be packed loosely and it's really difficult to store things if they are loosely packed.'

Karen called a number of people to tell them what she heard and what she was doing, but she couldn't convince the Pikes to take any action. Jodi recalls the phone call: 'She was saying the farmers in the catchment had a ridiculous amount of water, four hundred millimetres or something like that and they'd never seen anything like it. Karen said she was going to empty her house and leave. I think she was panicking.'

Karen says they had a nervous laugh together. 'I think I said, "Well, either you'll be laughing at me for packing up or I'll be laughing at you because you didn't evacuate."'

Jodi said to Karen: 'If you're right, don't laugh too hard.'

Rod Pike was not worried. 'It's always been a good thing when the dam is full. Everybody's happy when it rains out here, even if there is some minor flooding around and properties, because then there's years of good crops afterwards.' Jodi operated two hairdressing salons in Emerald and Rod worked in the coal mines. Though they have a few cattle grazing on their 40 hectares, they don't describe themselves as farmers. 'But we felt the same as the farmers about the rain — it's a good thing,' he said.

Like thousands of other people, Jodi went to look at the Fairbairn Dam and arrived shortly after it started spilling. 'I saw about twelve centimetres of water going over the wall,' she says. What no one could see from the dam wall was how much water was entering the lake or the upstream catchments.

A few colleagues and neighbours of the Pikes headed out to Selma Road and had a look at the water going across the wall. Rod was adamant that even though the water level had risen, they would be fine. 'None of them seemed too concerned,' says Jodi. 'We all talked about other years when dams flowed over, but we didn't mention flooding.' Rod went into town for the night.

Interest in the water was growing throughout the whole district. The focus was on the spillway. According to SunWater spokesman Glen Pfluger, quoted on ABC's online news, the overflowing water was not expected to cause any problems.

Queensland's second largest dam has filled for the first time in seventeen years, after a week of heavy rain in the catchment area near Emerald in the state's central-west.

SunWater spokesman Glen Pfluger says the 1.3 million megalitre Fairbairn Dam spilled over about an hour ago.

Mr Pfluger is at the dam wall and says it is a welcome sight in the drought-stricken region.

'It looks fantastic. I'm totally saturated, we've got probably 1000 or so people lining the roads watching it go over.

'Obviously many of them are young kids; they've probably

never seen it happen before so it's really an event that's happening in Emerald that hasn't happened in seventeen years.'

The overflowing water is not expected to cause any problems.

On Saturday afternoon Karen called Jodi again. Karen's husband Peter was still convinced there was no need for evacuation.

'Even when I spoke to Karen I wasn't overly concerned,' says Jodi. 'Sometimes people panic in situations like that, but nobody else was saying anything. I certainly listened to the radio after that, and then I rang SunWater and told them what I'd heard — that there was a great heap of water coming down — and they said, "No, it will be fine. Don't worry about it."'

Karen called Jodi again, late in the afternoon. 'She was really worried and by about four o'clock she told me she was ready to leave.' Now Jodi started to become anxious.

'I rang SunWater again. They said there was no reason for concern. They told me the dam spillway was going to peak on Sunday afternoon.'

Jodi had a coffee with her sister that afternoon, and went to bed alone and relatively comfortable. The kids were allowed to stay up late and watch a movie, as the Pike family usually slept in late on Sundays.

'I woke up at 5.30am, something which I never do on a Sunday morning, and I went down to look where the water was.' It was about 100 metres from their back door, having quietly but steadily risen throughout the night.

Jodi found a tomato stake, drew marks on it at about fifteen-centimetre intervals and placed it in the ground at the water's edge.

'I watched it for a couple of hours and realised it was rising quite fast — about seven centimetres an hour. That doesn't sound like a lot, but it's seven centimetres rising everywhere, right across to the river.

'It had a bit of movement to it and there was debris as well. I didn't want my kids in it.'

By mid morning Jodi was becoming very worried. She now needed to understand the context of what SunWater had said. 'They said it would peak on Sunday afternoon. That would be five or six hours away, so water was going to rise another half metre or more. That meant it was going to be close to the level of our verandah.

'If SunWater wasn't exactly correct, and the water rose a few more hours, or peaked at midnight, then the water level would be higher.' For the first time Jodi began to consider the possibility that the Nogoa River would enter her home. She started to wonder what that would be like.

'Every time we looked at it, I thought, "Shivers, that water's really moving." I rang Rodney and said, "Look, you have to get out here. This water is rising quite fast." Rodney could not conceive of any water through his house; he did not think the problem was urgent.

Jodi's parents Pam and David dropped in and Rod arrived soon after. Rod and David and Rod's daughter Hayley went for a walk, getting their feet wet. 'They walked in water to cross one of the house tracks, but an hour later the water was up to their knees at the same place. Dad was getting concerned ... that made me think, All right, we've got a problem here ...' said Jodi. 'He took a photo of the water. It looks so gentle, doesn't it? It's not roaring. It looks quite nice, actually.'

At this point Rod still believed what SunWater said, the worst-case scenario was that the water would rise until about early evening, then start to fall. By his calculations that would mean 'a splash of water across the floors'. He could cope with that.

Jodi's family went home.

At lunchtime Jodi sought further reassurance from SunWater. 'I said to them, "I've been measuring the water all morning and I need to know exactly what you mean by peaking in the afternoon. Is it going to be four o'clock or is it going to be six o'clock? Because by my measurements the water's going to be in my house by six."

They said: "Oh, the peak's changed and it's now Monday afternoon and it may be as late as Tuesday."' Jodi clarified with them that they meant the peak would arrive later because that would mean the water would be much, much higher.

By Jodi's calculations the water would reach the house at about 6pm Sunday but it would keep rising at 7 centimetres an hour for another twenty-four to forty-eight hours. Another 1.7 metres of water at the very least and maybe much, much more.

Their home would be inundated. At worst, the water could reach over the roof.

Jodi and Rodney were shocked. There was no time for hesitation — they had just six hours to empty their home of possessions. Every cupboard in every room; the garage and workshops, the containers; the cars, animals and assorted farming equipment. Clothes, books, pots, pans, cutlery, crockery, linen, tables, chairs, ornaments, mats, rugs, carpets, wall hangings and pictures, documents, books, doors, kitchen appliances, whitegoods, furniture, curtains, toys, school books, CDs, magazines; laundry products, garden tools, barbecue, camping gear. Everything in the house, the sheds, the paddocks.

'We don't throw much stuff away. We've lived here for so long and stuff just seems to build up,' says Jodi.

'We'd been in this house for only a year. We'd only put the curtains up the previous October and one room was still full of unsorted goods and possessions.'

'How do you shift it?' was Rod's first question. 'Because we didn't have a whole yard full of trucks and trailers to help.' Their next thought was: 'We need bodies.'

Jodi called her parents, who quickly returned, but it was a 40-kilometre drive. 'We rang a couple of friends and said, "We're going to go under. Can you help? Do you know anyone who can help? Can you bring some rubbish bags and boxes or something to pack things in?"

'My cousin sent a text message to everyone she knew in town. It was a great idea. But the message went round and round. One of the girls who works with me got it eight times! We ended up with a lot of people out here with camping boxes and trailers.'

But how many people is enough? As the afternoon wore on it became apparent what a massive job it would be to remove and then store all the belongings and things of value from a property in just six hours.

'One of my former schoolteachers, Jo Rosenblatt, turned up with her husband, Errol, although we hadn't seen them for years and years. I thought: Oh no what a disaster. She was the deputy principal and I had to go to her many, many times. I was very naughty! They brought sixty yellow grape-packing boxes and a ute. The neighbours offered to let us store things in their shed.'

The first deadline was 6pm. Everybody worked desperately, putting things in boxes, moving the items to storage at other properties. Rod drove the restored 1952 Hudson Pacemaker and the 1929 Chevrolet truck up the hill, loaded with gear at about 3pm.

There was no panic, but it was disorderly. Nobody really believed that worst-case scenario. They opted to assume that the water would reach the height of the cupboard doors. Given the information they had it was an irrational assumption, but few people can really grasp the idea their home will be completely submerged by floodwaters, roof and all. So items were stored on the top shelves of cupboards. Boxes were placed on the top shelves of the storage containers outside, and high up in the sheds.

Despite everybody's hard work, it was clear there would not be enough time to save everything. They could handle the movable items, but in a flood if you have enough time you could maybe salvage some doors, floor coverings, windows, cupboards and other fixtures and fittings.

The children were asked to clear out their bedrooms, but Hayley and Casey were too young to help much, so they played on the trampoline. 'They thought it was great being on the edge of the slope bouncing into the water. Yeah, bouncing into the water! That is exactly what we would have done if we were kids in the same circumstances,' says Jodi.

Every so often Jodi and Rodney would look at the water rising on the stakes in the backyard and, each time, the impact of their decision to ignore Karen Bray's advice confronted them. They knew they would lose their race against time. They knew their wonderful home would be flooded and damaged. It was almost too much to contemplate.

'People started thinking for us. We just kept going. We became the workers. They became the thinkers,' said Jodi. The willing helpers needed direction, but Jodi was struggling. 'At about five o'clock we were in the kitchen pulling things out when one person looked at the oven and asked, "Do you want me to pull this out?" I replied, "Aren't they wired in?" He said, "Yeah, I'll just cut the wires."

"I said, "But then I'd have to get an electrician to put them back in." I was thinking about the cost of it, and he said: "Jodi, where do you think the water is going to come to?" I pointed to the top of the door and he just ripped the whole thing out.'

All the while the people who had come to help were confronted by the uncertainty of their own situation. The floodwaters were heading for their homes in Emerald. They watched as water crept higher and flooded the tracks around the house until there was only one road out. They decided to let the youngest kids leave with friends, but thirteen-year-old Daniel opted to stay with his parents on the property until they could do no more.

Six o'clock came and went and the water hadn't yet reached the floors, adding more doubt to their tasks. It was going to be a long night.

But by 10pm, water was lapping the floor. The flood had covered all the property's roads and they needed to move the vehicles a bit higher up the road. Rod and Daniel hopped in the ute. Daniel yelled: 'Ouch, I've been bitten by a spider.'

It was one of Jodi's worst nightmares. When he was three Daniel had had a severe anaphylactic shock caused by an insect bite. Now Jodi, exhausted, bewildered, anxious, heartbroken, had to drop the evacuation and get him to hospital.

Rod stayed to remove more possessions in his ute and Jodi raced to town in their other car. She expected to take Daniel to her parents' place to recover while she returned home to be with Rod. But on her way to the hospital she was stopped by police at a road block. 'They said they were about to close the road and asked me to decide right now — which side of the bridge did I want to be on?' Jodi had no choice but to stay in Emerald. She left the hospital at 2.30am and took Daniel to her parents' house.

Rod, alone on the property, saw the water come into the house at 10.30pm.

'The first thing it did was start blowing up through the drains. It was like a scene from a movie about sinking submarines. You see water starting to come in but it looks like it's coming from the inside, out.

'There was nothing I could do, nothing at all. I didn't even have a last look through all the cupboards. I just ended up leaving the house before the height of the water stopped me getting out.

'Under these circumstances, you find solace in the fact that your family is safe and save what you can.'

Rod camped the night in a shed with his friend Colin Jones. Early the next morning they returned to the house. 'It was gutwrenching. There was about a metre of water through the house and it was still rising. We got into our boat and began retrieving stuff from the river.'

At one stage they inched the boat right into the house and called Jodi. 'Rod said, "I'm in the laundry, in the boat, what do you want from out of here? The water's just hit the bench top."'

The flow of water was much more powerful than Rod had expected. 'I had to hold the throttle at half open just to get the boat to sit still.

'Inside the house, the force of the water blew out any wall that was opposed to its flow — timber framing and plaster board, all gone.

'Things were floating out of the shed. My uncle had passed away in May and he'd bequeathed me his tools and gear, some of which were ruined and some were floating away. It was very emotional to watch things go like that.'

The shipping container floated over the fence. 'They're insulated. They float like an esky. It ended up down the river. The boys tried to stop it by opening the doors to let it sit down, but as soon as the water got high enough, away it floated again.' The gear inside floated out. 'We collected some tractor tyres which were floating away and put them in our boat, which was a bit overloaded. Just then we noticed our bull, Quiberon, was swimming away so we tried to round him up in the boat and we nearly sank. We had to put to shore, offload the tyres and go back to look for the bull.

'Every time he hit trees he'd get dragged under. We thought we'd lose him and then all of sudden he'd plough back out of the water. It was terrible. We've had him for years.

'We did some pretty silly things in hindsight,' says Rod.

Jodi was worried about the risks Rod was taking at the farm. 'They didn't have lifejackets. It was raging and they were trying to guide a one-tonne bull out of the river by boat. I rang Rodney's family to ask them to talk to him about getting off the farm, as he hadn't slept in days.'

Rod and his mate went out in the boat again after lunch and ran out of fuel. They called Jodi to tell her and that was the last she heard from them for two hours.

'I called the police to let them know he'd been missing a couple of hours and the police asked the Channel 9 helicopter to look for them,' said Jodi. The men were found downriver. The SES got them some fuel and they headed back to the property at Selma Road.

Rod says, 'I didn't save anything in my shed: vintage cars, tools, some of the unrestored cars in the shed were in pretty good condition. We lost all my workshop equipment, because we were so focussed on the house.' Rod lost his unrestored 1925 Willys Knight, a 1936 Dodge Tourer, a 1928 Chevrolet Four and a 1926 thirteen–hundredweight Chevrolet truck.

Meanwhile Jodi, who had left Daniel with her parents, was dealing with her own problems. Her unit and hairdressing salon went underwater when the floodwaters reached Emerald. After cleaning up as best she could Jodi thought about insurance. But her broker told her she was uninsured. 'That was the most stressful part of all,' Jodi says.

The water in the Nogoa River peaked on Tuesday night. By then it had spread out over many kilometres. Inside the Pikes' home at Selma Road water reached the ceiling in some parts of the house, although in other parts items stored on the top two shelves of cupboards were saved.

Maurie Iddles's house was completely inundated too, but he had managed to move important family belongings and equipment. His insurer didn't cover the cost of the damage to the house.

Karen Bray's family had a party on the verandah before abandoning her almost-empty home. The floodwaters rose just above the floorboards and Suncorp paid for some of the damage.

"We were surprised there wasn't more damage,' says Karen.'The floorboards warped when they were wet, but this is an old house and they went back to normal when they dried out. We just stripped and polished them.

'The water soaked up into all the cupboards, which were wrecked and had to be replaced.'

When the Pikes returned to their Selma Road property on the following Friday there was still water in the house. 'We started chasing the mud out but in the end we had to pull the house to pieces,' says Rod. 'It was demolishing, not cleaning.'

'My brother is a concreter who has done a lot of demolition work and renovation. He said we could just cut the Gyprock with a Stanley knife from the cornice down, so the dampness wouldn't get into the ceiling, so we did that. The timber floor expanded and is cupped, and where the timber was attached to the concrete it had to be demolished.

'The French doors had to be replaced. We got the doors off before the flood, but a lot were damaged during transport. We made the doors usable by planing them just after the flood; and for a while the door jambs were swollen, but they recovered.'

Rod's employer, Kestrel coal mine owned by Rio Tinto, had suffered its own problems but allowed all the employees to help with the clean-up in town. That meant Rod didn't have to go back to work immediately. 'My employer sent help out in the clean-up. They were very supportive and I can't speak highly enough of them.'

Unfortunately Rod and Jodi had to work long hours to rebuild after the flood; and the extra stress associated with the recovery resulted in Rod giving up his management job for a lesser-paid position, making money much tighter. 'I burnt up all my long service leave, which was for a family holiday. We used it up rebuilding the house.'

The recovery was slow and painful. There was no money, no insurance, and it was exhausting coping with a myriad demands. Jodi and Rod eventually lived in the partly reconstructed house. The ceiling wasn't finished, for example. 'Everything lives in our house. Bugs, bats and green frogs. I'd given up cleaning the windows until the ceiling was sealed,' says Jodi.

In the rebuilding they changed the design of the home in preparation for the next flood. 'Experts told us if the dam had been full, there would have been another metre of water through here,' says Rod. 'We thought about levee banks, but if you build them and they get breached, you end up with silt through the house. I think you are better off letting the water run straight through.

'Instead we tried to floodproof the house. All the internal walls were demolished and replaced with block and render. All the interior door frames are aluminium. I've mounted skids under the shipping containers so we can drag them up the hill. The kitchen is all removable, including steel frames and granite bench tops.'

The Pikes realised almost too late that while they were forced to focus on rebuilding they were sacrificing quality time with their children: 'The kids aren't allowed to leave home until they are forty!' says Jodi, laughing.

'I wasn't able to work and that affected my end-of-year income at the hairdressers. Rodney had to stand down from his position because of the stress.

'The flood changed us.

'Rodney and I have been fortunate. Neither of us had to cope with anything major. Neither of us grew up privileged. We always wanted our dream home here. We had twelve months of it, which was nice, but in the end we discovered our dream home was really only a kitchen and walls.

'It has been tiring and frustrating and in my thoughts I tend to be critical of others who might not appreciate what they've got. And we're tired.

'We worked too hard on the house in the years and months leading up to the flood. We realised now that you can't do that and give a hundred per cent to the kids.

'I am over it. When we finally got where we want to be, we had a huge setback. When we get the house fixed, I said, "I don't want to work like that any more."

'We don't want the kids to remember that the last five years was just about building and rebuilding the house.'

Their loss, like that of many farmers who lived on Selma Road, was heartbreaking, but Jodi chooses her words carefully when describing her feelings.

'Devastating? No, devastating is when you lose a loved one,' she says.

Through it all, the one thing that still frightens her most was the memory of Daniel and Corey going missing in the boat before the floodwaters arrived. 'I've got four children, and we've had many scary things occur, but I have never come that close to losing a child in my life,' says Jodi.

'The flood that destroyed my house means nothing to me. Of all the things that happened to us on that weekend, what could have happened to the boys is what makes me emotional.'

And what happened when Jodi and Karen Bray saw each other for the first time after the floodwaters went down? Who laughed at whom?

'We were cut off and I couldn't see them for a few days,' says Karen. 'When we first talked I asked how are you going, what happened? We didn't laugh. We weren't in a joking mood.'

* * *

On 27 December 2010, Jodi and Rod were holidaying on the Sunshine Coast with their family when they received a desperate phone call to come home.

The Nogoa River was going to flood again. And higher. The information had come from Geoff Kavanagh, the same farmer who years earlier had warned the Iddles and the Brays.

This time Jodi and Rod didn't hesitate. But all the planes from the coast to Emerald were full because of the holidays. Their brother chartered a small plane, which they really could not afford.

They raced home and started again.

This time with two days' notice and a heap of experience, the Pikes and their family and friends pulled everything out of their home. Everything.

The Nogoa River peaked a metre higher than in 2008. 'Water went up into the ceiling this time,' says Jodi.

She remains stoic. 'We know our neighbours better and we support each other better as a community. I think these things happen for a reason. You learn from them and other generations will learn from this.'

After two floods in three years, Jodi is sanguine about moving off the property. 'We have no choice: we can't afford it,' she says.

'But this isn't a frightening place to be. No one died here. We just think, this is what Mother Nature does.

'But my kids are growing up here and they're happy.'

'You were flat out seeing the street lights'
Mackay, North Queensland, 15 February 2008

Mackay in tropical north Queensland has seen some tremendous downpours over the years. The Bureau of Meteorology has reported twenty major floods in the years of known records since 1885: an average of one major flood every six years. The area is cyclone-prone, often experiencing torrential thunderstorms that dump massive rain on the city.

Mackay sits at the mouth of the Pioneer River, known as one of the most dangerous in Australia because it rises and falls quickly, is tidal and gives very short notice of an impending flood. While much of Mackay now sits behind levees, residents know that the system may be overtopped at high tide with cyclone-intensity rainfall. Like most towns in north Queensland Mackay has no cyclone shelters, only relief centres to cope with recovery.

At five in the afternoon on Thursday 14 February 2008, the Bureau of Meteorology issued its first severe weather warning. There were warnings about flash flooding all through the night. The warnings were accurate, as they usually are, but without context: what sort of flash flooding? What would the likely impact be? However, the bureau cannot give this detailed information. Warnings were issued in the middle of the night, but no local radio station played them until dawn.

Errol Coombs, the emergency management coordinator at Mackay Regional Council, had a gut feeling that the rainfall would be serious. At his home in Rural View, twelve kilometres north of the city, conditions were unusual. 'At about midnight it started to rain really steadily,' he says. 'I was woken up by it at two in the morning, and then by three it was still ridiculously heavy.

'The intensity was something I hadn't experienced before in my life. I have a corrugated iron roof and the noise was a massive roar, even though there was no wind. You were flat out seeing the street lights.

'I got up at three and said to myself, This is getting very serious. I thought I should get to work to start carrying out emergency procedures and to prepare for some inundation in the morning.

'I got dressed, went outside, lifted the roller door and knew it was too dangerous to drive. I hadn't experienced this sort of thing before. The rain was constant and I knew there were a couple of places between home and work where I wouldn't get across.'

Coombs contacted ABC Local Radio to broadcast a warning that everybody should stay home until further notice. 'That was a gut feeling,' he says. 'I didn't know what was happening, but I thought it best to alert the community.'

The rain had started just as Barbara and Trent Turnbull were driving home to Seaforth, a coastal village 44 kilometres north of Mackay, after a night shift in town. They were about halfway home when they were forced to stop at the Constant Creek causeway. They were unable to see the road because of the torrential rain.

'There was no water on the road,' says Barbara. 'We were just saying that Constant Creek could be up. Then we heard this loud noise to our left and as we looked out the passenger side there was this wall of water coming. It smashed into us, lifted us and threw us around.'

'It was like being in a boat,' says Trent. 'Just getting swept away, but it felt as if we were on top of the water.'

'The car was filling up with water, really quickly,' says Barbara. 'We knew we were in real trouble. We pretty much did the whole big I love you and if we get out alive … yeah.'

Eventually the car wedged high up in a tree. Trent kicked out the window, climbed onto the bonnet and lifted Barbara out onto a tree branch.

'We were up there for about an hour and a half, communicating with Vicki from triple zero, in the pouring rain,' says Trent.

Harry, a postman who works in Mackay, was the first to come across the stranded couple. He heard them screaming and called back that he would have to go and get help. They did not hear his reply.

'How he heard us yelling is beyond me,' says Barbara. 'So when he turned around and left, we thought we were dead,' adds Trent.

More than two hours after they had been swept up, the swift-water rescue team arrived. Barbara and Trent were still hanging onto the tree with all their might. Mackay Fire and Rescue station officer Dave Russo says that when the rescue team arrived they could hear voices, but couldn't find the couple at first. They waded into the creek system and found a high bit of land fairly close to Barbara and Trent. Then they set up some rope systems. Two of the technicians jumped in again and were carried down to the tree.

Trent and Barbara watched as the team risked their lives. 'One of the guys who came out got swept off first and then got pulled back and smacked into a tree before getting to us.

'I know they were rushing but it seemed like it was taking forever because they had to go from tree to tree and anchor themselves,' says Barbara.

Before the rescuers could get the safety ropes to Barbara and Trent, their branch snapped. 'We were both on a branch not much thicker than Trent's arm,' says Barbara. 'It was bending and creaking as well. We just thought they are so close but we're going to die ...' The rescuers managed to hook the Turnbulls onto lines and drag them across to the bank before carrying them out to a waiting ambulance.

Trent said later: 'If it wasn't for those guys we'd have probably been swept to Vanuatu and be dead on a beach somewhere.'

Justin Englert was the SES local controller from the volunteer team that, just after 4am, sent the swift-water crew to the Turnbulls. Rescues like theirs are not uncommon in Queensland during the wet season. After the team was despatched, Englert went back to bed. He woke an hour later and went downstairs to open his grocery store.

'I found a few things were out of the ordinary,' he said. 'Water was dripping from the top of the fridges and coming in the back door. That happens when we get a two-hundred-millimetre downpour, but there was more water coming in than I had ever seen before. I found myself having to mop the floor a lot, and started worrying about customers slipping over. I rang my dad and said I couldn't maintain the safety in the shop, so he came round.'

Englert's father arrived just before 5.30. 'More water started coming in through the back door, which we couldn't stop, so we decided not to open the shop. Dad's car was parked in the middle of the road because the gutters were overflowing. We went outside and saw water up to the door handles!'

At about dawn the SES phone began ringing off the hook. Englert says: 'I got a call from Errol's assistant, Bruce Chester-Master, who had somehow managed to get into the council offices and set up the coordination centre. He shouldn't have gone in, because he had to put himself in some danger to get there.'

Mackay Regional Council has a well-prepared disaster plan and a formidable disaster coordination team, but the water level meant that most of the team were unable to get to the centre until about ten in the morning. Stuart Holley, executive officer of the disaster management group, and ABC Local Radio manager Craig Widdowson tried to monitor the situation from the Northern Beaches police station, issuing warnings to ABC Local Radio listeners.

Then disaster struck. Just before seven in the morning the power in a large part of Mackay went off. The police station was plunged into total darkness.

'That,' says Justin Englert in something of an understatement, 'threw a lot of things out. There was a total loss of telecommunications: mobiles, landlines, everything.

'This was Murphy's Flood: anything that could go wrong did. The disaster management group has a satellite phone for emergencies like this, but it was in the office. The SES has another one at the headquarters depot. Neither was in a place where we could receive or distribute information about the flood.'

More than 3000 Mackay residents woke up that morning to discover they had no power or phone. They had plenty of water, but none they could drink. No help was forthcoming to most people because authorities were overwhelmed, roads were closed and, in any case, given the telecommunications system failure, many people could not call for help. Very little information was being distributed either.

Errol Coombs was at the police station, where the UHF radio was the only working means of communication. 'Which is how I found out that police were walking people through chest-high water in Bradman Drive. I knew then that things were real bad.'

Coombs thought the worst. 'I was expecting a report of deaths. The amount of water that came down so fast created tremendously hazardous conditions. If people are trapped, if they can't open the door because it will open out into floodwaters, they are effectively locked in their flooded houses.'

Bradman Drive in the northwestern suburb of Glenella bore the brunt of the flooding. The road lies alongside two small creeks that join nearby and then flow into the Pioneer River. There are paddocks all round, which are good for growing sugar cane. These may be earmarked for development, but are often subject to minor flooding.

Patrick and Dawn Hunt, who are retired and lived in Bradman Drive, confronted the same problems as did most people that day. Patrick says they woke at dawn, without thinking anything was particularly amiss. 'Up here you get heavy storms; that's life.'

The Hunts' small neat brick house sits about a metre and a half above road level. 'I got up just before 6.30am and the road was completely flooded and already water had risen more than an inch over the front patio,' says Patrick. 'I woke Dawn and said, "You had better get up — we may have to get out." The water was rising very quickly.'

Dawn is very frail, with a fading memory, and she cannot move fast. 'Getting up took her about five minutes. By the time she came out the water had risen another six inches, covering the patio and heading for the doors.' It eventually rose to the bench tops in the kitchen.

Patrick started to panic. When he calmed down after a few minutes, he said to Dawn that they had better get some clothes together.

'Then the water started coming into the house. We got some clothes, I collected papers and put our little TV on the bench top. By the time we'd done that, the water was up to our knees and still rising.

'I rang triple zero or the SES, I forget which one first, but I rang one of them and they said to try the other number.' Clearly the call centre was overwhelmed.

Patrick was fearful: by the time he finished the call, the water in his house had risen to forty centimetres. It would have been nearly two metres deep in the street. The backyard was now awash; the Hunts were effectively trapped in their own home. And it was still raining.

'So I called the other number and told them we would have to be rescued because Dawn can't swim.' He got the same reply as everyone else: 'They said they'd be a couple of hours. I wasn't happy, but I didn't have any options.'

Neighbours at the back of their house shouted to the Hunts to get through their backyard, over the fence and up to the slight rise at the back of the houses. 'I couldn't see myself getting up there,' said Patrick. 'The water was moving too fast and was too deep.'

Now the water was so high that the furniture began to float. The Hunts' little terrier Max had trouble finding a safe place.

The Hunts' son telephoned to see if they were all right, but clearly he could not get to them. 'He rang the local commercial radio station 4MK and reported that an elderly couple at Bradman Drive were trapped. He appealed to anyone with a boat to come and get us.'

This was the start of a flotilla-like rescue operation, where anyone in a flooded street who had a boat set off to begin rescuing others. Out of the darkness and rain came Terry, a neighbour of the Hunts', to the rescue. He helped both of them to get into his boat, carrying their clothes, their money. And Max.

Patrick said: 'On the way around in the boat, all you could see was the roofs of cars. The bloke driving the boat was just sticking to the middle of the road. We worked out where that was by the roofs of the cars.'

Two houses higher up were taking people in. A nurse looked after Dawn, who was shivering uncontrollably and in shock. 'The whole thing was terrifying,' says Patrick.

In the same area Mary Alderton, who describes herself as a 'sensible everyday person', woke at six that morning, heard the rain and went to see what was happening. She gazed at her glass sliding doors in disbelief. 'The water was rising on the other side like water in a glass. I didn't have time to do anything at all.'

A neighbour from across the road 'with quite an authoritative voice', saw her and yelled, 'Get out!' Mary's children, seventeen-year-old Jarrod and Jasmine, aged fourteen, were sound asleep. 'I shook them awake and said we would have to leave. By then the water inside was up to my knees.'

Jasmine grabbed clothes, a phone, her battery charger and her purse. Discovering her handbag would not take the battery charger, she left the phone on the table and it was lost. The family were still quite calm.

They watched as their Holden, parked in the street, started to go underwater; they realised that they would have to scale the back fence in order to escape. They would have to haul their overweight Labrador, Toby, over too, but he was nowhere to be found. Mary and her children climbed over the back fence and joined a group of about twelve who were seeking refuge together.

It bothers Mary now that, despite feeling calm at the time, they didn't think straight. 'We didn't even help our elderly neighbours,' she says.

The water in Mary's home eventually reached chest height. Freezers and fridges toppled over. Mary recalls: 'The stuff we don't use much — the Christmas tree and party plates — was high up in the cupboards and it escaped. The stuff we use all the time was lower down and it was damaged.'

Cheryl and Tony Haupt, who live on the highest corner of the same road, were woken at 6am by their daughter Jade, who according to her mother was 'in a state of high excitement'. Cheryl says: 'We could see water had filled the cul-de-sac and was still coming down all around. Tony said, "This doesn't look too good."'

Cheryl had no idea what to expect, never having experienced anything like this before. Not anticipating any problems in her own house, she went next door to alert her neighbour. 'I said you'd better get some clothes and come over to our place. We lifted some books up higher, then saw water coming up her sliding door.' Cheryl opened the door and the water gushed inside. 'The water was running really fast and it was hard to walk. A car in the street had water over its bonnet and there were wheelie bins tipped over and floating everywhere.'

Another neighbour of Cheryl's, an elderly woman, had water up to the windows. 'I carried her out,' says Cheryl.

Her own house was in difficulties, so Cheryl decided to go home across the street. 'I had to swim across,' she says. 'My feet wouldn't touch the ground.' Still in their pyjamas, soaking wet and chilly, the Haupts tried to protect what they could. 'Water was coming up the driveway, right up to the front patio.' They decided their best plan was to get over the back fence: at two metres high, that was not easy. Tony went to find ladders.

Water gushed into their home and quickly rose to just below knee height. 'We were resigned to it then; and we got a bit calmer,' says Tony Haupt.

Cheryl decided that it was not going to get much worse or be very dangerous. 'The water inside was very cold but still,' she says. She decided to stay inside with her two tabby cats Missy and Rosie.

On the other side of the tidal creek, some of the residents had previous experience with flash flooding because their suburb, Valetta Gardens, is at the junction of two creeks. Maree Smith woke at two that morning because the rain was relentless. Everything seemed all right so she went back to sleep.

'At about seven I hopped out of bed. It was still raining heavily but outside looked fine,' she says. 'But within half an hour the drains started gurgling, which I thought was really strange. So I went to the front of the house, thinking that something was wrong.

'Water was edging up the driveway. It was filling like a bathtub. I thought the water would come in through the bathroom drains, so I got some towels to block them. Five minutes later water was lapping at the front door.

'Half an hour after I got out of bed, I had a metre of water and sewerage through my entire home.'

Maree began to wonder what might happen when the tide rose. 'I grabbed my phone and clothes, put photos in a box and hauled them onto a high shelf. Afterwards I discovered that the box was really heavy: I don't know how I got it up there.'

Water rose to knee height. Because it was full of sewerage, Maree stood on a chair. She stayed there for the next thirty minutes. 'I saw locals evacuating their houses and then the SES arrived in the street. They were taking people up to the two-storey house further along.' Finally they came for Maree. Normally resourceful, not one to make a fuss, she was in shock as she trudged through the slime, water and mud.

Donna Dougan also in Valetta Gardens, was woken just after 5am by a phone call from her son Aaron. He had seen the rain and heard the radio warnings, and he wondered whether there was any water in the street yet. He was already flooded in, at the industrial estate, and he couldn't get out, but he was worried about her.

Donna, who comes from a family of fishermen and campers, is used to watching the weather online and she went to check the Bureau of Meteorology radar site. Rain registered on the site with blue for showers, darker blue for light rain, red for rain, black for torrential tropical storms. 'There was a black dot over Mackay,' she says, 'and it wasn't moving at all.' Outside it was still dark, but getting lighter.

'It was rubbish day. I looked out and saw a black garbage bag by our letterbox. A car was parked in the road I said, "Oh my God" when I realised water was coming over the tyres.

'My other son needed the car to get to work, so I banged on his door to get him to move it. By the time he got there it was too late.' The car was swamped, along with two others parked in the street.

Donna tried to think what she needed to do. 'I had to close the roller door to keep the water out of the garage if it got any higher. I started to think about our belongings inside. We had a low entertainment unit in the lounge, so we put the TV on that and the video on top of the TV. The kids' room was full of electronic stuff so we put that on the beds. We put chairs on the tables and the computers went into the ceiling in the shed.

'When the water came into the house the TV started floating, even with the video on top. The lounge chairs and my bed were floating too.

'I saw the water outside at a higher level than it was inside. Water started coming in through the power points, which are thirty centimetres above the skirting boards.'

It was time to retreat. Donna's daughter Lauren, more than eight months pregnant, and the children climbed out the window and went to the shed in the backyard. This was at the property's highest point; it was dry for the moment. 'We had to walk through thigh-deep water to get there,' says Donna. 'There was nothing else for us to do and once we got there we had to support each other. We used the gas cooker from the camping gear in the shed to make a cuppa.'

Retired child carer Kerry Carroll, who also lived in Valetta Gardens, had received a phone call the previous day from a friend who told her that Mackay might receive 900 millimetres of rain. 'I didn't know what she meant. I'm into inches. If she'd said we were going to get twenty inches of rain, I would have known what she was talking about.' Her husband Wayne pointed out that with a lot of rain nobody would be able to get to work, because the nearby Heaths Road would flood, as it often did.

Expecting quite a lot of rain, the Carrolls were having breakfast the next day when Kerry happened to look out the window. 'I noticed some rubbish bins strewn around in the street. I went out to get one and saw the water in the road.

'Five minutes later the water had risen to the letterbox. Five minutes after that it was at the front door. Then it started to come inside.

'Your first instinct is to try and hold it back, maybe by holding your hands outstretched! You say to the water, "That's enough, I can see you're serious, now go back ..."'

Kerry Carroll said it all happened much too fast for them to be worried. They watched the water rise and, not knowing how high it would get, they decided to go outside. Standing on the back porch, they realised that if they had to get onto their roof, that might be difficult.

'We were quite calm,' she says. 'I never felt in any danger. It was daytime, we had no small children or pets. We only had each other.'

And so the Carrolls watched from outside as their home was gradually wrecked. 'We watched through the windows as the TV started floating, then the lounge chairs were pushed over. We realised the water was higher inside than in the backyard, so we opened the door and water rushed out. The pressure must have been enormous.

'The garage door was down and my car was inside. The back seat got pushed into the front seat by the force of the water. Our upright freezer full of food tipped over.'

The Carrolls were relatively safe. Wayne went to see what he could do to help the neighbours.

Over in East Mackay, one of the city's oldest suburbs, life was growing chaotic. The houses there are set close together, often on piers with wide verandahs, the types of houses usually known as Queenslanders.

Tony Kaye, who lives in one, realised that his road was underwater. 'It was quite scary,' he says. He trudged through the rising water to help his friend and neighbour Tina who suffers from a disability that seriously affects her balance and coordination. Tina can barely walk, and would certainly be unable to lift anything.

By the time Tony got to her house, the water had risen to the top step and was about to come inside. He picked up fridges, frezers, dryers, the stereo, even Tina's four-wheel scooter (which she fondly calls 'my scooty'), her ticket to independence. He managed to get most of it out, despite the fact there were 12 centimetres of water on the floor, and that wet lino is very dangerous and slippery.

Justin and Afton Bianchi, who had settled into their home a little more than a year before, lived nearby. They listened to the rain on their roof from their upstairs bedroom. 'It was deafening,' says Justin, 'but we never thought of flooding.'

At 6am, their parents, who had heard weather bureau reports on local radio, called to warn them of rain and possible flooding. The Bianchis' first thought was for their instruments. They are well-known musicians; their lower living area held their equipment, including guitars, amplifiers and a PA system.

'We panicked a bit,' admits Afton. 'We saved all the expensive gear by moving it to the kitchen, up a couple of steps. Then as the water got higher we moved it to the bench tops, and then eventually right upstairs to the second level.

'We sandbagged the doors to the upper level with old sheets and plastic bags. In the end we only suffered silt on the bottom level.'

Afton has a peculiar interest. 'I breed snakes,' she says, 'mainly pythons. They had to be put in a pillow case and we dropped them into the bath upstairs. They get all snuggly if they are in a bag together.' They lost one of the baby pythons.

Despite all the activity their son Jack, a toddler, slept soundly until 10am.

The floodwaters rose all over Mackay, peaked at about 9am and started to recede by noon. The high tide prevented the water rushing out to sea earlier, but in the end it created no more real problems.

The first out to rescue people were the SES volunteers. The Regional Council despatched its work crews in their 10-tonne trucks. Altogether about 400 people were rescued; and there were also dozens of people who owned small boats and went to rescue their neighbours. By noon state emergency agencies had mobilised, overcoming lack of communication, closed roads and power failures. Emergency Management Queensland sent rescue and recovery teams, who scoured the city for residents trapped in their homes.

Relief centres were opened. However, of the 1000 people who needed immediate relief, only about 60 sought relief there. The rest went to family and friends, following the Mackay Regional Council emergency action plan.

Errol Coombs, emergency management coordinator of the Regional Council, was able to get into town to assist with the rescue and recovery. 'We were all in it together,' he says. 'SES teams were out going door to door; and by lunchtime EMQ had twenty urban search and rescue personnel up from the south who were going door to door looking for possible casualties. We didn't know if anyone had been drowned.'

Residents, wary of the Pioneer River, didn't know whether the worst was over even after it stopped raining: many began thinking of the following day's high tide. Justin Englert's sixty or so SES volunteers were needed for a variety of jobs. 'People wanted sandbags early on, even when water was already through their houses,' says Englert. 'They had this misconception that it would somehow stop what was happening. Others just wanted to get away because they were fearful and some felt really threatened.'

There were other problems. Englert says the rescuers were confronted by locked doors, particularly in places owned by elderly people. 'At one stage I contacted the police superintendent for confirmation that our local government staff and the SES volunteers had powers to enter people's properties.

'In many places the water was above the kitchen benches, which was where people keep their keys, and people couldn't get out of their houses. I told the team to force entry.

'We had council guys in trucks force entry into a couple of homes and neighbours were ripping off screen doors with hammers. Those locked doors were definitely serious threats to lives.'

As the morning unfolded and the rescue crews received more and more calls for help, Errol Coombs continued to be amazed at what had happened.

'I was expecting a report of deaths. One girl from council told me the first she knew about it was when she woke up and put her arm out of bed and felt water. She was in a high bed. She opened her eyes and saw a TV set and fridge had floated into the bedroom. The fridge was bobbing around, and still running.'

Justin Englert recalls it as a very stressful period. There were about two thousand calls to the SES for help. 'I had to put a couple of members through psychological debriefing. Some of our younger volunteers had people screaming and crying at them, panicky because the water had risen so quickly. Many people were wondering when it would stop.

'We rescued people from their rooftops and roof cavities. I was expecting a large number of electrical deaths. There are a lot of old homes without earth leakage circuit breakers, and I was waiting for that. When you have so much water, the water is the earth ... you have to turn it off at the main switch before it gets to power-point level.'

Checking every house was a nervewracking task for authorities, who were anxious to see the rescue end and get on with recovery. 'Three days later some people were found sitting at home on a box, in shock, in the stench of a flooded house,' says Errol Coombs.

In fact, there was one death: a seventeen-year-old boy disappeared in the swollen Pioneer River west of the city.

Among the injured was Kyle Attard in Valetta Gardens. His house was not flooded, but that morning the seventeen-year-old cut his finger making sandwiches and had to be evacuated by the SES rescue boat and taken to hospital!

In some parts of Mackay, sewerage had backed up and entered the floodwaters. Authorities also issued a crocodile warning: there were unconfirmed reports of sightings near homes.

By the end of the day, the water had gone down.

Cheryl and Tony Haupt started washing their home out even as the water was falling. This helped get the silt and slime out, as it did not have time to settle. 'We only had twenty centimetres of water through,' they say. 'All our friends descended and we cleaned out quickly, then we went to help others. All the people in our street just grabbed brooms and mops and washed out house after house. We worked as a team.'

The Haupts spent that night in their own home, using the gas barbecue for cooking and wishing they had more batteries for their now useless mobile phones and portable radio.

Patrick and Dawn Hunt's entire home was trashed. They moved into a one-room self-contained unit at the Mackay Motor Inn for nine months. 'It wore a bit thin, I can assure you,' says Patrick.

Donna Dougan's husband Mark hitched a ride to the street in an SES boat that morning. 'The water was over the height of the toilet,' says Donna. 'The water was black. The carpet was black. We threw that out when the water went down and washed the walls with disinfectant, but the mould was amazing.

'It rained the next night and I dreamed about the water and woke up and couldn't sleep for another two days.' The Dougans had to leave their home and did not return for nearly six months.

Maree Smith and her husband Andrew got help from Andrew's friends. 'Andrew was a Vietnam vet and all his mates came around to help with the clean-up. We came back to live in the house two weeks later, but we couldn't get to some of the mould in the walls and cavities. That made my asthma play up; and we moved out for another twelve months.'

Kerry and Wayne Carroll were also out of their home for a longtime, eight months in their case. They stayed with friends, lived at motels and briefly rented accommodation.

Mary Alderton and her two teenagers were able to return when their house had been repaired three months later. It was a rental property and Mary had no contents insurance. 'The local church and the Lions Club helped with furniture, and someone donated $2000 of kitchen appliances,' she says.

Errol Coombs says that insurance was a major drama for many people. 'I spoke to Jenny Macklin, the federal minister, when she and the prime minister visited, and expressed the need for a national all-hazards insurance policy, similar to an ambulance or fire brigade levy, to cover all types of loss. We had people sitting in their houses not prepared to take anything out until the insurance company could see what they would pay for. Some said take a few photos and get out, others said don't touch anything.'

Justin and Afton Bianchi say: 'We have universal health insurance — why not flood insurance?' It's an interesting question.

Once the water stopped, Justin Englert's shop got busy. 'People needed their food and cigarettes. There were lots of young people and others in kayaks, and the four-wheel-drive tourists started after that.'

The coordination centre was open for two weeks and the recovery operation lasted for months. Errol Coombs says: 'There are no shelters in Mackay for a cyclone: you need friends and relatives who aren't affected. We tell people we can't protect them. We try of course, through disaster awareness, but people are responsible for their own safety.

'We always tell people to prepare in advance, not to wait for the event. Prepare in May for next January.'

Emergency Management Queensland estimated damage in Mackay at $350 million. EMQ chief Frank Pagano, who has since retired, said emergency authorities had been surprised by the intensity of the rainfall. 'I think it would be very difficult for the Bureau of Meteorology to predict falls of more than two hundred millimetres,' he said. 'It would be great to say to the public, brace yourself, you're going to get six hundred millimetres of rain, but it's impossible.'

Mackay received six hundred millimetres of rain in five hours! Bureau of Meteorology senior engineer Jeff Perkins told the media at the time: 'We expected heavy rainfall. I don't think we expected it to be quite as heavy as this.'

How did we survive?
Mt Ive, Gawler Ranges, South Australia, November 2008

Joy and Len Newton bought the Mt Ive sheep station in South Australia in 2002. The station is in the Gawler Ranges; Lake Gairdner is its northern boundary. Tourists come here to experience the remote but beautiful Gawler Ranges and the outback.

Like everyone else who calls this part of South Australia home, the Newtons are self-sufficient and good in a crisis.

In November 2008 they needed all their experience and determination when they got caught up on a flooded road which almost brought them to grief.

The day began simply enough — they were travelling back from Port Lincoln and had stopped for dinner at the community hotel at the tiny settlement of Kimba, where they were part of a group giving a presentation about tourism facilities in the area, including those at Mt Ive.

With them were Nathan and Nicky Prosser, and their eighteen-month-old son, Ned. Nathan and Nicky had worked at Mt Ive for the past seven months and were about to return home to Marree in the far north of the state.

It had started raining midway through the afternoon. Mindful that even a small amount of rain can make roads in the outback sticky, the Newtons had a quick dinner and asked to make their presentation early so they could get on the road and home without any problems. As the presentation progressed the rain grew heavier, the storm lashed and a power point crackled and sparked. The overhead audio-visual flickered off. 'It was bucketing down,' recalls Nicky, 'but with a room full of people we just had to make do. Everybody crowded round to see the rest of the presentation on the laptop screen.'

The Mt Ive group phoned home and found there was less rain up that way. And so at the pub they considered their plan. 'We decided to give it a go to head for home that night,' said Nicky. They knew that there was much less rain further north and the sooner they got onto the road, the safer they would be. 'But we changed the route to avoid the station tracks and instead thought we'd go back via Iron Knob. If the roads were bad, we could stay at the pub there, or with friends on the stations at Siam or Nonning.'

They had dinner at the pub and set off from Kimba about 9pm, headed east towards Port Augusta. Nearly an hour later they were at Iron Knob, where they turned northwest and left the bitumen.

Although it was still raining, there was no hint of drama. 'The conversation was pretty upbeat,' says Nicky. 'We were talking about the tourism event and some funny things that happened. The road was starting to get a bit wet. We were pulling a horse float with some furniture and other belongings, and started to think that maybe we should reach Siam Station and stay there for the night.'

The group drove through mud and occasional long patches of water, but the road presented no problems.

As they had expected, they were halted by a creek just before Siam homestead. As they had done many times, Len and Nathan climbed out, took their trousers off and walked barefoot into the floodway, checking all over the road for possible trouble. The cold water was running gently and it reached just below their knees. They agreed it was not going to present much trouble, as the road surface was all right, but it seemed sensible to wait for a bit and see what happened. The two men returned to the vehicle and, as they expected to check more water crossings, they did not bother to put their trousers on again.

The men checked the creek several times; and the level fell.

'We had decided to stay at Siam,' says Nicky. 'But when we got to the homestead, we found the creek running very fast between the buildings and the road, so we couldn't drive all the way to the house.

'We tried to raise the homestead on the UHF radio, but there was no answer. We thought if we waited half an hour the water would probably go down and we could drive up to the shearers' quarters and stay the night.'

But the water didn't go down, so instead they decided to remove the horse float and continue the drive home.

Soon afterwards they came to another creek crossing and Len and Nathan tested the water again. No problem. They drove on and decided to sleep in the shearers' quarters at Nonning Station, about 20 kilometres further on.

They reached Nonning at about 11pm, with the station in darkness. 'We could have slept there and left the next morning, without even waking anybody up,' says Nicky. They had no sleeping bags, but would have made do. However, the last creek they crossed had been dry and the rain was easing up. 'So we decided to drive on,' says Nicky. 'Home was only an hour away.'

About a kilometre west the road turned to the left and they came across water on the track, 60 to 100 metres long. 'We could see road markers and saltbush on the edge of the road,' says Nicky. 'It didn't look as if it was flowing very fast and it wasn't deep.' Len drove on.

They had in fact driven into a water course, but it was nothing more than a low area of the road.

Len drove slowly. The water was deeper than he had expected. 'Come on, Len, put some boot in,' said Joy, anxious to be out of the water. Nicky bent down to take off her boots and felt water underfoot, coming through the door seals. Momentarily distracted, she left one boot on.

The headlights showed the car had almost made its way through the water; and Len accelerated. 'We were virtually out,' he says. The headlights picked out reflecting signs that indicated a grid just ahead on a slight rise. The engine revs climbed, but there was no response from the vehicle. Len thought something was holding it back.

'The car dipped down again,' says Nicky. 'It was now quite

deep. We felt the vehicle lose traction, then the engine cut out.' The water had come up nearly to the running boards.

Len, worried, thought he had run out of fuel, something very much out of character. He switched to the auxiliary fuel tank and the car fired up immediately.

Nicky unbuckled baby Ned from his car seat. 'I started to get worried,' she says.

Len accelerated, this time with more 'boot'. The vehicle did not move forwards: instead, it seemed to slip sideways.

'I could feel the vehicle float and turn a bit,' says Nicky. 'I thought we should call Nonning for help. We did. But there was no reply.'

The front of the vehicle appeared to lift and move sideways to the right. 'You could feel the water push the car,' says Nathan.

The rear wheels caught something: Len thought at last he might get a grip on a hard surface, and he accelerated. But the engine died and this time could not be started. The front of the car started to rise again.

Len was confused: the weight of the vehicle was in the front, with the engine and gearbox. What was going on?

The front of the car was now clearly being washed sideways. The four-wheel-drive appeared to be floating, completely at the mercy of the water. This had all happened in a matter of moments.

Surprisingly the water was now up to the windows; the front of the vehicle dipped down again and water started pouring into it through the air vents on the dashboard. 'The car seemed to fill with water almost instantly,' says Nathan. The vehicle was now being washed downstream.

Everybody had the same idea: the engine was not working and the windows were electric, so how would they roll them down to get out? Could they smash them? But when Len hit his window button, the driver's window rolled down. By the time it took people to use their own window buttons, the car was half full of water. It started tipping over.

Len reacted first. He started to climb out the driver's window. 'Not that way, you'll be washed away downstream,' said Joy, who realised there must be some sort of hole under the vehicle. 'Get out my side and take the baby.' Len climbed into the back seat and out through the window into the water. The cabin was almost full of water but there was no panic.

The car continued to tip further over and fell towards the driver's window. Nathan pulled himself out into the water.

Outside near Joy's window Len couldn't find the bottom of the creek. His feet were tripping and tangling and he realised that he had been caught up in some wire, which was quite taut: he couldn't understand why. There was no time to think. 'I was being belted against the car, among all that wire,' he said. The floodwaters swirled chest high and he was being savagely bruised.

Nicky handed Joy the baby to pass out the window to Len. 'I was desperate to get Ned out,' says Joy. 'I knew the car was filling with water and was totally out of control.'

The car was rolling away from Len, but Joy shoved Ned out the window and into Len's outstretched arms. Len and the baby were in deep fast-flowing water. Len tried desperately to find some ground or a rock to steady himself on, clinging onto the baby, and they went under the water a couple of times. 'I was surprised how Ned held his air,' said Len. 'When I was under I could see the lights of the car shining through the water. I couldn't believe they were still on, with the engine off and the car being bashed and turned over.'

By now the vehicle was gyrating wildly. Nathan dragged himself to the water's edge and took Ned, who was screaming.

Len turned back towards the Landcruiser and saw only the wheels and underbody. Nicky had managed to scramble out, and was standing on the top as the vehicle seemed to gently turn over in the water.

Len thought: Where's Joy?

She was trapped inside the flooded cabin, with no perception of which way was up or down. Her lungs were bursting, but she had the presence of mind to try and breathe out as slowly as possible to stop the urge to take a breath. Finally she felt she could not hold her breath any longer, gave a final push, pulled herself out of the window and was immediately washed away downstream.

Joy continued to struggle, with no breath left. 'I thought, I can't do this, I just have to let go.' She did, mentally and literally, quietly resigned to her fate. But as soon as she relaxed she floated to the surface, her head broke free of the water and she started to gulp huge lungfuls of air.

Nicky, still perched on top of the vehicle and hanging on as hard as she could, yelled to Len: 'She's out! Joy's gone down the river. She's OK, she's OK.'

But now Nicky had to get off the rolling Toyota. She knew she would have to jump into the water and the idea terrified her: she cannot swim.

Nathan, out of the water and holding Ned, told her to jump. 'She had to get clear of the vehicle so she didn't get her feet stuck in the undercarriage,' he says. Nicky saw the hopelessness of Nathan's plan: she decided to try and jump towards Len. In a moment of blind faith she leapt, hoping not to hit the water. But one leg slipped as the vehicle moved under her and she fell into the creek.

'It was freezing,' she recalls. Len managed to grab her, though he too was pulled into the water. Both emerged gasping and Nikky scrambled up to Nathan and Ned.

Joy wasn't trying to fight the current. But every time she reached out to try and grab something — a small tree or a shrub in the water — it broke off or pulled her head under the water. She was exhausted.

Eventually she was washed to one side, among a group of trees, with water swirling all around. She heard Len yelling directions: 'I thought that if he jumped in to rescue me, he'd be washed away too,' she said. 'I told him not to come in.'

A little later, they were all reunited on the riverbank. Everybody was safe: wet and cold, but alive, and incredibly lucky to have survived. Len and Nathan were in their jocks with no shoes. Nicky, who had lost one boot, was shivering, holding a freezing Ned.

'We were exhilarated,' says Nicky. 'We all said we couldn't believe what had just happened.'

Joy says: 'We reassured each other and I quietly thanked God. It was amazing how calm we all were; and we considered each other, which helped us cope. I felt we all just did what had to be done to get out of the car and stay alive.'

They were not too far from Nonning and Len, who was worried about the baby getting hypothermia, walked off towards the homestead. The rest straggled up the road and eventually arrived at the gymkhana sheds. Angus McTaggert at the station provided welcome warm drinks and dry clothes and they stayed the night.

The following morning they came back to see what had happened to the Landcruiser. It was on its side, half full of water and silt, with the front window smashed, clearly undriveable. 'We looked for clues about what went wrong,' says Len. 'It was a shallow descent, not a lot of water across it, and it was hard to picture where the creek started and where the road stopped. The road was not washed out anywhere.'

But still attached to the chassis of the Toyota was a five-strand wire fence, still taut, dragging on the car. The fence had recently been replaced, with the old strands left along the road. Debris and water had washed it onto the track. Len said: 'It must have stopped the vehicle when we were driving across the road. That's why we couldn't keep going forwards.'

The wires tangled under the car and the momentum of the water made the Landcruiser wash sideways. Off the hard-packed road base, the water had washed away the sandy riverbed and, in effect, had dug a big hole that the car fell into.

If the fence had not been there, they would easily have driven through the water. Even now Len is not sure that, if they had walked across the river before driving, they would have come across the wires. They certainly would not have driven through if they had been aware of the fence.

Why the water had been flowing so fast remains a mystery. Angus McTaggert mentioned later that he thinks the water course is part of Salt Creek, the biggest creek between Iron Knob and

Mt Ive, but in all the years Joy and Len have lived in the area, they've never heard of the creek, or that this part of the track was a crossing of any sort.

The road was easily passable and there was no rain. Perhaps a cloudburst upstream resulted in a momentary wall of water hitting the car, but nobody is really sure.

Nicky still struggles to understand the whole event: what they did was so sound, so cautious, and they still got into trouble. She says: 'When we saw the car on its side and all smashed up, my first thought was, Oh my goodness, how did we survive?'

Struggling Against Nature
Kempsey, Northern New South Wales, May 2009

The northern rivers region extends from south Queensland to Taree, including Port Macquarie, Coffs Harbour, Lismore, Kempsey and the coastal strip loved by holidaymakers from Brisbane and Sydney. This is idyllic Australia — blue water and white sand coastal regions, verdant floodplains, dark rainforests, escarpments, peaks and gorges, subtropical weather, annual torrential revitalising rains, languid rivers and the rolling hills of the tablelands.

It's a mixture to confound emergency agencies frequently called on to prepare their communities for natural disasters. Unfortunately numerous complex factors conspire against effective flood response.

Rain depressions originating as tropical cyclones in the Gulf of Carpentaria or Coral Sea bring massive summer falls. Even monsoonal low-pressure systems from northern Australia arrive during the late summer and autumn months, although they are much less frequent. And at sea level the marshlands fill and the seaside communities are subject to inundation from storm tides. East-coast lows travel along the coast, usually in a southerly direction, during the cooler months and direct moist onshore winds over the Macleay River basin.

In addition to complex weather patterns, the topography of the region adds to the problematic nature of floods. The big rivers like the Macleay and Clarence rise on the tablelands in the Great Dividing Range, where water rushes off the granite bedrock, descending with considerable velocity. It flows down over the escarpments and through the forests to the soft, rich alluvial plains before running out to sea via the marshlands and floodplains of the deltas.

With every flood, riverbeds on the plains are scoured deeper and deeper, making the riverbanks steeper, increasing the velocity of the next flood. The damage along the riverbank can be substantial. This scouring has resulted in some parts of the Macleay River now lying below sea level; and the inflow of seawater is threatening the groundwater further and further upstream.

The history of Kempsey doesn't help either. It used to be a red cedar town, nestled on the river where boats could transport the timber to Brisbane and Sydney. Kempsey's CBD sits alongside the Macleay River — in the middle of a natural flood channel. In November 1949, winter snowfall runoff coupled with an east coast low resulted in flooding that rose up quickly in the Macleay River and smashed Kempsey and numerous other villages along the entire length of the river. Most buildings in central Kempsey were washed away.* Six people died.

Just eight months later a series of east-coast lows developed off the New South Wales coast, resulting in disastrous flooding of the Macleay. The heavily flooded Clarence River at Grafton literally carved a new path to the sea. Again there were a number of deaths and reports that houses were washed off their stumps. Kempsey was flooded again in 1963.

After 1963, in a paper 'Nature of Flooding in Kempsey Shire', the New South Wales government warned that even worse flooding was inevitable. 'An estimate of the Probable Maximum Flood (PMF) at Kempsey is that it would reach a height of 11.2 metres at the Kempsey traffic bridge gauge. This flood, the worst possible on the Macleay River, would peak more than 3 metres higher than the level reached in 1949.'

After the 1949 flood the council debated moving the CBD. They did not; and no government at any level has since been willing to consider moving it to the high side of the river.

Kempsey is a proud blue-collar community, not rich, with stubborn unemployment more than double the state average

---

* *Stormy Weather: A century of storms, fire flood and drought in NSW*, BoM 2008.

and higher in the Aboriginal community, and with many people depending on welfare*. These communities throughout Australia generally tend to have fewer volunteers in times of natural disaster, less infrastructure and more one-vehicle families whose members cannot afford to take time off from work.

Flood mitigation works seem to follow most disasters in Australia and some levee work was being constructed after the 1949 and 1950 floods, but when it all happened again in 1963, the community had had enough. Possibly under the influence of the success of such heady engineering feats as the Snowy Mountains scheme, and riding high on the belief that agriculture was the economy's mainstay, Kempsey people demanded that attempts be made to contain nature. The flood mitigation scheme was significantly enlarged and completed in the 1970s. It consisted of 182 flood-gated structures with 352 floodgates, 147 kilometres of drains, 34 kilometres of levees and 37 kilometres of bank protection. Around the Kempsey township, flood levees were constructed to provide general protection in the CBD for the one-in-ten-year flood.[†]

The community along the Macleay River has now come to understand the levees and catchment works will protect them from minor and moderate flooding. They watch the water levels in the automatic gauges of the towns upstream and try to guess how much water is coming down the system and how they should respond. They don't generally start really worrying until the levee at Kempsey is threatened with overtopping. The phrase everyone in the region listens for is '6.9 metres at the Kempsey traffic bridge'.

But this is the level of a major flood. Before this point is reached, all the floodprone regions are already awash. Roads will be cut, farmers isolated, some power and water switched off.

---

* Kempsey Employment Service Area: Kempsey Better Connections Workshop, 2 May 2008
† mhl.nsw.gov.au/www/2001floodreport.pdf

After the 1963 floods, the next major event occurred in March 2001, resulting in damage to ninety-four businesses*. Heavy rainfall saw the river peak at 7.43 metres. According to a study of those floods, a one-in-twelve-year occurrence, experience and preparedness were low. 'Once warned, 80 per cent of businesses attempted to validate warnings, either by listening to the radio, contacting emergency services, talking to neighbours, or observing river levels.'

This is one of the frustrations faced by emergency authorities. A 'wait and see' attitude prevails in most floodprone areas. It almost guarantees that losses will be greater than they need to be.

Minor flooding had occurred in Kempsey and along the river in February and March 2009; and then in winter 2009 the community was warned again.

On 20 May the Bureau of Meteorology announced that an east-coast low was forming over southern Queensland. The bureau issued the following forecast for the northern rivers area:

There is a current Flood Watch for Moderate to Major Flooding of NSW coastal rivers from the Queensland Border to the Nambucca this Thursday and Friday. Computer models indicate [the] system could produce falls in the range of 150 to 300 millimetres over this period with local heavier falls possible.

Moderate to major flooding is possible in the following catchments during Thursday and Friday [21 to 22 May]:

1. Tweed
2. Richmond / Wilsons
3. Brunswick
4. Clarence, including the Orara and Nymboida rivers
5. Coffs Harbour
6. Bellingen
7. Nambucca

---

* Andrew Gissing, Risk Frontiers–NHRC, Macquarie University, 42nd Annual NSW Floodplain Management Conference, April 30–May 3, 2002 Kempsey

A Severe Weather Warning is also current for the area. Across NSW, about 70 per cent of Flood Watches are followed by flooding."

The forecast was accurate. Local heavier falls did occur and some isolated gauges recorded 800 millimetres of rain over the four days. River levels throughout the entire region reached their highest levels since March 2001.

Kempsey residents believe they will have twenty hours' warning when the water reaches Georges Creek, well upstream. For well-prepared people with an escape plan who can move their belongings safely and quickly, this warning time is handy. In reality, time appears to pass much more quickly. Roads close, power shuts down, flood warnings change rapidly. And because the riverbank changes its shape and velocity after every flood, people are almost certainly going to be caught out.

On 20 May the Bureau of Meteorology issued its first flood warning: a minor to moderate flood was expected for the Macleay River that afternoon. Most people in the town didn't stir. A minor flood warning can be largely ignored, except by people who want to take advantage of the low-lying parks and gardens. Even a moderate flood warning is largely irrelevant to those who live behind the levees, though along the river farmers and property owners need to react quickly. They would be cut off by road and their pastures inundated: people who live in low-lying areas, along the riverbank or on the floodplain need to heed the warning so they can take steps to protect their property, machinery and stock.

Emergency agencies and government departments started to prepare their community for flooding. Bruce Morris was Kempsey Council's director of shire services. He says, 'Our residents are mostly aware of the preparations and planning we undertake. The historic yardstick is to watch water levels at Bellbrook [northwest of Kempsey and fifty kilometres upstream] but the gauges there failed in the last three floods! The trouble with this approach is that the community comes to believe that every flood will be similar to the last one. The community needs to understand that no two floods are the same.

'A lot of people have moved here since 1963; and they had never seen a real flood. Their kids had taken over the levees and everyone forgot what their fathers told them.'

Morris understands why people are reluctant to move early in the face of flooding in the town and along the river. 'We've got five low-level bridges which we'd close five times a year. Our people live day to day but a well-informed person should always have a flood cupboard stocked with five days' food. Most of them wait for the warning about the height of water at Kempsey traffic bridge. But there might only be another thirty minutes' notice before roads are closed.'

The council has installed small markers on utility poles in Kempsey which show the water levels from previous floods. They are a useful reminder that the town is floodprone and should encourage residents to be constantly prepared. But the markers are faded and some are obscured. And the council website has carried little information about floods, including how to prepare for them. This information is only available at the Kempsey Council library. Flood warning and response are the responsibilities of the New South Wales State Emergency Service, which has pamphlets on flood risk and evacuation available for the community. They are not easy to find and are not easily accessed online. All this reflects the mindset of the community about flooding in Kempsey.

Nevertheless, Kempsey Council has a well-organised flood plan.

When the river reaches 5 metres at Bellbrook, council gets to work.

'There are a hundred roads to close. We always run out of signs,' says Morris. This invariably annoys the community. Some roads disappear under water very quickly, but others appear passable, with just a few centimetres of water flowing over floodways and low bridges.

'People don't always understand what impact the river can have on a road surface and how little water it takes to wash a car off a bridge,' says Morris.

'The water can lift the sealed pavement quickly and you don't see that. Police can't be at every closed road, but the public needs to know we do that for their own safety.' Bruce Morris emphasises that if people drive on a road closed by the council, their insurance is invalid.

It takes many hours for council preparations to be complete. The barbecues in the parks have to be disconnected. Council buildings such as the netball clubrooms have to be cleaned out and, in some cases, entire transportable buildings have to be moved. 'In one flood the water twisted the chassis on a building,' says Morris. 'We remove the taxi stands, contractors disconnect water, sewerage and power to various buildings. At some stage we'd need to contact the SES to get their sandbagging machine.' This enables 5000 bags to be filled in a few hours. Council asks the local garden suppliers to deliver a few tonnes of clean river sand close to the CBD, so people can collect bags and not have to travel very far with them. 'We expect shop owners to sandbag all the shopfront entrances in the CBD. If the wall is built and shaped properly, sandbags will keep water out to a height of one to one and a half metres. But once they get a small breach, they don't hold water out for long.'

When the river reaches 5.4 metres at the traffic bridge, the council tries to defy nature altogether. Floodgates at the end of the river stop sea water flowing in and backing up the river at Kempsey. If the river is low they are left open. If it is high, they might be closed. As soon as the gates are closed water starts to spread out over the floodplain. 'If we can leave the paddocks dry, the stock will have something to eat,' Bruce Morris says. The choice is between leaving stock with food and dairy farmers with a livelihood — and flooding Kempsey.

'The farmers get very concerned about when we open and close the gates. But the water downstream will be higher than the town and will flow back into the drains if we don't close them. At 5.7 metres we'll usually close all the floodgates, although that depends on the tides.'

On the afternoon of Friday 22 May the Bureau of Meteorology, relying on information about water heights upstream, warned that at 1am on Saturday the river would reach a peak of 6.4 metres at the Kempsey traffic bridge. This would result in moderate flooding across the floodplains. An hour and a half later they announced that water levels would exceed this. They had not yet issued a major flood warning, which would occur if the water was going to overtop the levee. However, more cautious people in the Kempsey area began to prepare for possible major flooding.

One of the biggest businesses in the CBD is the historic Macleay Regional Co-op, which was formed more than 100 years ago and is now one of the biggest grocery stores in town. Chris Crilley, who had recently taken up the position of manager in the store during the floods of 2001, remembers being told the water would overtop the levee. 'We were expecting a trickle of water, but we got much worse. Rapidly moving floods brought more than a metre of water through the place, destroying stock, fridges, tills, food — everything. Water went over the top of the checkouts. All the shelves were smashed over,' she says.

Now eight years later, Chris has a plan to prevent a repetition of this disaster. 'On the Friday we contacted the transport companies and put them on standby to assist with an urgent evacuation of the premises. We called electricians, plumbers and IT people to be ready to disconnect everything.

'We asked builders to be on standby because we could brace the shelving and then store some non-perishable goods on top. The carpenters and builders could help us dismantle the showcases, which we could store upstairs.

'We needed six trucks — two for dry goods and four for perishables. We would have to dismantle the checkouts and showcases. It would take us about five hours. It's a big cost in wages.'

Chris could not afford to wait and see what level the water would be.

Despite the moderate flood warning and the continuing heavy rain, most Kempsey residents went to bed that night and slept easily. But Bruce Morris could not sleep. His instinct told him the water would be higher than the bureau forecast.

'It's a long catchment and we have twenty hours' warning. Our first main gauge is at Georges Creek, twenty hours away, and our second gauge is at Bellbrook, eight to ten hours away. The weather bureau listened and watched but it took them a longtime to twig to what was going on. I went home to bed thinking, there's something wrong. The BoM is never more than a couple of centimetres out, but in my heart I knew this flood would overtop the levee.'

Morris believes that the best approach to flood preparation is to get all the vulnerable people out of floodprone areas before the water arrives. 'If we don't evacuate, people become isolated,' he says. 'And in the worst cases they get stuck on roofs; and in the dark they get scared, then we have to ask others like the police and the SES to risk their lives to rescue them. It's much better if they voluntarily evacuate early.'

At midnight the Macleay River at Kempsey reached 6.4 metres as forecast, but according to Morris was still rising. It wouldn't take much more water to achieve the town's worst-case scenario: evacuation during the night.

Bruce Morris went into the office. He got on the phone to the council staff, the Chamber of Commerce, counsellors and emergency agencies. The message from the council was that though they couldn't be sure, they thought the levee might overtop. In New South Wales flood warnings are the responsibility of the Bureau of Meteorology and the State Emergency Services, but the council plays its part with informal warnings and advice. They know best the operation of the levee system. 'Water doesn't just come over in or two small places, it comes across its whole length,' says Morris.

At around midnight Chris Crilley received the call that the levee might be over-topped. She called every casual and full-time staff member at the Co-op and asked them to come in, bringing anyone they could with them. 'You can't really plan this because we need twenty or thirty people, or more if possible, but most people will want to stay at home preparing their own homes,' she says.

In a remarkable effort the contractors, staff and their families and friends prepared the Co-op for the flood. 'The refrigerator mechanics took out the fans, wiring motors, everything. The carpenters shored up the shelves and the tops were used for storage. The rest of the food, cans, assorted groceries, frozen goods, fruit and vegetables, meat and smallgoods, household and garden products, even clothes, were reboxed and trucked out. The store was dismantled in five hours,' says Chris. Any Kempsey resident assuming they could stock up on last-minute essential supplies from the Co-op on the Saturday morning would need to rethink their plans.

Ray Wells, the manager of the local community radio station TANK-FM, decided that their tiny team would begin broadcasting to Kempsey, withdrawing from nationally networked programs. This is an arduous task for any radio station, but an incredible effort for tiny volunteer-led community stations. 'The decision was taken at 2am Saturday to take the station off automation,' he says. 'The presenter who went live to air had just helped move computers to higher ground at the station's shop and office in the CBD, as a precaution.

'We're not immune to flooding at the shop but the studio is in a disused concrete water reservoir to the east of the town and the transmitter site is at another reservoir site five kilometres west. They're both flood free. One of the problems facing the station during a major flood is that the town can be cut in two, leaving just four presenters who live on the studio side of the river.'

At 2.30am Bruce Morris received information that the river had reached 7.2 metres at the Kempsey traffic bridge; and the peak would be at 6am on Saturday. Now even council offices had to be prepared for the flood and staff were asked to come in. An evacuation order was issued for Smithtown, Gladstone and Jerseyville, little communities downstream. Emergency agencies started to door-knock affected residents.

Dawn came to a wet, cold and very busy town. Some businesses tried to sandbag their premises and rescue their equipment and all along the riverbank most property owners began to move equipment, hustle stock to the higher paddocks, move machinery and vehicles. Everyone kept a wary eye on the river.

Bruce Morris described the water's action as nervewracking. 'The water came up to 6.2 and stopped rising, then went up another five centimetres and stopped rising, then it stopped near the top. It took five or six hours to rise the last twenty centimetres to the peak.'

Residents received an evacuation order to be out of any floodprone homes by midday. The water came across the levee mid-afternoon. 2000 people left their homes, although only 200 needed the support of the relief centre. The Kempsey CBD was placed on lockdown: local police ensured no one could enter.

Lower Macleay residents, including those at Smithtown, Gladstone, Kinchela, Jerseyville, Hat Head and South West Rocks on the coast, were now isolated. People couldn't drive to the town to pick up food, petrol, prescriptions or other essential supplies. The only way to move around was by helicopter and flood boat.

Within hours the first calls for help came in. The Ambulance Rescue helicopter evacuated three people from Gladstone: an old man with breathing difficulties, a twelve-year-old boy suffering a possible snakebite and an elderly woman who was extremely weak and dehydrated were flown to the Kempsey hospital.

The Kempsey SES was alerted to a child with breathing difficulties at Hat Head. A flood boat travelled along the Macleay to Gladstone with two ambulance officers on board. They were met by SES members in a four-wheel-drive vehicle and driven to Hat Head. The child was then taken back to the flood boat which took him back upstream to Kempsey hospital. A man needing dialysis was isolated at his home in South West Rocks. A flood boat travelled against the fast-flowing river, dodging floating debris, and he was retrieved.

A local farmer driving his tractor to higher ground got trapped in floodwaters and the SES found him clinging onto a cattle yard. Altogether, thirty people were rescued in the first twenty-four hours.

Debbie Schmidt had lived on the family property thirteen kilometres downstream from Kempsey for forty years. She had experienced floods in 1969, 2001 and two in the previous twelve months. 'My dad hated rain,' she says. 'He was here in the 1949 floods and when it started raining he'd always say, "Bloody rain, it can just piss off." In 1949 the house was flooded up to the eaves.

'In 2001 the floodwaters chased me through the house. We had ten minutes' notice and no chance to save anything. We had over a metre of water in the house for four days. When we started cleaning I burst into tears. The mess was unbelievable. We had ten centimetres of silt in every room; we had to hose down the floors and walls. But whatever was in the water seemed to just eat into the walls, and they all fell to pieces.

'We threw away nearly everything, including a lot of antique bedroom furniture, which was wrecked. The floor coverings were the worst.

'In 2001 it took us a month to clean the house and six weeks before we could move back in.' Debbie recalls that her eight-year-old daughter Samantha thought it was all very funny, having water everywhere, 'until she realised she'd lost all her clothes and toys'.

Debbie listened to ABC Local Radio for hourly updates of the water levels. 'We thought the water would reach no higher than the front steps. We started milking at 3am with dry paddocks; and by the time we'd rounded the cattle up into their paddock — in about forty-five minutes — water was filling the paddocks.'

But Debbie and her husband Paul didn't hear all the flood warnings and, in any case, the water came in different directions from before.

'We started moving our belongings at 3.30 in the afternoon. We still thought we had plenty of time, but the next minute water was in the house and by Saturday night we had a metre of water through the place. We had water views all around the house!'

The water came up so fast the family, cut off by road to anywhere else, climbed onto the carport roof and called the SES for help. 'The SES said they didn't have a flat-bottomed boat to get across the low-lying floodwaters, so we'd have to stay on the carport roof with the dogs, Princess, Tippy and Texas. We heard on the radio that the river would peak at 6.9 metres, then it was 7.2 metres. We thought if it kept rising we'd get up on the roof of the house. Paul had been to Melbourne but he thought that was the coldest night he'd ever spent anywhere.'

Next day the SES arrived using a boat belonging to an eel catcher who lived upstream. 'I started crying when I saw them.'

Even though the Schmidts had experienced floods before, the water damage was still heartbreaking. 'Everyone says it wasn't a big flood and I just ask them, "Did water go through your house?" It breaks your heart every time. You always lose all your kids' stuff.'

Debbie faced isolation of another sort. She believes theirs was the only property between Kempsey and the coast to go under water. No help came for days and no recovery money was made available. 'A bloke and his wife came from the Salvation Army at Grafton and asked if we needed help. He arranged for the St Vincent De Paul and Red Cross to bring us some hot food, groceries, water and toilet paper. He came back the next day with groceries.'

Debbie's problem was money. She didn't have any. The recovery agencies said Paul earned too much to qualify for immediate assistance, which puzzled Debbie as the floods would ensure there was no money coming in and bills would pile up quickly. 'It costs $150 to park a skip outside to take away all the rubbish.' Debbie complained to her local member of parliament and was eventually given $2000, but the whole episode left her with a bad feeling.

'I have always been brought up to expect to fend for myself. But at that time I wasn't asking for a handout, just a bit of help. I needed beds, pillows and blankets and something to put our clothes in. But I never let them see me cry.'

Roslyn Rowe lives nearby with her husband Milton. She's seventy-five years old. Like Debbie, she was looking for more local knowledge as a basis for her flood response. 'We didn't trust the SES figures. We have a friend at Willawarrin [fifty kilometres northwest of Kempsey] who tells us what's going on.

'In 2001 the water got to the top step leading up to the house, so this time we didn't think we'd be in any trouble. But this flood was different and the water gauges people relied on weren't much help at all.'

Her house was all right, but she lost animals. 'I am kicking myself we didn't ask more people what was happening on the properties; and then we wouldn't have lost so many animals and so much equipment. We should have a better network.

'In forty-two years on the river we've had six floods. You know damned well that no two are the same. Our house didn't even get flooded in 1949; and the 2001 flood was the scariest because it came at night.'

Roslyn's farm is a place for horses and cattle. The milking cattle stay next to the house and the rest can only go to a higher area in one paddock. 'It's not big enough for all of them. After two or three days they will want to lie down, particularly the weakest ones. But there isn't enough room. They crash the fences down looking for feed: we lost two on the road.

'Floods are very, very tiring. You are constantly wondering what else will go wrong.'

The scouring action of the river has a dramatic effect on some parts of the riverbank. Roslyn lost a big piece of paddock. 'The river created a huge hole. A cow disappeared into it. We needed eight trucks of gravel to fill it.'

Although the animals need constant attention, Roslyn is fairly self-sufficient. 'We can stay in the house for about a fortnight. We lose the power and phone, but we have a gas barbecue, and keep the hurricane lamps in good order so if we have to use them we can.

'We don't expect another flood of 1949 levels, but if it does happen we have a hole in the roof and we'll get up there. I'm not sure how we'd get the dogs and cats up. I'd be miserable if the animals were lost.' Roslyn is seventy-five years old.

Further along the same road farmer Fay talked about the differences in all the floods she's experienced — 1949, 1950, 1963, 2001 and again in 2009. 'We have lifted our house now and we take the cattle away for three months over the summer.' Her paddocks of corn and potatoes were destroyed by the 2009 floods. 'We're all pretty laid back out here. We all know the floods are going to come and we help each other. We lose bits of the farm every flood. It's washed away by the water, or silt is deposited on the paddocks,' she says.

Murray and June Williams have a little farm on the Macleay. Like many others they don't rely on official warnings to start to prepare. 'I've looked at the paper for years and realised they aren't always right,' said June. 'We have relatives up the top of the rivers who tell us what's going on.'

In town the damage in 2009 could have been much worse. One hundred shops were affected, but with most homes on piles about two metres above the ground, no homes got water above their floorboards. The Northern Rivers region had avoided a complete catastrophe by a small margin.

In Kempsey damage to the region's infrastructure was severe. Roads were damaged in numerous places and many bridges remained closed for days until they could be inspected.

The most dramatic sight, and one that reflects the complexity and danger of the flooding in Kempsey, was seen along the main road where river sand had been deposited along a four-kilometre length to the height of a metre or more. It required a massive earthmoving operation to open the road, remove the sand and mend the damage. Bruce Morris says he'd never seen anything like it; and it was yet another reminder that no two floods are the same. 'At Belgrave Falls the river shifted fifty metres, which means next time there is a flood, it will be felt differently everywhere,' he says.

Lismore, 316 kilometres north of Kempsey, is one of the Northern Rivers regions most floodprone towns. It is where the Wilsons River and Leycester Creek meet and, in May 2009, there was great concern there. Scott Hanckel, division controller for the

Richmond Tweed SES at Lismore, told ABC Local Radio the rain over the four days had fallen on an already saturated catchment.

'We started with very full dams and some of the statistics showing water coming out of them were absolutely mind-boggling,' he said. 'I think I saw one figure was 660,000 megalitres per second coming out of Rocky Creek Dam at one stage. I think this means that in a major flood a Sydney Harbour worth of water goes past Lismore every hour.'

About 200 kilometres north of Kempsey, 9000 Grafton residents living along the Clarence River were put on evacuation notice and told there would be flooding in Grafton and South Grafton. They were told to evacuate to Coffs Harbour. The evacuation notice from the SES encouraged people 'not to underestimate the danger to life which this flood poses'. Instructions were clear and specific.

Residents and business owners are to activate their personal and business flood plans and evacuate ASAP. If you leave later, the roads may be closed.

To prepare for evacuation you should:
- Raise belongings by placing them on tables, beds and benches. Put electrical items on top. Some items may be able to be placed in ceilings.
- Gather medicines, personal and financial documents and mementos together to take with you.
- Listen to radio stations for further information and to confirm this warning.
- If possible, check to see whether your neighbours need help.
- Make arrangements for care of pets or companion animals.

The immediate rescue operation took a further four days. Fodder drops couldn't begin until 25th and 26th May, meaning some animals were without food for five days. About 35,000 people were isolated by floodwaters in towns and rural areas on the north coast and mid-north coast. There was one fatality: a man's body was found in a flooded creek near a submerged vehicle at Raleigh near Coffs Harbour.

A recovery centre was set up in Kempsey. Margaret Motter came out of retirement to run it. 'Two thousand people needed immediate assistance and a further thousand sought assistance over the next four weeks,' she says. 'Initially the requirements were mostly from people in rural areas needing fodder, agistment, fences, and that sort of thing. Later came the human needs. Sometimes it doesn't become apparent to people who've been flooded that they do need help, but over time they realise they are short of something.

'Centrelink gave people $1000 if their home was a quarter damaged. This was means tested and, if the people had insurance, we couldn't assist.

'The majority of our work ended up being to help farmers get rural assistance grants. A lot of hardened farmers came in to us in tears. They say they don't really need anything, that they've coped before and they'll cope again.'

Three months later one farmer, who'd lived on the floodplain for years, looked around the soaked, black and ruined pasture on her property and declared: 'This is a disaster. The volume of water and mud was amazing. I am still getting over the shock. It's like death: you know it's coming but you aren't prepared. You don't know what you are waking up to.' The farmer, who didn't want to be named, watched cattle die. 'The cows cry — they get stuck in the mud — then they die and all you can hear is the silence.

'Everyone did their best to warn us, the council, the SES, police and volunteers. But this flood came as a shock to a lot of people.' The river's behaviour surprised as well. 'Once in a flood you could drive into Yamba [the closest town] during a flood, but now you can't. Now it's just helicopters.

'We keep a shovel near our rear door now, because even minor floods bring silt and we can't open the doors.'

Before the damage in May 2009 had been repaired, another minor flood swept through the Macleay River in July. The following year 2010 was drought-stricken by comparison, but then a La Niña pattern emerged. Kempsey and the Northern Rivers copped a massive series of floods in June 2011. Six communities were evacuated and 16,000 people isolated in the Kempsey and Taree regions, with more than fifty flood rescues.

Kempsey remains in the same place; farmers still eke out a living on the floodplain. The community winds down, waiting for the next flood. As Grafton SES controller Dave Mackey is fond of saying: 'Water never gives up.'

Losing the Battles; Winning the War
Ulmarra, Northern New South Wales, May 2009

At first sight thirty-seven-year-old Deb Wallace seems an unlikely superhero. She had joined the navy as a hydrographic systems operator, and was based in Cairns for five and a half years, but she suffered from seasickness. She then decided to study climatology and perhaps work at the Bureau of Meteorology. And so she came back home, to Ulmarra on the Clarence River, to live with her parents. Ulmarra is a former river port about thirteen kilometres north of Grafton in northeast New South Wales. About forty homes line the usually idyllic riverbank: here the Clarence is about 500 metres wide.

With a can-do attitude that typified people joining the Navy, Deb volunteered at the SES at Ulmarra when she got home.

In May 2009 Deb was feeling like every other university student facing mid-year exams, with only two days to complete assignments in astronomy, climatology, maths (algebra and calculus), and physics. Too much to do; too little time. And there was also flooding rain. The extremely intense rainfalls that typify the north coast of New South Wales can temporarily raise the flow of the Clarence to massive levels.

In addition to her study, every second Sunday Deb was doing work experience at the Bureau of Meteorology office at Coffs Harbour. In mid-May she began taking a little more interest in the weather charts. 'I saw the charts and thought, we're going to get hammered, but of course that was just my student's perspective,' she says. 'I couldn't help feeling we were in for something big, though.'

On the 18th there was some suggestion that an 'east–coast low' might form off the coast. This low eventually affected a large portion of the northern New South Wales coast. The system provided ideal conditions for very heavy rain over a large part of the northeast.

Some east–coast lows cause great consternation because while most just blow back out to sea, some stay virtually stationary over the coast and dump massive amounts of rain. Emergency agencies prepare well. The SES Controller at Grafton, Dave Mackay, needed as many people as possible to help if the system did form up, and he asked Deb if she could come into Grafton for operational centre training.

Deb was the only remaining active Ulmarra resident at the town's State Emergency Service unit. 'Our unit was closed. There was no one to run it, so technically we weren't operating. We were winging it.'

Dave, the local SES controller in Grafton, admired Deb's determination and commonsense, and trusted her to help her little community downriver.

Despite being very busy with her study, Deb agreed and attended the Grafton headquarters for three days. 'I thought, oh crap, I have five assignments and four exams.' But because the situation looked grim, and because the SES was understaffed, she agreed. She did the training course from Monday to the Wednesday.

The rains came on Monday 18; storms started on Tuesday accompanied by significant winds. 'I didn't sleep much that night,' recalled Deb. 'I'd planned to do my reading for the exams at night, but on the Wednesday the storms really picked up even stronger. I couldn't sleep, so by the Thursday I was exhausted.

'Then we really got hammered by the weather. The rain was loud and really annoying. I knew I was getting crankier and my patience with people was wearing thin.

'By Friday I was really tired. That's the thing with storms ... everyone is already tired before they have to do anything. Then if they are like me they start to do embarrassing things.'

The floodwaters didn't wait for Deb to recover.

The Clarence River rises on the Queensland border. After flowing south and then northeast for almost four hundred kilometres, it flows into the Pacific Ocean in a delta formation with Yamba on the south side and Illuka on the northern side. It is one of Australia's big waterways: the only river in Australia south of the Tropic of Capricorn that carries more water is the Murray. And now the river was stirring; and the Bureau of Meteorology was issuing warnings.

Most towns on the river sit behind levees. Grafton is on a hill but still it has a massive wall between the town and the river. Ulmarra too sits on a rise. The main street runs perpendicular to the river and is home to some substantial nineteenth-century buildings. There are a few bed and breakfast places, a coffee shop, a newsagent, a store and a couple of commercial businesses.

The wider community lives on the alluvial floodplain. It's lush and green and dairy cattle are usually knee deep in pasture. Nearly all homes are on stumps about a metre high. Minor floods happen most winters and moderate to heavy floods every six to ten years. Theoretically residents in a resilient community should be ready. They should be active members of their communities, preparing, safeguarding, training and helping newcomers.

Emergency authorities and the council began preparing for flooding on the Tuesday and emergency crews were brought to Grafton to help with planning and possible rescue. The level of the Clarence was predicted to be above 5.7 metres at the Ulmarra gauge. At that level, surrounding farmlands would be flooded and properties isolated, roads cut, and perhaps power turned off. 6.1 metres was the level at which water would enter the town.

Deb returned from Grafton on the Wednesday night, preparing for the weekend peak, and began to assess the situation. The Ulmarra SES was effectively a one-person unit (Deb), plus a volunteer from a neighbouring unit, a shed and a tiny flat-bottomed punt with an outboard. In previous years it had been busy, but now it was much less so. There were fewer people in the region as dairy farms amalgamated. Increased bureaucracy, new legislation and a largely ungrateful public had undermined the unit to the point where it effectively did not exist. This sad state of affairs has affected volunteer emergency units throughout Australia.

Although some of the volunteers were still living in the community, it was hard for Deb to approach them and ask them to help. 'They had been disheartened previously.' There was no time to try to pull a new team together.

The police, rural fire brigade and ambulance staff all met in a room at the SES shed at Ulmarra to start planning. No one had any operational centre experience, so Deb, despite just three days' training, began to set up a place to plan, take phone calls from residents and distribute information. 'It was organised chaos,' she says. The river rose quickly and the first requests for assistance in the form of sandbags came on Thursday, but the Clarence Council couldn't get the sand to Ulmarra until mid-morning Friday.

People confronted by serious flooding began to vent their frustrations, which was Deb's first inkling that perhaps this task wasn't going to be simply about SES rescues.

The community's lack of preparation started to become apparent. People would ring Deb and ask for sandbags and, because they were frantically trying to put their belongings in a safe place, or because they didn't have cars capable of transporting the heavy bags, they explained they couldn't come into the depot to get them. In any event elderly people wouldn't have been able to lift them; and others with no experience in using them to build a useful barrier wanted someone to show them what to do. The SES didn't have enough people to help supervise the sandbag filling: people had to fill their own. 'I didn't like sending them away, but I seemed to have no option,' said Deb.

A swift-water rescue crew arrived and based itself in Ulmarra, but they were tasked for urgent rescues and couldn't get involved in things like sandbagging. It seemed to be the highest priority; Deb was getting increasingly desperate calls for more sandbags and from people who wanted help with them.

Eventually she abandoned the SES shed for a moment and asked rural fire brigade staff to help with the sandbagging. They refused. 'I felt really disappointed,' says Deb. 'I knew it wasn't their responsibility, and they helped in all sorts of other ways, but at the time I was totally disheartened.'

Deb had just had her first taste of the powerlessness that comes when community leadership has no assets and no authority. Over the next few days not much would make her feel better.

It was raining heavily and the wind remained strong. A drain collapsed along the river's edge, letting water into an area around the back of Ulmarra, which would have cut off road access. A team of SES volunteers from Bathurst turned up to fill the breach. It took all day.

Police arranged a door-knock to advise residents of the likely onset of the flooding and encouraged people to evacuate. They arranged the bus that took eight people away on the Friday. 'I thought most people in the town would go,' says Deb. 'One woman just arced up. She crossed her arms and refused to take their advice. I asked one family who had young kids why they wouldn't leave, and the husband said "looters". I hadn't thought of that. The majority of the people in the town were like that. They didn't leave and they didn't cooperate.'

The Pacific Highway was cut by the rising floodwaters on the Friday afternoon, effectively isolating the town from major service centres.

A big wooden river cruiser disappeared from its mooring at Ulmarra. The owner came and asked for help to find it. Deb only had one little boat in the shed, the punt, and she said she couldn't let him have it to look for a boat. The search might take hours and probably wasn't safe in the punt. 'I told him we might need the boat to rescue people and that was my highest priority, not searching for his boat.' The owner and his wife were very disappointed and made their feelings known to Deb.

Deb stuck a picket into the open space on the riverbank at the end of the main street and noted that at about 8.30pm on the Friday night the water was at about 5.1 metres. By 9.40pm it was 5.5 metres, a jump of 40 centimetres. In a river kilometres wide and hundreds of kilometres long, that's a massive increase in the volume of water. And it was churning.

'The water was very erky. It was full of debris. I realised that our little boat was going to be no use for water rescues in the main river, but it would probably be OK across the floodplain. But I felt if someone was washed away in the river, we wouldn't be able to help.' Deb was worrying about things over which she had no control. Sleep deprivation, stress and inexperience do that.

The picket became a gathering point, with many people from the community making numerous visits to see how far and how fast the water was rising. 'I was really nervous about a night-time evacuation.' There was a brief flurry of excitement when the big river cruiser chugged back into the town mooring. It had been found floating downstream, the mooring line having broken. The jetty was now well under water, so the boat was tied to a tree.

Apart from the logistical difficulties of not having a boat to rescue people, and not having any volunteers, Deb had already experienced errant behaviour that would get in the way of an orderly evacuation. Friday night in the pub meant too much drinking. It would usually lead to friction she and the town could well do without. They certainly didn't need it when the flood was coming.

'When a 'colourful' local resident started playing up in the pub that night, I just started crying. I was so emotional and really tired. I called the police to come and get him, but the highway was closed. I wanted to put it all out of my head and sleep.' Someone eventually shut the resident up.

According to one resident, Deb was pretty generous with this description: apparently the man 'just cut loose'. The same resident also described the communication problems Deb was having. 'There was a lot of tension between people. All the different characters and personalities had different opinions. They assert themselves even if they have no right to voice their opinions because they have no background or knowledge. There is a lot of that around here in general!'

The Bureau of Meteorology now advised residents that the water would peak at 6.1 metres at 1am. Deb, and most of the people in the town gathered at the water's edge watching and now expecting that the flood would threaten the homes and buildings in the main street — and along the riverfront.

Just after 1am, Deb left. After a full day and most of the night arguing, pleading, organising and running on adrenalin, she had had enough. 'I was exhausted and had to get some sleep.' The river's rise had slowed considerably and it hadn't reached the forecast levels. Deb went home to bed. The heavy rain continued all night. There was no respite; she tossed and turned, worrying about how things would unfold the next day, wondering if she would meet the expectations of the community, worrying what she should do about the exams and assignments. Hungry and very nervous, she had a fitful few hours of sleep.

Deb woke at 5.30am, feeling a little better. She went for a walk around town and looked at the water in the river. The level was 5.7 metres. Deb was mightily relieved, but not for a moment did she think the worst was over. She just felt that it would be easier to deal with the flood during the day than at night.

The day wore on and the water continued to rise slowly. The streets and roads on the edge of town filled with water, marooning residents in an ever-decreasing area of high ground in the main two streets. Deb watched as the surrounding farmland became lakeland. Any travel now would be by boat.

She had her first phone call wanting assistance on Saturday afternoon. Someone had run out of asthma drugs. Another call came soon after with a resident wanting food.

'We got a call from two females who were in their farmhouse. They argued with us previously that they would stay, but then their house got invaded by snakes and they wanted to get out in a hurry. They ended up some time later getting into a fight at the pub. I called them the Medusa girls.' Someone called for more insulin for their diabetes. An SES boat from Grafton was arranged to bring food and medical supplies down the river.

Deb couldn't believe it. The warnings and encouragement to evacuate, education campaigns on the radio and in newspapers and the community's previous experience of floods meant nothing to these people. They just thought the SES had a duty or responsibility to help, even though by doing so they were putting themselves at risk. Arranging for delivery of items kept Deb and the swift-water team busy all day. At least the river stopped rising, even though it didn't start to fall.

Night came. Someone reported that a man was trapped in his car. It was dark and this was the sort of exercise best left to well-trained and experienced rescuers. The swift-water rescue team was called to assist elsewhere. Untrained, tired and emotional, Deb had to make a decision about going to help. 'There seemed to be a sense of urgency in the voice of the person who called and there is a horrible feeling when you think that help may not get there quick enough,' says Deb.

The task was extremely dangerous. It meant crossing unseen fence lines, ducking under single-strand power lines, avoiding objects in the dark water. It was still raining, the river was full of debris and the boat was flat-bottomed. Sensibly Deb asked Scott Chard, a local service station owner, for help.

Scott had been the SES Unit Coordinator in Ulmarra, one of the people Deb says 'got disheartened'. He was quick to help. 'He knew all the fence lines and gates and he also knew the right angles for the propeller. He is worth his weight in gold.'

That rescue was successful but another, much more demanding on Deb's stressed emotional state, was now necessary. An SES rescue boat had become hopelessly lost on the river. 'You could tell from the voice of the operator that she was really frightened,' says Deb. The boat had been lost for some time and fuel was running short. Having no fuel in a fast-running river would have been dreadful. If a large log or submerged item hit the boat, they might well be tipped in.

Deb had no idea where the boat was, but she promised the voice on the radio she'd stay on the riverbank and talk to them until they were safe.

She felt if she could get a spotlight of some sort to scan the river, the SES boat might see it, and be guided into the shore safely. The only decent light was on the previously lost cruiser. Deb asked the vessel's owner to put the spotlight on to the river to see if the little SES boat could see it. The owner was happy to oblige but the woman with him wasn't.

And so began one of those inexplicable episodes that tend to occur only when people are under stress. Deb said, 'I felt people's lives were more important than her boat, but she was screaming and getting hysterical and I was in tears saying, "There are five people in a boat right now who need our help."' A group of friends arrived to calm the woman down. Deb walked away and composed herself.

The boat owner scoured the river with his light and the SES boat crew saw it. 'There was enormous relief in that boat then — you could hear it in their voices,' says Deb.

All day Sunday food and medical drops were made to isolated farmhouses in the community. Deb, Scott and the two swift-water specialists handled most of it. It's easy to understand why Deb wanted to be out of town. But she found the water rescue and supply equally difficult.

'We weren't trained for this. People got cranky with us really quickly. We picked up three civilians and dropped them off and only one said thanks. I don't think people understand how dangerous it is,' she says. Apart from the risk of hitting fences and other submerged structures, being struck by debris or getting hopelessly lost ducking under live power lines, there are other problems.

'We went under a tree and snake fell into the boat and curled up and went to sleep! Later we were travelling along and had to stop at a house to get some petrol. We heard gunshots, which we thought were aimed at us to keep us away from the house, but it turned out it was a farmer shooting foxes that had found sanctuary in a tree.

'I got bitten by something, a spider or a black ant, it was really painful and the welt lasted a week. I am such a girl sometimes.'

Eventually the water receded, the roads opened and people began to help themselves. Little water entered Ulmarra but houses all round suffered flood damage and people's livelihoods were threatened until their pastures grew back. Three weeks later it rained again and the low-lying areas were hit by more minor floods. These things were bad, but nothing like they had been.

Upon reflection Deb is philosophical. 'It could have been worse if the water had reached its forecast height,' she says.

She spent a short while debriefing over the events of those two weeks, much of it shaking her head about aspects of human behaviour. 'Some people didn't behave well. For many it might have been their first time in this situation. I was pretty hard on myself on how I handled all that, but I didn't expect that people would get so upset with me, when all I was doing was the best I could.

'I was already stressed from lack of sleep and worry about my exams, but I wanted to help because there was no one else.'

Deb got her astronomy and two physics papers in on time. Climatology was three days late. She got 70 per cent for her astronomy exam, and 90 per cent for physics. She achieved her goal with her university studies and soon after began working for the Bureau of Meteorology. She remained a member of the SES. Of the 2009 floods she says, 'We were all in this together. In that sense we were all equals. This flood might have been a first-time experience for some people, but it won't be the last. We have to educate the community to learn to help themselves.'

The Ulmarra SES unit grew over the next year to have eight members, who were initiated with the January 2011 floods. But that's another story.

'It was fantastic, what they did'
Condamine River Catchment, Southern Queensland, December 2010 to January 2011

The rains came early to the Condamine in 2010. Indeed, the La Niña weather pattern brought rain all year and, after a long drought, it was very welcome. Ray Brown, the mayor of the Western Downs Regional Council and a broad-acre crop and cattle farmer, says there was never a season like it. 'My father says we had the best grain crops ever,' he says.

The Condamine River is a tributary of the Darling, Australia's longest river, which rises in the Great Dividing Range southeast of Warwick in southern Queensland, about 140 kilometres west of Brisbane. Rainfall from these ranges generally makes its way into the rivers, which run inland. The Condamine itself begins at The Head near Killarney, literally falling straight down via the beautiful Queen Mary Falls and then dropping another 200 metres in less than 10 kilometres: a very sharp gradient for a big river.

Water flows out into the Condamine valley, 50 kilometres wide in some places. At Chinchilla the river then flows in a narrow valley only 5 kilometres wide. The water picks up speed as it rushes through this pinch at the little town of Condamine before it eventually enters the Balonne River system and finally goes to the Darling in New South Wales. The water will travel 1200 kilometres along the Condamine–Balonne river system. It is so flat through the valley and on the floodplain that the broad-acre farmers sometimes have to create a gradient on their land to allow the water to flow away. The Condamine catchment contains some of the most fertile soils in the world and is one of the most productive agricultural areas in Australia.

The 2010 rains kept coming, saturating the soil, replenishing the aquifers, the tributaries and the rivers. Finally there was run-off and people in the southern part of the Murray-Darling system began to wonder if, after ten years of raised hopes and disappointment, there might be enough water in the top of the basin to reach the Murray and the lower lakes. It turned out there would be more than enough. Ray Brown and the farmers on the Darling Downs knew that as early as October. They watched what looked like a record grain crop flower, promise a massive yield, and then rot in the water-logged paddocks.

'We never harvested any of that wheat. We should start to get it off in October. That's how wet it was. It stayed wet right though,' says Ray Brown.

In November the Western Downs Regional Council, which takes in its regional centre of Dalby and extends to Chinchilla, Condamine, Moonie and almost to Surat 238 kilometres west, conducted a disaster exercise. The council based its scenario on what the disaster experts believed was a realistic assessment of how bad flooding could become in the region — isolating towns for a number of days, making emergency response difficult. The second part of the scenario involved a man falling off a bridge into a river and needing rescue.

'We were ready for anything,' says Ray. 'We tested it, created a template and updated some of the shortcomings.'

It rained throughout November and into December. The region receives most of its rainfall in summer so disappointed farmers locked away their barely used machinery, tidied up their paddocks and yards and houses and began the holiday period. They hoped Christmas and New Year would bring new beginnings.

Despite the heartbreak from the poor cropping season, Ray says the locals felt like they always do: 'She'll be right. The season will be good next year.' But it kept raining. And the rain was widespread, from the escarpment to the Great Dividing Range and through the outback. The disaster of the 2010–2011 season had begun. 'People were feeling a little bit disillusioned because they lost all their income.' For many, it would get worse.

On 20 December the Bureau of Meteorology began issuing moderate flood warnings for the Condamine and its tributaries. Infrastructure and agriculture have been built into the floodplain to ensure that water travels across it gently. Roads, for example, can't be more than 10 centimetres or so above the ground, to ensure they don't act as barriers to water flow. This means that when the plain floods there is water as far as the eye can see. This is a normal pattern through summer and the locals expect isolation. It is not unknown for them to drive across forty or fifty kilometres of floodplain surrounded by water.

The town of Condamine, about 125 kilometres west of Dalby, is right on the river, a tiny farming community of about 350 people, although only about ninety live in the town itself. There are just nine businesses, the biggest of which is the Condamine Bell pub across the road from the caravan park and truck stop. There are only about two dozen streets. Most homes are high-set, although a number are on small stumps. The river is for the most part not particularly attractive: a murky, dusty brown.

Large-scale flooding within the area's main towns such as Warwick, Dalby and Chinchilla does not happen regularly. On the floodplains it's a different story, with big floods occurring on average every two years. The weather bureau advice for the Condamine valley says flooding 'can result from heavy rainfall in any of the large tributaries which enter the Condamine River. Under these circumstances flood forecast lead times may be short'*. If farmers move too slowly they will lose fencing, pumping and irrigation equipment, machinery and stock through drowning. Residents in towns expect to be isolated for brief periods every summer. The roads are cut every year and there are occasional problems with electricity and phones.

But, as Ray Brown says, floods in residential areas are unknown to the people of Condamine. 'No one in town had any memory of a decent flood; and they all knew that the previous

---

* bom.gov.au/hydro/flood/qld/brochures/condamine_cotswold/condamine_cotswold.shtml#PreviousFloodingCondamine Town

record was 1897. A few talked of the 1983 floods, when nearly all the homes were marooned, but damage was minimal. Initially this became the reference point.' In the face of these regular moderate flood warnings, which usually only affect agricultural land and farming properties, and with no recent experience of what serious floods can do, only a handful of people in town responded to the first bureau warnings.

Ray Brown knows his community. He's been in local government for more than twenty years. He understands floods himself, remembering the big Dalby floods of the early 1980s. 'We copped an absolute hiding where I live on the Weir River that year.'

On 26 December the Bureau of Meteorology increased its warnings to 'major flooding'. Very quickly, in Dalby 200 homes were inundated, and dozens more in Chinchilla and Miles. Evacuations in both towns began as people moved out of low-lying areas and went to their friends and relatives. In the east of the shire, towns were cut off by rising floodwaters.

'I ended up with eight towns in trouble and all had major concerns,' said Ray Brown. Dalby, Jandowae, Warra, Chinchilla, Miles, Condamine, Flinton and Tara were all isolated. 'When towns are completely cut off, all our supply-chain networks shut down. We rely solely on helicopters to get emergency services and supplies in and out. Our SES crews were stretched to the limit.'

At Condamine the community got busy. People started lifting their furniture and packing boxes to be stored in safe places. Those who had been through the 1983 flood felt they knew where the high points in and around town were and people banded together to move the furniture of low-set homes to the school or to a number of farming properties where the owners had agreed to let people use their big empty grain storage sheds.

It was felt that if the water rose as high as it had in 1983, the low-set houses would have water across their floorboards, but the high-set homes would be all right.

Bill Power, the SES controller at Condamine, says the young people pitched in and did much of the backbreaking lifting and carrying. The SES group consisted of about seven people, but it grew a bit. 'It's typical of Australians, isn't it?' says Bill. 'When someone's in trouble, everyone helps out, but you only see some people when there's a major problem.

'It was pretty busy, but no one was panicking.'

Some residents still didn't believe the flood forecasts; and others were worried about their pets. Some were worried about personal security and looting.

Up until this point everything was unfolding as expected. Then later on 27 December the Bureau of Meteorology issued a chilling warning that was frankly impossible for most people to contemplate. 'Early that morning we were made aware that we had a serious situation,' says Ray. 'Every river and tributary of the Condamine was running at record heights and we were having trouble understanding the ultimate impact of that.

'Then the bureau told us the river height might exceed the record at Condamine, set in 1896, at 14.25 metres. The major flood level at Condamine in most people's memory is ten metres. The bureau was forecasting more than fifteen!'

Bill Power says the forecast was received with total disbelief in Condamine. 'No one could envisage that amount of water coming down the river. I've lived here more than thirty years. In the '83 floods my house didn't get wet at all. I never dreamed my house could get flooded.'

'No one believed it,' said Ray, 'Every river that was flowing was now well above record height and we couldn't get a defined final height. The local SES controllers said it wont be that ... and we said yes it will.'

Ray Brown had to contend with this skepticism. 'All the locals said it would never go above the record. No one in living memory in that town could remember a house being flooded.' To understand the mindset you have to view the situation as the locals did. Condamine is flat country. For the river to rise by a metre or more than the previous record, the flood would have to extend to the far horizon, 10 kilometres on either side. 'There was a sense of disbelief, but there's also the Australian nature, the "she'll be right" attitude.'

At 8am on Tuesday 28 December the council's disaster management group met to discuss the situation. 'We had everyone around the table — police, EMQ, rural fire brigade, Red Cross, roads, health — and we were connected to the district disaster management team and state disaster management team,' says Brown.

Initially the conversation focussed on all the issues of dealing with the eight isolated towns — how could they be resupplied? How could people be rescued if they got into trouble? They decided on voluntary evacuation. The people of Condamine were notified that Black Hawk helicopters would arrive later in the day. The local disaster committee at Condamine met at the pub and discussed the situation with the people of the town. About twenty people decided to leave. Preparations began.

The next day, just before 11am Ergon Energy advised the Dalby team that the water level would result in their three-phase high-tension power lines going under water within about twenty-four hours. The power would be switched off, because it presented a local danger but it would have also taken out the power to other towns in the region, including Miles. This advice changed the situation significantly.

'No water. No sewerage, no communications,' says Ray Brown. 'We'd lose our Telstra tower, no road access. Once you lose power you lose fridges. And power drives water supplies and sewerage. Then there is no communication. Once you lose communication you are in big trouble.' The shared belief around the disaster table at Dalby was that the situation would not change for ten days.

At 11am acting Inspector Simon Chase, who chaired the district disaster committee, called for a mandatory evacuation of the entire town. Even though the decision had been slowly gelling as the morning unfolded, it was still a shock to everyone when it was actually made. Such action had only ever been taken in Queensland once — two days before, when 300 residents of Theodore in central Queensland had been evacuated. This was an entirely new environment for the emergency agencies.

'To evacuate the whole town is a big call,' said Ray Brown. 'We didn't not want to, but there was an enormous amount of water upstream and our first priority was to protect life. It was a safety order.

'I felt terrible. How do you feel when you tell someone whose home is their castle, who's lived there safely all their lives, that they have to leave?

'The decision was made by about forty people. No one was saying, hang on hang on.

'We consulted the group leader at SES, Bill Power, in Condamine. He was busy organising his troops. And we went through Helen Thomas, the local disaster manager at Miles, the nearest big town, who is responsible for emergency management in Condamine.'

Bill Power hesitated, thinking his people were being overwhelmed. Ray Brown thinks they couldn't have been asked to do any more. 'It was getting too big for them. They were coping well, but just how do you look after a whole town? We could see it would take ten days to get back in there, to get the power on, the water and sewerage plants fixed and operating, but it was something the people in the town couldn't comprehend.'

The residents of Condamine baulked. 'They were hostile,' said Ray. 'We took a lot of heat from that decision.

'We knew we had to protect life. They were not going to do it themselves. When we decided to evacuate we had a commitment from Queensland police commissioner Bob Atkinson to maintain a police presence in that town for the whole time.'

Bill Power says the problem was the way the decision was changed from voluntary to mandatory evacuations. 'It was just dumped on us,' he says. 'I was absolutely astounded. One minute we were told there was a voluntary evacuation and an hour later we were told it was mandatory.

'People were up in arms.'

Another meeting was called for 2pm to explain how the evacuations would take place. People would be allowed to take one small bag on the helicopters with them.

People had a choice. There were homes just on the outskirts of Condamine that were above the flood threat line and many farmers in the area were well out of harm's way. Many families moved in with their neighbours or those in rural areas. They knew they would be isolated from the town, but they would be closer than the evacuation centre in Dalby and these homes had their own generators, septic systems and food supplies.

The planning began for an evacuation on the 30th, twenty-four hours later and just two and a half days since the first "major" flood warnings were issued. Restoring confidence among the townspeople was a priority.

'We decided to send four police officers who would be staying in one of the high homes. They probably got eaten alive by mosquitoes and sandflies, and I think every snake and spider in the world would have turned up. One SES crew stayed with them too. It was a tremendous effort.' On 30 December two Black Hawks from the Army Aviation Training Centre at Oakey, near Toowoomba, were tasked to evacuate 86 people from Condamine to Dalby 125 kilometres east. The operation included moving a defence refuelling team to Dalby.

The defence force advised the evacuation would begin at about 5pm and be finished by 10pm. 'We would like to have had all the evacuations completed by dark,' said Ray Brown. 'But there were plenty of other things happening across Queensland and that was the only window we had with the Black Hawks.'

People began to realise that Condamine would be abandoned. That meant leaving belongings and pets and animals, including horses. 'Animals are a part of people's lives,' says Brown. 'There was a lot of discussion about this. The defence force told us they wouldn't allow animals on the Black Hawks. We kept telling them, and the locals told them, they wanted to take any companion animals. The officers changed their tune, which was a credit to them because they have rules to abide by. In the end they allowed small companion animals and one small bag and we got people out of there.'

The two Black Hawks would evacuate the residents to Dalby, 125 kilometres away. The first helicopter landed just before 7pm, the last at 10pm. The helicopters, fitted with external fuel tanks for the long journey, travelled at about 120 knots [260 kilometres] an hour. For some people, Ray said, the experience was 'terribly frightening'.

The blackhawks departed Oakey: one went via Miles the other via Dalby; picking up several police before heading to Condamine. The aircraft arrived at Condamine at 6.45pm and the last evacuees arrived in Dalby at approximately 11pm. Ray was waiting at Dalby airport when the first flights came in. 'There was a lady, well into her eighties, who'd never flown in her life, and she was just plucked out of her town, the town she loves and lives in, and moved to a completely new place. That woman became a medical case. That was just severe stress. That's just heartbreak.

'The first ten who came off were greeted by a media scrum. When they got into the buses they all picked up phones and rang Condamine and said, "Bloody hell, there's a lot of water out there." That's when the penny dropped and then everyone queued up ten deep at Condamine to get on the next Black Hawk, because reality did hit home. They saw an ocean of water and realised we were correct to call the mandatory evacuation.'

Although still dry, the town was all but abandoned. By the next morning water had risen out of the river and was inching through the streets. Homes on the low-lying riverbank areas already had water through them and, when Ray Brown inspected the town, the water had reached the footrails in the Condamine Bell hotel. It was still rising.

'I flew back in to make sure we had everyone out. SES crews were going from house to house picking up animals and pets. There was bugger all land left sitting out of the water.

'I also wanted to reassure residents we had every dog, cat and bird and that every home was protected. I gave my word. The police commissioner gave his word. Everything was protected.

'I went into the SES shed when water was just starting to come in. That's where they stored many of the dogs and cats and birds. There was a very large police officer wearing nothing but his budgie smugglers and police shirt. These guys were up to their knees in water for days.'

The SES volunteers had to feed all the animals, which was something of an effort. 'To see these SES blokes in a boat, which already had three or four dogs on board, and they would pull up next to a house on a landing and try to coax stray dogs they'd never seen before, onto the boat … and those animals on the boat didn't seem to like each other … and there are four or five snakes on the landing … you tell me if it's a good job being on an SES crew!

'Inside the SES shed there was a talking parrot among the dogs and cats. You can imagine the mayhem. Every time a dog or cat moved the parrot would say, "What you doing, what you doing?"

'I spoke about that when I got back to the evacuation centre at Dalby and a fellow broke down in tears and he said, "That's my parrot." He just wanted to know he was OK.'

Months later it was this anecdote that forced Ray Brown to blink back the tears as he remembered the bewildered Condamine people so far away from their homes, unable to comprehend what was going on around them, worried about their pets, their homes and properties.

'I can remember the horses too that were left in the town. The owners left all the gates open and the horses had to fend for themselves. There were about four horses standing on the top of a truck-loading ramp, surrounded by water. It was the highest part of town.

'I always wonder: How did those horses know it was coming and where to stand to keep out of the water?

'They never moved off that all day. They stayed out of water for the whole time. Pity we couldn't tap into their thoughts. We've got all this technology predicting things, but the horses didn't need that to know they weren't going to hang around in their paddocks.

'I am getting emotional now.'

The SES team and police continued the clean-up in town even though the residents were all gone. 'I saw these young fellas lifting clothes dryers above their heads and walking up to their arms in water to save people's belongings. It was fantastic what they did.'

Those four police and about seven SES crew who were alone in the town were ordered not to travel at night. 'The river was getting to pretty extreme heights. At one stage we couldn't travel on it at all for fear of running into the Ergon power lines. And there was a lot of debris being washed downstream too. Big trees and shrubs and bits of buildings.'

As Ray Brown inspected Condamine in the flood boat, he listened in awe to the noise of the water, but his mind was always on the people. 'I had my heart in my mouth because everyone's left their homes. I was confident we would protect the town and, anyway, I'd given my word. Nothing untoward could happen to those empty properties.'

As predicted by the bureau, the water rose to 15.2 metres. Of the sixty homes in town, forty-two went under water, and all nine businesses, the school (where many people had stored their furniture) and the church. Sixty-nine rural homes were also flooded in the Condamine region.

'The floods affected every bit of the whole region. Those rural properties copped an absolute hiding. Homes a hundred and forty years old which had never been flooded had two metres of water through them.

'In hindsight the evacuation was the right thing to do,' says Ray. 'That elderly woman who went to hospital for stress, when she came back she discovered there were two and a half metres of water through her home. You tell me, did we do the right thing? Of course we did.'

But as soon as the evacuation was complete, the next phase began. 'We had our plan for re-establishment. For two days I never went to bed. I was waiting on water heights. The peak came at midnight or one in the morning two days later. When it started to fall we had information from upstream and we knew when it would be OK to return to town.'

A convoy was arranged. Non-residents were told to stay out. 'There will be no entry to the town apart from this convoy,' Brown said on ABC Radio at the time. 'There will be a media blackout on the first day of return as residents want time to express their emotions in privacy. They're coming back to something they might not like to see.'

He adds: 'By then we'd organised hygiene, as the sewerage still didn't work, so we trucked in portable toilets and water. We had to talk to the residents about how to take care of themselves. We got the power connected back to homes and flew in twelve electricians to check every house. Twenty homes needed major electrical work. Red Cross, Lifeline counsellors for support, EMQ. The rural fire brigade had to bring in fire hoses to clean houses. There was a huge workforce with nowhere to stay.' The coal seam gas mining companies allowed the residents to stay in their nearby accommodation cabins, provided them with food and transport. "They even gave us their helicopters,' said Ray.

Seven days after the flood the townspeople returned in a bus. Some were greeted with the sight of a relatively untouched home. Some properties, like the pub, were smashed.

'It's devastation,' Shane Hickey, the publican, told news agency AAP. 'Even though we've had days to prepare for it, it's still extremely hard.

'It's just flattened everything; all the grass is mud; all the plants have been torn out of the ground; the trees have gone over and are just covered in silt and mud.'

A metre of water through the hotel had left the place a wreck and repairing damage to the building alone would cost about $200,000. The hotel's proximity to the normally sedate Condamine River meant it couldn't be insured against floods.

'The big walk-in coldroom came off the wall and landed about three metres behind the pub and the next door's coldroom was lifted up and dumped on our hotel,' Hickey said. 'The hotel sheets were black, the pool table swollen with moisture. Beer kegs were swirled around as if they were in a washing machine. All the fridges went, the washing machines, the freezers, all the laundry. Cartons of rum were found about a hundred metres down from the pub.

'Everything smelled awful. You thought the best way to fix this up would be to just bulldoze the lot and start again.'

Ray Brown says the volunteers who descended on the town lifted spirits.

'We can be proud to be a part of the western downs, and a Queenslander and an Australian most of all. It was a tremendous effort. There was support from every Australian and from all over Australia.

'We had a coal seam gas industry exploring here, which attracted a lot of objectors, but the number one objector to the industry was pushing a mud mop alongside the main men from Origin and British Gas. That was a wonderful sight.

'All the problems were put aside. It was unbelievable. All credit to the people and the companies involved.'

The clean-up was exhausting, the hard work only broken by a visit from the governor-general, Quentin Bryce, who arrived via army helicopter to inspect the town.

The recovery didn't go smoothly. Initially there were concerns about hygiene and Ray decided no children would be allowed back. 'That was a problem for many families and caused a lot of heartache. But disease was a big issue and the last thing we wanted was kids playing in the mud.'

The atmosphere remained humid; the flies, sandflies and mosquitoes were vicious. But gradually damaged homes were emptied out and, with doors and windows all open to air, residents felt they were getting somewhere.

It rained every day, everywhere. A couple of residents returned to their homes, although most remained in the camp or with friends outside town.

On 10 January residents heard with horror about Toowoomba and the Lockyer Valley, where a wall of water had cascaded down the escarpment east of Toowoomba and smashed homes and whole towns, killing twenty-two people.

Ray was talking to the state disaster committee when news of the deaths began to reach Brisbane. 'When you hear the Premier of the state upset, I heard her crying, and then I knew we had a problem. Anna Bligh was deeply upset, no doubt about it.'

Although not all the residents would have been able to see the unforgettable images of the roads awash in Toowoomba and the debris piling up on bridges at Grantham, they all knew what had happened. 'The residents of Condamine and the rest of the shire realised that no matter how bad they felt, no lives had been lost, and they gave thanks for that.'

That wall of water had been created by massive and unprecedented storms in the Great Dividing Range. People in the Condamine Valley began to realise that the water on the range usually flows west and that more flooding in Condamine was possible. And inevitably the weather warnings started to flow in, going from likely to moderate to major flooding. With data from the first flood able to confirm river heights, the bureau was more confident of its warnings. Condamine was going to be hit again with another record-breaking flood.

With the town infrastructure not repaired, homes empty and being aired, exhausted people and problems throughout the shire, the decision was taken — the town would have to be evacuated again. But this time, when the call came on the 13th, it didn't have to be described as mandatory. Another meeting was called involving the few people remaining in town and the large number of volunteers. Ray Brown says, 'As soon as we explained the warnings, there was a brief discussion, the meeting lasted fifty-five minutes, and twenty minutes later everyone was ready to leave.'

The air of resignation was felt throughout the community, which had already exhausted its supply of superlatives to discuss what was happening well before the new horrors occurred.

Andrew Smith from the Western Downs Council put the second flood in some perspective. He told people, 'Certainly the damage this time around will be less because you can't lose something you've already lost.'

Thirty homes and businesses in Condamine were inundated for a second time. 'Any outbuildings and garden sheds left after the first flood were destroyed in the second. They'd already lost what was in them. The water was a lot cleaner and didn't seem to bring so much mud back with it,' says Ray Brown. 'There is nothing worse than cleaning up mud. It is really shocking.

'The river was much noisier the second time. The big flood at 15.25 metres carried all the first debris and took everything. The second one was 14.6 metres, well above the old record flood height, but the water was running much quicker, the velocity was huge because there was no debris in front of it. It had all been cleared.'

The town was reopened for the second time on the 17 January 2011. Council engineers were worried that the scouring would undermine the homes; and many were checked by the shire before the residents could return. Although some had stumps almost completely exposed by the water, no homes were declared unsafe. But Ray Brown recalls that homes in the path of the second flood were scoured inside as well. 'The people emptied their houses and left all the doors and windows open to dry them out. There was nothing to stop the floodwaters then.

'Everyone was pretty exhausted. They'd done a massive clean-up but this was heartbreak number two.

'In our re-establishment plan, the new inspector of police, Mick Bianci, made a call to request help from the army.'

A 'Joint Task Force' of helicopters and ground vehicles in convoy seemed to descend on Condamine. The helicopters delivered temporary tent accommodation know as 'flexible habitat shelters' owned by Queensland Fire and Rescue Services, to provide emergency accommodation for the residents of Condamine.

For three days, army and aviation regiment personnel supported the residents of Condamine. They established a water purification point to provide fresh water and dozens of defence staff helped with the foul task of cleaning buildings, roads and farms.

Ray stopped retelling the story at this point. 'Now I'm upset,' he said. Perhaps he was thinking that calling in 'the cavalry' was a sign that the floodwaters might have broken the spirit of Condamine, that rebuilding would be too hard, that the town was broken.

Actually he wasn't thinking about the hopelessness, just the outpouring of goodwill as he recalled the wave of fresh-faced volunteers descending on his community to help those who were really struggling to help themselves. 'That's the call that touched the hearts of everyone. To see them come in, drive through Dalby, troop carrier after troop carrier, it was just amazing.

'It was such a wonderful community before. That's the heartbreak. But the army brought a sense of relief which lifted the town and, although many people were dejected, when the army arrived everyone was proud. To be Australian and not too proud to ask for help.'

The Condamine River remained above the major flood peak level for the twenty-nine days between the 24 December and 22 January. The water purification plant was finally dismantled on the 31 January, when all infrastructure was reconnected.

The town slowly recovered. Appeals raised funds and donated goods flowed in. The community asked that as a sign of recovery every home would get new floor coverings, even the rental properties.

The media arrived and were sometimes surprised to receive a pretty cool welcome. 'They'd had such an ordeal, and the media seemed to turn up every second day. They wanted to be giving out warm hug sessions, but the residents just wanted to get on with life.'

The farmers began to plan for the forthcoming season, and crossed their fingers that they would be able to get their next crop in. 'It will take years for them to recover. They need the cash flow.'

Six months later most people had returned to their homes. 'There are a couple of people not back, but I think deep down they don't want to come back either.'

Ray Brown had his first day off in July. Then a month later he had two weeks off. He had to return after that to implement the recommendations of the commission of enquiry in the Queensland floods and get ready for another summer rainy season.

He has no regrets about the way his team and the people of the shire handled the disaster. 'I wouldn't do anything differently. We had a plan in place and stuck by it: to protect life.'

'We will do what we can for the community to help them. The farmers got some financial assistance, and the shire can help with the new three 'Rs' — relocate, remove or raise, or whatever is required.

'But we'll leave it to individuals to make those decisions in their own good time. They don't want us to tell them what to do. We need to give them counselling and financial support to help them in the process.

'Everyone's closely knit here. They will reassess their own life, and move on.

'I have no doubt Condamine will survive.'

An Inland Tsunami
Grantham, Lockyer Valley, Southeast Queensland, January 2011

Peter Row, captain of Emergency Management Queensland helicopter Rescue 510, thought he knew what to expect. From the last few weeks of 2010 he had been working throughout central and southern Queensland, helping evacuate residents stranded at a time when two-thirds of the state had been declared a flood disaster zone. But now in January 2011 he was about to face his greatest test.

Peter grew up on a cattle station and completed a diesel apprenticeship — but his eyes had been on the sky since he travelled in a Fokker as a little boy. 'I can still smell the kerosene and feel the sense of excitement from that trip,' he says. He began flying in 1978, but a friend took him for a joyride in a helicopter, and he was mesmerised.

'That first flight was unbelievable. I knew then I just had to learn to fly one.' It took a few years to first learn to fly a plane, then the helicopter. In the meantime he joined the water police, and did some motorbike work as well. He earned his helicopter pilot's licence in 1986 and in 1988 was employed by the National Safety Council doing search and rescue work in Townsville. He worked for five years flying out to oil rigs in Karratha and Bass Strait, several years with Channel 9's news helicopter and three years with the Surf Life Saving rescue helicopter in Sydney.

Since 2000 he has been employed in Brisbane where he's conducted hundreds of search and rescue missions. He's got 8500 flying hours under his seatbelt. 'People come out of the military with two–and–a–half–thousand hours,' he says, to put things in perspective.

On 10 January 2011, he was unaware that the disaster about to unfold would demand every bit of expertise he had.

It was Peter Row's day off and he went into the office to undertake some night-vision-goggle training. He arrived just before 5pm and a few minutes later the 'phones started going mad.'

'It was the other helicopter pilot saying, "We need help out here, this is crazy." Then the police said that at Withcott near Toowoomba at least five people had been washed away. At Grantham in the Lockyer Valley ten people had been washed away. There were people on roofs; it was chaos,' he says.

EMQ has only one helicopter based in Brisbane: Rescue 500. Rescue 510, the other helicopter, had been undertaking rescue work in Rockhampton. Both have been in operation since 2007 and are AW 139 aircraft. They can seat up to fifteen passengers, though there may also be capacity to carry a stretcher for medical rescue. Both helicopters can travel up to 310 kilometres per hour, with instrumentation, navigation and autopilot systems that are the same as those of a Boeing 777. They are state-of-the-art rescue helicopters.

Rescue 500 had been sent to the Lockyer Valley and the pilot already had his hands full. Because the Bureau of Meteorology was forecasting a massive flood in Brisbane, Rescue 510 had been flow to the city. It had arrived that morning and was sitting partially fuelled at the EMQ hangar at Brisbane airport, known as Archerfield. It was not ready for operational tasks.

But Rescue 510 needed to be airborne — and quickly. The crew who had brought it to Brisbane were ready to go, but it was decided that because of Peter Row's local knowledge of the area, he would be captain. 'Because of low cloud there was a question mark whether we could get out there, but I knew the low level routes we could take and I was pretty confident we'd make it,' he says.

'It took us twenty-five minutes to get airborne, which is quite quick. There was definitely a sense of urgency, but we had no rescue equipment, we weren't the crew scheduled to fly it and we had to get our rescue gear together. Rescue 500 had both of our rescue strops, so we had to meet them out there before we could start to rescue people.'

Rescue 510 can carry 1600 kilograms of fuel and it burns about 400 to 450 kilograms an hour. However, it was only carrying 1044 kilograms when Peter decided not to fill its tanks completely. 'The extra time spent refuelling was less time we could rescue people. It's a difficult balance, but I know the area and I knew the light was fading.'

It's a decision that still troubles him.

Air crew officer (winch operator) Brett Knowles and two rescue crew came as well. David Turnbull from Brisbane and Stuart Wark from Cairns familiarised themselves with the circumstances as the helicopter headed west along the Cunningham Highway to the Lockyer Valley. 'We communicate a lot so everyone knows what's going on, what's their job,' says Peter. 'We'd never worked with the Cairns crewie before.'

They were racing against the helicopter pilot's two biggest frustrations: visibility and fuel supply. But as they flew over the ridge into the Lockyer valley, the sight which confronted them momentarily stopped all the usual planning.

'We saw an inland ocean, a brown moving mass of water. We said, "Holy shit, look at this." It was unbelievable. None of us had seen anything like it before. And it was moving fast. Several miles before we got to Grantham we were flying over water and that was all, as far as the eye could see.

'Towards Grantham you could see these houses in the middle of the moving water, and gunk and trees. It was phenomenal.'

The task of rescuing people looked beyond them. 'Police said, "If you can get to Grantham do what you can and if you can get to Withcott see what you can do there." Withcott is at the base of Toowoomba range. We decided we'd get to Grantham and if we had some time later we'd go towards Withcott.

'We were prepared for anything and that's part of the job we all like. Not knowing what's happening and making decisions on the run is what I'm trained for. I'd be thinking all at once about fuel and reserves and turbulence in the area behind the hills. It keeps your brain working hard.'

But no one had ever come across what the Bureau of Meteorology called an 'inland tsunami' before and, because of the reports from Rescue 500, Peter Row knew this wasn't going to be like any other day.

In a rescue helicopter it is the captain's job to assess all the information coming in, take input from the crew, try to make sense of it all and put a plan into action.

Peter says: 'The hardest of all are water rescues. In a helicopter your area of vision is huge ... at five hundred feet you are seeing many square kilometres of land or water, and a lot of our searching is at a thousand feet. From that height you can see from Moreton Island to Mt Gravatt and up to Bribie Island. To see one little head in the water is extremely difficult. It's the same on land. You are seeing the big picture.

'The problem at the Lockyer valley was that the cloud base was very low and heavy showers kept moving through. So the light wasn't great. Once we got to Grantham we could see the houses and people on the roofs. We could see some of the houses had been moved and washed into other houses.'

They dropped down beside Rescue 500, on a paddock about a kilometre out of town. By then the first helicopter had retrieved twenty-eight people from roofs and in the water. The 510 crewies ran over and grabbed the strops and rescue gear and they took off again immediately. They decided to start at one end of town and move through.

The rescue operation itself is quite straightforward, if nothing goes wrong. The crewies harness themselves to the cable, drop down beside the people they need to rescue and accompany them back up. 'The crewie has to go down to place the strop over the person and under their arms. They come back up to help control the survivor and help them into the aircraft hovering overhead. If things go wrong, they can control the person, or stop them swinging. If they start flailing their arms around, there is a chance they can slip out of the strop, so the crewie has to keep them calm and make sure they keep their arms down.' The strops are now pretty safe, although for terrified people being rescued from houses in floodwaters, they don't appear to be.

'Survivors have fallen from rescue strops in the past, but the new ones have a clip across the chest, so it's extremely rare for anyone to fall out nowadays.'

Each rescue can take about three minutes. 'We rarely bring people up one at a time, but we do if there is threat to our crewie. There was a rescue a few years back of a man standing on a submerged dinghy that was being battered by a tiger shark. We lowered the strop down to him because it would put our rescue crewie in danger if they both ended up in the water.'

Part of the skill of the pilot is to determine how far above the rescue the helicopter should hover, says Peter Row.

'It's a balancing act because we've got a six and a half tonne helicopter so there's a massive downdraft. We don't want to blow people off roofs and, if we are winching over trees, we don't want to break limbs off. During the rescue of a family from a tree at Leyburn two weeks before we got to Grantham, we snapped a branch off and it hit our crewie right across the head.

'Anyway, we were about eighty feet above Grantham, which was ideal for the conditions. It minimises downwash on survivors, and was good for me to see reference points so I could hold a stable hover.'

The rescue of people started just forty minutes after the calls came through. There was less than an hour of light left. Fuel would last a little longer than that. They couldn't afford to scour the floodwaters for people who might have been swept away. Rooftops were the priority.

'We knew people had been swept away, but trying to find them in floodwater is virtually impossible. If you go for people clinging onto trees and roofs you might save forty, whereas if you look in floodwater, you might save one.

'Once we got to the roofs, we could see some people were quite safe, so we flew over them. Some houses looked unstable and we didn't know if they would move or not and some had steep, slippery roofs, so we thought we'd get those people first.

'We started at one end of the town and worked our way downstream, winching people up. We usually take the kids first, so they aren't left alone, and then the mum. But we saw a mother with a baby and brought them up together. The mother was in a strop hanging onto the baby; and the rescue crewie had his legs around the mother and his arms around mother and the baby together.

'We can't take pets. I've done it in the past, but there is a directive that we aren't allowed to, even if they're in a box. We do take police dogs and ninety per cent of the time the dogs just sit down quietly, overwhelmed by the noise. But when you need to get as many people off as you can, and you're trying to secure a dog in a harness at the same time, and you don't know if it will create a danger to people, it is difficult.

'But we did rescue a cat at Grantham. We were winching someone up and the cat launched onto her body and just hung on. That cat wasn't going to be left behind. When they got to the aircraft, the air control officer said, "No pets" and then the rescue crew said, "Pet, what pet?" And when he saw it he said, "I can't see a pet!"'

Rescue 510 flew over another house, collected two more people and raced back to the landing paddock. The Rescue 500 crew had left a doctor and paramedic at the site. They came over, escorted the survivors off the helicopter and took care of them at a nearby farmhouse while Peter and the crew flew back.

Although there were clearly many people stranded on rooftops, and they were going to be easiest to rescue, the crew kept one eye on the water. 'We didn't know if there was going to be any more flooding. The water had gone down from the initial flash flood but we didn't know if there was any more coming.'

The tension began to grow. Peter felt it in his legs and shoulders.

'Once we get to a scene I'll pull up to a datum point [imaginary vertical point from which horizontal distances are measured for weight and balance purposes], normally back and to the left of the rescue, and then I'll give control to the air control officer (ACO) in the back.

'Winching is difficult; to hold a very stable hover for any length is difficult. You are using both feet and both hands. You are controlling the helicopter but the ACO in the back calls the instructions — forward right, right now, back one; drifting forward, steady, winching out cable ... He's giving you directions, painting a picture in your brain. You can't see what he's doing because the winch is behind you. You are focussing on a tree or building in front. You can tell by the rate of closure where you are moving, when he starts to count three, two, one.

'In training when you learn to fly you exhibit what we call the death grip — the white knuckles. When I'm winching I do tense my legs a fair bit and, I have to keep telling myself, relax your feet, relax your feet. I get tense across the shoulders and, if you winch for an hour or two on end, by the end you are really stuffed. And even if it's freezing cold, you are sweating.

'It's absolute mental concentration: you have to move the helicopter minutely, so we can put the rescue crew in the right place. It was difficult to see to get a reference on anything.

'It's OK as long as you've got good visibility.'

But now it had started to rain. 'Relatively low cloud and heavy rain showers were coming through. And when it's raining you can't see outside, only through the chin bubble under your feet. Often you've got no visibility, so you look through your feet to get a reference, which is extremely hard.

'Instead of having the big picture, you work on a fifteen or twenty per cent picture through your feet or outside the side window.'

Each rescue takes about two or three minutes. At a height of 25 metres or so above the ground, the crewie slips down in fifteen to twenty seconds. It takes a moment to slip the strop over the head and onto a person's body and give them directions. A minute or so to winch up. The captain then adjusts the power of the rotors as the machine takes on weight.

'It means holding the helicopter steady for twelve to fifteen minutes. Then you move onto the next house, or breathe a sigh of relief and head for the drop zone to let them off.

'When the showers came, though, it was very hard to hold the hover.

'We came over one roof and the people were pointing to a nearby tree. There were two people in the tree who couldn't make it to the roof, so we dropped the rescue crewie off and went on to the next rescue, while our crewie helped them out of the tree. Then we went back to rescue them.

'We could see people walking in water above their knees, but we left them as it seemed they could make their own way out safely.'

Some of the houses were tilted at alarming levels. 'One house we weren't sure about. Water was really racing by and we weren't sure if it was going to move or not. We saw one house with another washed up right onto it.'

There were four or five adults at that house. 'I thought, my God the force must be unbelievable. I hope it hasn't moved the house we were going to be winching off.'

Grantham is a small settlement. Peter could see the railway bridges where debris metres tall and deep had been washed up and around. Embedded in that were cars, tanks, trucks, trees and more than likely bodies. 'We all assumed there would be people in the cars. The water was still flowing through and we all said, "My God, how many people are under that?"'

The light faded. It was now dark and the helicopter was navigating by its searchlight. Fuel was running low. Peter decided to abandon the idea of the twenty-minute flight back to Archerfield and instead hoped to reach the RAAF base at Amberley, ten minutes closer.

He gained precious minutes to extend the rescue effort, but now regretted not adding fuel before he took off. 'We were going to have to make a low-level flight out of the valley in the dark. There would be no room for missed landings or navigation errors.

'By quarter past seven I was saying to the guys, this will be our last group and we've got to go. I swung the searchlight around the house in front of me and saw a guy standing in floodwaters clinging onto the tree.

'I said to the crew, "We have got to get him before we go." He had been hanging on to the tree for some time. When we met him several weeks later at the base, he told us he kept having to break off limbs and push the snakes away, there were so many trying to get into the trees with him.

'I hadn't thought about the snake issue in floodwaters, even though I'd seen them on the cattle property I grew up on in central Queensland, which used to flood every January. I hate snakes. I really, really hate snakes.

'We went over and rescued him and as he came up to the aircraft and I heard this scream in the back. It was from one of the women we'd rescued earlier, she realised it was her husband. She flung herself across the cabin and we had to prise her off him so we could get the strop out and get him inside.

'She told me later the last time she saw him, he'd been running off down the road saying he'd rescue the dogs. She thought she'd never see him again. Ironically, if the man had rescued his dogs, he would have had to leave them behind.'

The women who had hurled herself across the aircraft cabin to cling onto her husband had had a number of narrow escapes herself. 'She almost got killed several times that day,' says Peter. 'In the floodwaters she was swept against a power pole and because of the water pressure couldn't get off it. Then the water dropped and she got off, but then got swept towards a big steel electric gate. The water was flowing twenty-five to thirty knots, absolutely flying, and when she came within a few metres of it, it fell over. She was sure she'd have been killed if she'd hit it.

'She was washed into the yard of a nearby house. She got caught in an eddy and was swept around and as she went past the railing she hauled herself out of the water and up the steps.

'There were people on the roof and they pulled her in.'

Leaving Grantham was, Peter says, incredibly hard. 'We had just dropped our last load of people when the paramedic and doctor told us they had a pregnant woman who needed to be taken to the Princess Alexandra hospital in Brisbane.

'They said she was twenty-five weeks pregnant and had been hit in the stomach. We thought we'd get some fuel at Amberley and fly on to the hospital after, but when we got there, we found it would take a while to get fuel, so she went by ambulance.

'The woman was sitting on her verandah with her husband and two year old daughter when they saw the water coming for them. As the father was going inside, the woman was hit by the water and she and her daughter were washed away. She had the little girl in her arms, but was swept up against railway sleepers and she lost her grip, and the child was washed out of her arms. That was very sad.

'The father was washed away too. We picked him up off a roof and dropped him in the paddock. When he returned to his home, he found his son still clinging desperately to the showerscreen in the bathroom.'

In ninety minutes Rescue 510 saved fifteen people. Peter flew back to Amberley, refuelled, and did an instrument landing out of the clouds over Archerfield. The job wasn't over yet.

'Flying on instruments is mentally demanding. We got back and packed the aircraft and left work at ten that night.

'When you do a job like that it takes a while to wind down. Your brain's going at 10,000 rpm. You ask yourself for a longtime: What could I have done differently? You are self-debriefing the whole time and you ask: Could we have got more people off, should I have put more fuel on?'

Peter had the next day off. 'I was so tired I was numb,' he says. The following day he was back on duty, his job being to try to find or rescue some of the dozens of people reported missing in the Lockyer Valley, and thought to have been swept downstream. In an arduous nine-and-a-half-hour flying shift, he did not find a single person alive. 'We found one body, but no survivors,' he says.

Some of the survivors shared a barbecue with the rescue crews a few weeks later. 'They are all amazing people for what they endured. It was phenomenal. They had a positive attitude, which was really good.' It made Peter reflect on events of that day in Grantham.

'Basically we went in and did what we had to do, what we're trained to do. It tears your heart out to leave people still on roofs, but the decisions have to be made and they are really hard; and we have to live with them. On the day we did the best we could with what we had — with the light we had, with the fuel we had.'

Peter still worries over the decision to take off without the extra fuel. 'We could have gone to 1300 kilograms, which would have been great and would have made things less stressful. If I had to do it again, I'd probably put it on. These are the decisions you have to make in the heat of the moment.

'It's always good to have that little bit of fuel — for mum and the kids.'

Epilogue
Chas Keys, flood management specialist

Chas Keys is a wise old man of floods and he doesn't like what he sees. He puts it this way: 'People have to own the threat from flooding. It's like giving up smoking. You can't do that unless you absolutely want to. And you can't do anything about managing your flood or your fire or your earthquake risk until you own the problem. You have to face up to it, accept the reality of it, be prepared to work at dealing with it. And in doing all that, you may well have to make some difficult choices about what to do.'

Keys might occasionally get people offside with his views, but he speaks from enormous experience. Originally a social scientist specialising in urban and regional development, he spent 14 years managing floods for the NSW State Emergency Service, including seven years as its Deputy Director-General. He has written extensively on flood mitigation and flood management. When he talks about managing warning systems, evacuations and property protection, he knows what he is talking about.

He retired in 2004 and has since been a consultant on the emergency management of flooding. His most recent book dealt with the efforts of the community in Maitland, New South Wales, to manage periodically disastrous floods over a period of 190 years. He is an honorary associate member of Risk Frontiers, a natural hazards research organisation at Macquarie University, and holds the Emergency Services Medal (ESM) for his work with the SES.

'I was born in New Zealand, but spent my early adult years looking for the perfect climate,' he says from his home on Queensland's Sunshine Coast. 'I tried Fiji, which was too hot, Canada (too cold); then found the east coast of Australia in 1975 and decided it was nearly perfect.'

He is still frustrated about the inability of emergency agencies to manage floods as well as they might. He feels that, especially in Queensland, local government does not mitigate the threat properly — and he is exasperated with members of floodprone communities who, he says, sometimes steadfastly refuse to take responsibility for their own safety.

'We are not very good at this stuff,' he says. 'People generally are complacent about floods. They say it's never going to happen or they decide to worry about it at the time. And when it comes to the time they've never done enough. Preparation is not something you can do solely on the day. It's got to be ongoing. Much of it has to be done before you realise a flood is coming.

'I mean you've got to understand that flooding is a threat, and if you live in a flood liable area it will happen one day; and it might happen sooner than you think. There are things you can do that will soften the blow, and it's worth doing them.

'You can plan to save things you need to save. It's dumb to try to do this solely during the event because you'll miss things out. If you organise yourself beforehand you'll get a reasonably complete list.

'What do you need to save? Precious sentimental items, photo albums, family heirlooms. Things of monetary value. Things that you can raise or move offsite. Kids should be encouraged in the planning process to take ownership of their important things. It might only be a teddy bear, but it matters.

'But a whole lot of bureaucratically important items count too: passports, wallets, title deeds, insurance, wills, your driver's licence are really painful to replace. It's not that they can't be replaced, but it takes a lot of time and effort which could easily be avoided.

'You should think about the steps you will take to save things. Put them up high, depending on where you are. There are places which get flooded over their roofs so there is no point in putting items in the ceiling if there's a really big flood coming.

'So ask yourself, am I going to put them up high, or off the floodplain altogether? A refuge on a hill, like a relative's home, can take stuff too.

'The second thing is to work out your behaviours. There is a difference between people who behave effectively and those who don't.

'Everyone who is at risk of flooding ought to have a flood plan, but most don't. I know of very few who have a flood plan, and even fewer who've got a written one. And that plan should be informed by an understanding of the vulnerability of the place you are in for different levels of flooding. You can come to grips with the nature of that vulnerability by finding the history of flooding in your area.

'If you know the highest flood reached twelve metres at the local gauge and it was over your roof, and you've been told the levee will be overtopped at say, ten metres, then you should assume if there is a warning that says ten or more, you are going to get some water.'

Keys believes strongly in plans and even more strongly in the activity they require. 'Stick to the plan. Don't be distracted. Stick to it, drill to it. Do it periodically. All your thinking has already been done, so all you then have to do is do it.

'If people are leaving, they should know what they will save in the house and what they will put in their car. Their plan needs to include what route should be taken to avoid driving through floodwaters, as that can be dangerous, particularly if there are surges that can sweep cars off the road.

'You should have a destination, which often will be the home of friends or relatives on higher ground nearby.

'The emergency services will very likely ask you to register your evacuation. That's a really good idea, because other people will then know you are not stuck in your house and they won't come looking for you. It can also help in planning to protect from looting.

'And whatever you do, you should do it early. Don't wait until you can see that the water is about to get into your house before you act. Start moving when you hear a flood warning.'

Chas Keys believes local government in Australia is reluctant to acknowledge the risks of flooding. 'Councils don't like the flood word. Nor do businesses. They don't want to talk about it because of the alleged economic effects, which are not important but are usually overstated and a whole lot less serious than drowning people or having them lose important items unnecessarily.

'For example, in Maitland there are markers all over the place which indicate the flood levels that were reached in 1955. They're fading and falling off the power poles, and I've challenged council to maintain them, but they haven't. They obviously don't want to. They are fixated on the assumption that having flood signs on the power poles is bad for property values and the economy. There's precious little evidence of that, as it happens: what damages property values is flooding, not signs about it. Houses in Maitland sell at perfectly good prices.

'If you've got a house or a business or an institution you should know about its vulnerability in relation to a riverine flood or, if it's on the coast, the storm surge potential. You can do your own research too. Look at the flood history and at your own house relative to that history. Look to see if there are flood-level markers on the house, or mud inside the walls.

The prevailing wisdom in modern Australia is to evacuate towns and homes when the floods come. There is much debate about the value of this.

'As a general rule it's best to evacuate if there's going to be water in your house. But for flash floods, with water arriving with very little warning, the best advice is usually to stay inside your house,' says Keys, who confronted this crucial decision when leading the response to the 1998 Wollongong flash floods for the NSW SES.

'In Wollongong, with its spectacular escarpment, heavy rain could lead to landslides, in which case it would have been best if people were not anywhere near the place, but you need to get out before there is any water in your vicinity or any landslide damage.

'In places like these, when flash floods arrive in a hurry, by the time you are motivated to leave there is already water around your house: it's too late to go. The streets will already be flooded and dangerous.

'Same in Adelaide, with water coming out of the Adelaide Hills, where there's going to be high velocity because of the gradient, and there will be a debris load including bits of houses and trees and rocks.

'It can get very nasty. In that situation, by the time the threat is recognised, you might be advised to stay. But in general the SES should take the default option that it is not good to have people in houses in floods.

'So if you know or have a reasonable indication from flood intelligence and flood warnings that houses are going to have water in them in the next few hours or days, in places on the western plains of NSW like Moree or Forbes or Narrandera, or Cunnamulla or Charleville in Queensland, I think it's a good idea to encourage people not to be there.

'They should move stuff up, or out, and then leave.'

But how safe are buildings in a flood? Experience in Queensland's Lockyer valley in January 2011 suggests that some houses are at risk of being washed away. 'Depends on the environment,' says Keys, a common refrain when talking about floods. 'Plenty of houses in Maitland in 1955 and Emerald in 2011 were not safe because they were wet up in the ceiling cavity, but they weren't washed away. In very few environments do modern Australian houses fall down. If you go back to the nineteenth century they were wattle and daub and they fell down a lot — for example in Gundagai in 1852, when ninety people were killed and many houses were simply washed away.

'Mostly houses don't get washed away in floods. In Wollongong they could, because of the flow velocity and heavy debris load coming off the escarpment, but very few did in 1998.

'In Mackay in 1918, houses were washed away by wave action when the sea invaded the town as a result of storm surge. And on the shoreline you can get waves causing erosion and houses on sand dunes being undermined. Years ago, near Byron Bay, a street and several houses disappeared as the coast retreated as a result of erosion. That threat exists in several places in Australia.

'But in general in riverine floods near the mouths of the rivers which flow to the east coast of Australia, or even in most of the floodprone parts of Adelaide, by the time the water gets to the densely built up areas there isn't the velocity to cause too much damage to the structural soundness of a house.

'At the same time, if there are going to be houses with water in them, it's a good idea not to have people there.'

So if most houses aren't going to fall down in a flood, why evacuate?

'Look at Rockhampton in 2011. People will say, "I'm OK, I don't want to be rescued, it's only water, I'm not leaving." But they'll get sick of staying and they will call out for rescue and the emergency services will then have to get them. And for the rescuers, there can be real danger in that.

'People don't understand, they will soon get sick of being floodbound. It's horrible. You lose power, phone, you will have to have candles. Someone will knock a candle over and start a fire, and those fires are very hard to put out. A flood brings a lot of water but it's not very usable. Firefighters can't get there.

'You can't communicate, so if you change your mind you can't tell anyone. You'll be cold. It will be uncomfortable, it will stink, and anyway, do you really want to sleep in your house with a lot of water in it?

'Your house will be invaded by snakes, spiders, insects and other nasties. Lots of snakes come out of the woodwork in floods. They're looking for dry ground. And even without being bitten by snakes people do get injured in floods. There are always spikes in admissions to the accident and emergency departments of hospitals as a result. And if you're hurt when you're cut off, you might have to wait a long time, perhaps in great pain, for treatment.

'I've always found the threat of snake invasion is a pretty good way of convincing people to leave. There was a house after the 1955 floods in Maitland that had five brown snakes in it.'

There are other problems too. There is a genuine risk of serious illnesses breaking out when there's prolonged inundation — gastric illnesses, for example. 'There could be sewerage-infested water and the houses might be sitting in it for ages, which poses a serious public health problem. In Nyngan in 1990 we evacuated virtually every house. There were 990 houses and 970 were flooded above floor level. They're pretty quiet waters out there and they stay around for days. And while the duration of inundation is usually less near the rivers which drain to the east coast, the problem is not insignificant.

'There is no safe period of isolation. The longer it lasts, the more things will go wrong. People will fall down or slip over and break bones. If they do that at night, rescuers can't get to them so they have to wait until the next day in huge discomfort.

'Or people cut themselves, or there will be medical issues made worse by the fact that you couldn't get to hospital. So people have to put up with more discomfort than they should. And sometimes what might otherwise be not all that serious can become life-threatening.'

Keys prefers a layered model. 'You shouldn't have elderly people in flood zones when a flood is coming; you shouldn't have mothers with kids; it's a legitimate technique to reduce the population by getting them out; and it will encourage the blokes to go as well. Once you start the others will follow.'

Chas Keys has had experience in cleaning up after flooding.

'Clean quickly,' he says. 'If you allow mud and silt to bake hard it's impossible to shift, like concrete. Hose it out quickly if you have a water supply. Hose the walls, squeegee the water out, dry the place out as quickly as you can.

'The longer you leave it, the harder it gets and, remember, it's possibly sewerage-tainted. Mattresses and bedding are largely irretrievable and chipboard stuff breaks up, so most people find they have to rebuild their kitchens.'

Chas feels the recent approach to flooding, in which the state and federal governments provide immediate cash assistance and massive flood appeals are set up, has had some unfortunate side effects. 'The generosity of the public system means you can get stuff reimbursed.' He wonders, however, whether this causes some sort of welfare mentality that actually prevents people taking action. 'People learn dependency, not self sufficiency.'

Utilities? 'Turn them off as you leave. You don't want power on in your house that will create shorts; and if gas lines rupture there will be a serious problem. Turn off water, power and gas at the meter box.'

All of this is simple enough and sensibly reduces the risk to life. So why do people ignore the basic planning and safety procedures?

Complacency is a modern trait, born of the fact that in most areas floods are infrequent and most people don't have to respond often. The exception to this are the farmers, who own land right down to the rivers with fences, livestock, pumps and other equipment and crops to protect and plans to implement before floods arrive.

'They have good economic reasons to save their stuff and they get quite a bit of practice, so they are good responders. And they plan, and they correct former mistakes — like under-responding. Farmers are amongst the best flood managers.

'Most people in towns don't get flooded very often, and in one sense we've inadvertently made that situation worse with mitigation projects like levees and retention basins.

'Levees are really good things, but there is something called the "levee paradox". An area gets flooded, so the community builds a levee to keep the water out and people think all is now OK. So they put more investment into the land behind the levee with more houses and factories, and then the levee gets overtopped in a bigger flood than it was built for, so there is actually more damage than if the levee wasn't there.

'Flood mitigation can encourage people to intensify the use of land. We create more vulnerability, more to lose. We need to mitigate the threat without encouraging the unfortunate side effects.

'We are complacent anyway because we think the water comes up, goes down and who cares? We compare our strategies with bushfire safety. Many fewer die in floods now than in bushfires.

'That's true of the last thirty to forty years. There are probably more people living in fire–prone areas now than on floodplains.

And, especially with mitigation, floods have become almost theoretical and abstract in people's minds. This feeds the pre-existing level of complacency and, anyway, people think no one dies in floods.

'This is largely true, but not entirely. Maitland's been there since 1820; and since then about sixty people have died because of floods — and fifteen in the last century, including eleven in one day in 1955. Yet Maitland hasn't had a really bad event like Gundagai in 1852 when ninety died, or Clermont in Queensland in 1916 when about sixty-five lost their lives.

'We are nakedly complacent and that doesn't encourage people to plan or to think what they would do. We underestimate the damage that floods — even routine ones — can do. People can be financially ruined by flooding, even though the recovery processes and the fundraising efforts are quite generous. The problem is not just about deaths. It's about livelihoods and property too.'

People will do inappropriate things when floods approach, he says. 'I get the jitters when I hear people are sandbagging the town levees, as happened in Nyngan in 1990. When floods punch out the sandbags it's like a dam failure.

'You can suck the community into this heroic effort to save the town by sandbagging and they ignore their own houses; and when the heroics don't work these people have done nothing to lift or move their belongings.

'At Nyngan you could say that virtually one hundred per cent of the potential flood damage was achieved. Because what they did was not useful. They did this heroic community thing, and I'm not minimising this, of trying to save the town by piling sandbags on top of the levee. Hindsight tells you they would have been much better off in their houses lifting stuff off the floors. But sandbags are really useful for Telstra exchanges, or the doors and vents of shops when the flooding is not likely to be deep.

'People need to understand that levees are built to a design standard and are not intended to be raised beyond that level, for economic, hydrologic and aesthetic reasons. It's almost never possible to build them so high that they'll keep out the really bad floods. Which means that every flood levee in Australia will be overtopped one day — but only in very bad floods, whereas many now-leveed areas used to be inundated over and over again and even in floods that weren't particularly big. The message is that if you live in a levee-protected area you'll get flooded occasionally — but much less often than you used to be.' The levee is a good thing, but it can't solve the entire problem.

'Most town levees in NSW are built to keep out the one per cent flood — a flood so big that the probability of it happening at a specified location in any given year is only one per cent. That's the real meaning of the so-called "one-in-a-hundred-years" flood. In bigger floods — those with an even lower probability of happening in a given year — levees will be overtopped. And that's without even considering the question of inadequate levee maintenance. There are places in NSW whose levees have gone to rack and ruin and are virtually not there any more. They could fail even in quite small floods, well below those which they were designed to keep out, by what's called piping — the water will get inside the levee and bubble under to the dry side, and the levee will collapse.

'Levees are designed to be overtopped, but people don't realise that. On the day of a flood they want to protect them, to protect themselves, so they want to put sandbags on the banks. There are situations when that will work, but many times I've heard towns sandbagging the spillways on levees, which is really dangerous because the lower portions of the levees are designed to take the water away to protect the rest of the system and the rest of the town.

'These are complex engineering devices with bits and pieces all designed for a purpose. People don't understand them very well. We need to do more to explain how levees function and let people know that their operation should not be tampered with.'

Overall, Chas Keys believes that we know a great deal about flood mitigation and management in Australia, but are reluctant to use it or learn from experience.

'Sadly, we have allowed the problem of flooding to accumulate for decades and it damages us repeatedly. Strong policy and community-protecting decisions — statesmanlike decisions, even — are needed from governments and councils. A larger, more coordinated effort is needed.

'Many of the approaches are politically difficult and governments and councils frequently shy away from them after the hue and cry of a bad flood and the inevitable inquiries have died down. But if we do not make some hard decisions, after all the suffering at the beginning of 2011, we will condemn ourselves to more suffering, over and over, when floods strike. We've always done this in the past, and I fear we'll go on doing it.

'Australia's most manageable natural hazard is rarely well managed. We could do so much better, and we should aim to.'